OXFORD READINGS IN PHILOSOPHY

Series Editor G. J. Warnock

PRACTICAL REASONING

Also published in this series

The Philosophy of Law, edited by Ronald M. Dworkin
Moral Concepts, edited by Joel Feinberg
Theories of Ethics, edited by Philippa Foot
The Philosophy of Mind, edited by Jonathan Glover
Knowledge and Belief, edited by A. Phillips Griffiths
The Philosophy of Mathematics, edited by Jaakko Hintikka
Reference and Modality, edited by Leonard Linsky
The Philosophy of Religion, edited by Basil Mitchell
The Philosophy of Science, edited by P. H. Nidditch
Aesthetics, edited by Harold Osborne
The Theory of Meaning, edited by G. H. R. Parkinson
The Philosophy of Education, edited by R. S. Peters
Political Philosophy, edited by Anthony Quinton
The Philosophy of Social Explanation, edited by Alan Ryan
The Philosophy of Language, edited by J. R. Searle
Semantic Syntax, edited by Pieter A. M. Seuren
Causation and Conditionals, edited by Ernest Sosa
Philosophical Logic, edited by P. F. Strawson
The Justification of Induction, edited by Richard Swinburne
Locke on Human Understanding, edited by I. C. Tipton
The Philosophy of Perception, edited by G. J. Warnock
The Philosophy of Action, edited by Alan R. White

Other volumes are in preparation

PRACTICAL REASONING

Edited by
JOSEPH RAZ

OXFORD UNIVERSITY PRESS
1978

Oxford University Press, Walton Street, Oxford OX2 6DP

OXFORD LONDON GLASGOW
NEW YORK TORONTO MELBOURNE WELLINGTON
IBADAN NAIROBI DAR ES SALAAM LUSAKA CAPE TOWN
KUALA LUMPUR SINGAPORE JAKARTA HONG KONG TOKYO
DELHI BOMBAY CALCUTTA MADRAS KARACHI

© *Oxford University Press 1978*

British Library Cataloguing in Publication Data
Practical Reasoning—(Oxford readings in philosophy).
1. Reasoning—Addresses, essays, lectures
2. Human Behaviour—Addresses, essays, lectures
I. Title   II. Series   III. Raz, Joseph
160   BC177   78–40255
ISBN 0–19–875041–2

*Filmset in 'Monophoto' Times 9 on 11 pt. by
Richard Clay (The Chaucer Press), Ltd., Bungay, Suffolk
and printed in Great Britain by
Fletcher & Son Ltd., Norwich*

CONTENTS

INTRODUCTION

THERE was a period during which many philosophers almost lost sight of the unity of practical reason. The perennial problem of the foundations of morality was compounded by doubts cast on one's ability to reason in moral matters at all. It was realized of course that similar doubts could apply to other spheres of practical reasoning but no special study was devoted to them. Attention was held by the 'more important' argument about morals. This state of affairs could not last. After all, the source of the new doubts on the role of reason in morals lay outside moral philosophy. They were engendered by the birth of modern logic and the philosophy of logic which accompanied it and made it possible. Thus right from its beginning the modern philosophy of logic saw little to distinguish moral reasoning from other areas of practical reason. Whatever special difficulties moral reasoning presented derived from the old difficulties about the foundation of morality, not from modern logic. Philosophers began to turn to a serious consideration of practical reasoning outside morals in order to draw analogies between these and moral reasoning. At the same time interest in practical reasoning was stimulated by growing awareness of the special features of explanations of human action and by the development of the mathematical and psychological study of decision-making.

As a result of these developments much writing was devoted to practical reason in its generality, although it was not denied that different areas of practical reason may have their own peculiarities. Still, the conception of practical reasoning as a unified field of philosophical inquiry is not yet firmly established and the contours of its problems are far from being generally agreed upon. I felt free to use essays written as contributions to moral philosophy which throw light on general problems of practical reason. I have been unashamedly partisan in selecting those articles which seem to me either to have made significant advances or to have signposted major alternatives. The following remarks attempt briefly and rather dogmatically to outline some of the main problems of the philosophy of practical reason and to take sides in some of the disputes.

1. REASONS—GUIDING AND EXPLANATORY

The most-discussed problem concerning practical reasons is that of their role in the explanation of behaviour and in particular whether reasons are causes. The problem of causality lies at the foundation of all the sciences which attempt to provide a systematic explanation of human behaviour (such as economics, sociology, psychology, and history). It is also central to an understanding of the foundation of personal responsibility for action. But the disagreement at the bottom of this dispute is a disagreement about the nature of causal explanation rather than about the nature of reasons. I make this point partly to explain why relatively little of the material included in this collection bears directly on these questions but mainly because overlooking this point so often leads to or is combined with a misunderstanding of the nature of reasons and their very special role in the explanation of behaviour.

We invoke reasons in several different contexts. Consider the following somewhat artificial situation:

Lucy waits in her flat for Mary. She bought a book and intends to give it her as a present hoping that this will help to cement their recently begun friendship. Edward happens to call on Lucy just then, she tells him her intention. 'Isn't it a good idea?' she asks. 'No,' he says, 'there is absolutely no reason why you should give her a present and several why you shouldn't.' He is always a little long-winded and likes being mysterious. Before he can explain Mary arrives and Lucy gives her the book. Later that evening Lucy asks Edward, 'You really don't understand why I gave Mary a present, do you?' Edward: 'Oh I knew your reasons but you didn't know that she hates presents.'

There is nothing wrong here. We understand not only what Edward meant but also what he said. It was perfectly in order despite the appearance of contradiction between his statement that (1) there was absolutely no reason for Lucy to give the gift and his statement that he knew her reasons, which entails that (2) she had a reason: her desire to please Mary. This suggests that there are two separate standard uses of 'reason'. The one exemplified by (1) is typical to contexts of guidance ('You have no reason to . . .'), the other exemplified by (2) to contexts of explanation (The reason you did it (or wanted to do it) was . . .).

Reasons are the corner-stone of all explanation of human actions, indeed of the very notion of human action itself.[1] Apart from several categories of involuntary, semi-voluntary, and semi-automatic action (such as breathing, hiccupping, automatic doodling, etc.), which are on the borderline between what we do and what happens to us, all action which is not itself intentional (for example, acts done by mistake, inadvertently, negligently, or recklessly) is done through doing or attempting an intentional act. Intentional action itself is action performed by an agent who knows what he is doing and does it for a reason. Thus all non-intentional action is explained by reference to intentional acts performed or attempted and these presuppose the notion of a reason for action. The reasons referred to in these explanatory contexts are normally mental states of the person whose actions or desires are explained (for they figure in the explanation of desire as well); either his beliefs or his desires. Whether an action is intentional depends on the agent's state of mind which led to its performance. Here a very important warning is in place: to ascribe to a person a certain state of mind need not involve the ascription of a conscious episode which can be given a phenomenalist description (such as the thought occurring to him or his feeling the pull of the desire).

In this sense, then, it is the person's belief that it will rain, his fear of punishment, his view that promises ought to be kept, or his desire to please his friends which are his reasons for taking an umbrella, obeying the law, keeping his promise, or throwing a party. Not so when one looks for reasons for guidance. Though one's fear of punishment or desire to please serve as guiding reasons, one's belief that it will rain does not. It is the fact that it will rain which is a reason to take one's umbrella, not one's belief that it will. I should take this medicine because it will alleviate my pain, not because I think that it will do so. The fact that it will help is a reason for me to do so even if I do not believe that it will—that is precisely why my G.P. informs me that it will alleviate my pain—so that I shall know that there is a reason for me to take the medicine. But his bringing this fact to my knowledge does not create the reason. It merely informs me of its existence and makes it possible for me to take it into account. Contrariwise, if my belief that the medicine will help would have been by itself a (guiding) reason for taking it then there would have been no gain in telling me that I am mistaken and that in fact it will harm me. If belief is by itself a reason, then even though had I come to believe that it would harm me I would then have had reason for avoiding it; so long as I believed it to be beneficial I had all the reasons I could have had for taking it and was in no way wrong in doing so.

A third important kind of context in which we refer to reasons is in evaluating action. We evaluate by guiding reasons whether the action was the right one or the best. We use explanatory reasons to judge the agent's rationality in doing what he did—rationality is measured in light of the agent's own beliefs and goals. But there are other evaluations as well—his conscientiousness or aversion to risk may depend on his care in investigating all the relevant facts, etc. Thus judgements of a person's rationality or reasonableness presuppose the concepts of guiding and of explanatory reasons and do not give rise to a third kind of reason.

We seem to have reached the conclusion that we distinguish guiding from explanatory reasons. Guiding reasons are facts[2] which affect what one should do; they include facts about the world (rain, trains timetables, etc.), the validity of certain moral principles (promises ought to be kept, etc.), the having of certain desires (to be rich or loved, etc.), and others. Explanatory reasons are all states of mind of the person whose actions are to be explained. They include his having goals, desires, factual beliefs (that it will rain or that the train will arrive at 9.30), and moral convictions (his belief that promises ought to be kept, etc.). The two classes overlap in certain areas (the agent's desires) but diverge in others.[3]

What is the relation between these two uses of 'reasons'? It is plain that explanatory reasons presuppose guiding reasons. My belief that it will rain explains my action of taking the umbrella only because I believe that in the circumstances the fact that it will rain is a reason (i.e. a guiding reason) for doing so.[4] Hence we cannot explain the concept of explanatory reasons without using that of a guiding reason. The reverse is not true. This is a very important fact about the explanation of action. Intentional action is one which was, whether successfully or unsuccessfully, guided by reason, i.e. by the agent's desires or his beliefs of what reasons apply to him. Reasons are those facts by which behaviour should be guided and we refer to the agent's belief in reasons in explaining intentional action because its peculiar feature is that it is an attempt, successful or otherwise, to be guided by reason.

Hence the theory of practical reason contributes to the explanation of action by describing those standards of reasoning which the agent was trying to follow. Whether his reasoning explains his action causally or otherwise is not within the proper sphere of that theory but is a problem about the notion of a cause and of the alternative patterns of events—if there are any. From now on I will be concerned exclusively with guiding reasons.

2. REASONS AND REASONING

That the room's temperature is approaching 0° C is a reason for switching on the central heating. So is the fact that people suffer in such low temperatures. So is the fact that I want to test whether the central heating is still in working order. Assume that all these facts obtain, do I have three distinct reasons for switching on the central heating? Clearly not. I have but two distinct reasons. The low temperature in the room and the fact that people suffer in such temperatures somehow belong together and make but one reason, each being merely a part of a reason. My desire to test my central heating forms a second and distinct reason for the same action, separate from the first yet somehow reinforcing it. What is the test by which we determine which facts belong together, each being a partial reason while all are but one complete reason, and which do not and form a part or the whole of distinct reasons? The mere use of the term 'reason' does not help. As the example shows it is used to refer to partial reasons as well as to complete ones.

The answer lies in the relation between practical reasons and practical reasoning. A practical inference is characterized by having an appropriate practical conclusion (the nature of which will be considered below). The premises of a valid practical inference if they are all true (or justified) state a reason. All of them together state a complete reason. Naturally an inference can contain redundant premises, namely premises omissions of which will not invalidate the inference. We could define *an atomic complete* reason as the fact(s) stated by the premises of a sound practical inference with no redundant premises.

The relation between practical reasons and practical reasoning is crucial to the understanding of both. What then is practical reasoning? It is the transition (not necessarily conscious) from belief in the premises to acceptance of the putative conclusion of a practical inference. The explanation of this process is not our concern. But it is crucial that it is intended by the agent to conform to logical standards. That is, the agent regards the conclusion as justified only if it is adequately supported by premises which are themselves true, valid, or justifiable. To explain a piece of practical reasoning we must refer to the putatively sound practical inference by which it aspires to be justified. Valid practical inferences are ordered sets of statements the last of which is a practical conclusion adequately supported by the others. But in considering their nature it is important to remember that they are meant to justify practical reasoning, i.e. to show that the reasoner's conclusion is well supported by premises he relied upon.

The character of an inference as a practical one is determined by the nature of its conclusion. The extant explanations fall into three main types; (a) the view that the conclusion is an action or an attempt, (b) that it is (the formation of) an intention or an expression of an intention, (c) that it is a deontic statement, for example that the agent ought to perform a certain action. It is common ground that correct reasoning by the appropriate person would lead or tend to lead him to perform the relevant action. Clearly, an intention leads or tends to lead to action and so do one's beliefs as to what one ought to do. The second view, unlike the first, allows for failure to act in the way entailed by the premises which is not a failure of reasoning but is due to inability, forgetfulness, weakness of will, etc. So one way of describing the difference between them is that the second view is better able to represent the difference between non-action owing to failure of reasoning and non-action owing to other factors. Another way of representing the difference is in terms of distance from the act. If the conclusion is an action then the inference can only be drawn at or just before the time of action. If the conclusion is an intention then it can be drawn long in advance. Both views regard the conclusion of the inference as the determination of a person to action. Therefore according to both only the person whose action is in question can engage in practical reasoning and every single practical inference determines an action as conclusively necessitated by reason. Supporters of the view that conclusions of practical inference are deontic statements may well base their position on an objection to these two features. They may feel that there is no essential difference between a man reasoning about his own course of action and his reasoning about his friend's action. A person may even put himself in another's shoes. It seems artificial and unjustified to exaggerate the difference between such cases. Sometimes the distinction is even more difficult to draw: it is in virtue of our reasoning about certain general or hypothetical situations that we know how both we and others should behave in those situations and it is by the same reasoning that we judge ourselves and others. The view that the conclusion is an action or an intention exaggerates and misdescribes the difference between the first person and the third person reasoning.

It could further be argued that there are at least two basic types of practical inference (though the difference between them is often obscured). First, argument as to which action there is a *prima facie* (atomic) reason to perform. Second, in case of there being conflicting reasons (i.e. reasons to perform incompatible acts) argument over which way the conflict should be resolved. If the conclusion of the argument is a deontic statement (or any fiat including one representing a desire or volition which is not necessarily overriding—as in Kenny) these types can be easily separated (more on this below). Their separation is more difficult if the conclusion is an action, or an attempt, or an intention or its expression.

I have been referring to 'ought' sentences as used to make statements. This is of course yet another controversial view which it is impossible to justify here. It is commonly contrasted with the view that such sentences are or express prescriptions such that their endorsement or acceptance by a person entails his having not a belief but a volition.

Two main reasons are advanced to support the view that 'ought' sentences express volitions. First, there is the view that 'value or deontic judgements' are neither true nor false and hence cannot be stated. The point is not a terminological one and one cannot get round it by saying that 'value judgements' can be justified or not justified, correct or incorrect, valid or invalid. The point of the argument is that none of these applies if it implies some objective and public way of ascertaining the validity or invalidity, etc., of 'value judgements'. The argument does not deny that there are logical relations among 'value judgements' including relations of entailment and incompatibility. It does not, therefore, deny the possibility of inferences providing relative justification to 'value judgements': p is entailed by q and therefore it is irrational to accept p and reject q. The argument is thus an argument about the foundations of 'value judgements'. The examination and evaluation of these arguments falls beyond the scope of this collection. Nothing in this introduction supports the view that there are, for example, moral values binding even on those who do not adopt them or that such values are reasons for action for those who reject them. Our concern is merely with the concepts we employ in practical reasoning, not with the truth of statements made by their use if there are any such. The only point I am pressing here is that even if these sceptical arguments are sound they do not establish that value or deontic sentences are not normally used by people to assert that which they take to be valid, correct, or perhaps even true.

The second argument, which with some philosophers supplements and with others competes with and supplants the first, turns on the connection between volition, beliefs, and actions. The conclusion of a practical inference if not an action must at least be non-contingently related to the appropriate action. This is no doubt true of prescriptions. Assent to them is non-contingently related to action. But is not the same true of assent to certain judgements such as 'I enjoy swimming', 'It is in my interest to lose weight', 'I have a (moral) duty to look after my son'? Three basic positions with many variations have been canvassed in recent writing: first, assent to these statements does not include commitment to the acts they relate to and they are not statements of (complete) reasons for performing these acts. Second, these are not statements but fiats, i.e. expressions of different volitions (in some or all of the examples perhaps mixed with statements—for example, slimming will prolong John's life and he wants to prolong his life). Third, these are genuine statements, assent to which commits one to the appropriate action (in the common jargon they are not purely 'descriptive' statements).

The dispute around the first basic position concerns the role of such statements in practical inferences where there is no doubt that statements like those in our examples often appear unsupported by any fiats. Are these ever valid as they are or are they enthymemes valid if at all only because of some suppressed premisses which are perhaps always fiats? But this is a problem concerning the logical properties of certain concepts which though important does not go to the heart of the divide between 'cognitivists' and 'volitionists'. This is reflected in the disagreement between the second and third positions which, it seems to me, reflects at bottom a disagreement about the very fundamental distinction between cognitions and volitions. The dispute is whether volitions are by definition the only active principle in a person. Cognitions by themselves are thought to be inert as are sensations and perceptions. Active feelings are analysed into combinations of emotions and volitions. This way of dividing the active from the passive has the advantage of simplicity and the drawback of a contrived and artificial device. One of its results is that certain beliefs are always conjoined with certain volitions: we always desire (other things being equal) to protect and further our interests; we always desire to avoid that which is painful, to have that which is enjoyable, etc. I am not suggesting that these statements are false, merely that it is misleading and mysterious to interpret them in a way which makes a sensation of pain separate though conjoined with a desire to avoid its cause, or a realization that a certain activity is of a kind we normally enjoy, or that it is in our interests, separate though conjoined with a desire to engage in it. But these are large issues which cannot be settled here.

3. IS THERE A SPECIAL 'PRACTICAL LOGIC'?

One fairly common objection to viewing a practical inference as inference of a deontic statement from a set of statements is that this is not really a *practical* inference at all but a theoretical inference, for it governs reasoning which leads to a modification of a belief and not to action. We have already seen that this objection is based on a restrictive view of cognitions. On other views some categories of cognitions are related to action in the same way as are volitions. But this retort only reinforces the view that practical reasoning is but ordinary theoretical reasoning. If so, well and good: but is it so?

It has been claimed that practical inferences differ from theoretical in being open in some special sense. Professor Anscombe regards practical reasoning as proceeding from premisses which indicate that a certain action has certain desirability characteristics to that action itself. But the action is not 'entailed' or made inevitable by the premisses. The agent may fail to desire the action despite its desirability. That an agent desires an action is not itself a premiss in practical inferences. It does not explain the action but merely indicates that it was taken or was intended for a reason. It is the fact that the act was desirable in virtue of some desirability characteristic it possessed which explains why it was desired or taken, but as we noted a person may fail to desire it despite its desirability. The reasoning is open in this special way which marks it as practical reasoning.

Professor Anscombe is of course correct in insisting that reasons do not render action inevitable, nor does the agent's realization of the facts which are reasons make them so. But, as we noted above, Professor Anscombe's account does not enable one to distinguish failure of reasoning from other factors leading to failure of actions. Besides, it obscures one central fact about the relation of reason to action, namely that people who have certain beliefs or beliefs and desires cannot fail to realize that they are committed by them to certain actions. This logical determination of action by reason is expressed by the practical inference leading from premisses to the conclusion that a certain action ought to be performed and being such that a person who accepts the premisses of an elementary inference necessarily accepts its conclusion.

Professor von Wright regards a statement that the agent has certain goals as among the premisses of a characteristic type of practical inference. His conception, therefore, is not meant to facilitate representation of one way in which reason may fail to guide a person, i.e. where he rejects the view that a certain goal is binding on him in a way other than as a means to another goal he already has. His formulation is more suitable for explanatory purposes and for showing how acceptance of one goal necessitates another. At the same time he is anxious to insist on the open character of practical inference in another respect: human action is incapable of causal explanation and practical inferences do not point to facts which causally necessitate action. In that respect explanation of action by the practical inference of the agent is unique.

This aspect of von Wright's account, however, does not establish that practical inferences are anything more than a special application of ordinary deductive logic. Anthony Kenny's account of practical inferences does establish their special features. He regards them (or at least some of them) as governed by the logic of satisfactoriness not that of satisfaction. It is common ground that the premisses of a practical inference specify a goal; either a goal the agent has (that which he desires) or one which we should have (being valuable or desirable morally or in some other way). According to the logic of satisfaction it follows from the premisses that one ought to perform an action whose performance is *necessary* for the achievement of the goal the premisses specify. By the logic of satisfactoriness the conclusion specifies an action performance of which *suffices* for the realization of the goal. The logic of satisfaction has to overcome two difficulties.

First, such a logic may lead to a conclusion that a certain action ought to be performed even though it is known that the goal on which this conclusion is based will not be realized even if the action is performed. Let us call the goal G_1 and assume that actions A and B are severally necessary and jointly sufficient for its realization. Assume that G_1 is a valid or justified goal. It follows that one ought to do A. It may be the case that (1) it is impossible to do B; or (2) B ought not to be performed because it leads to G_2 which is very bad; or (3) only other people can perform B and it is known that they will not whatever our agent does. In all these cases it is pointless for the agent to do A. How can the logic of satisfaction avoid the conclusion that A ought to be brought about? If B cannot be performed G_1 might be declared an unjustified or an invalid goal on the ground that ought implies can. If B is undesirable because it leads to G_2 then this again should reflect on the desirability of G_1. It shows that G_1 and not G_2 conflict and since we are assuming that preventing G_2 is more important than securing G_1, G_1 is invalid and the desirability of A cannot be soundly deduced from it. The third case (where B is both possible and desirable but its occurrence depends on other people who will not perform it) should be assimilated to the first. G_1 is impossible *for our agent* unless the others do B. Hence G_1 is a valid goal for him only if they do B. (I am overlooking cases of uncertainty since they do not affect the principle.)

In all these cases the conclusion that A ought to be performed because it is necessary for a valid good G_1 is avoided by the logic of satisfaction only by introducing further principles to modify our conception of a valid goal in a way which makes it logically necessary that every action one ought to do is not only necessary for a valid goal but also sufficient for it. Suppose, for example, that the agent could at t_1 perform both A and B. At t_1 he should do A. Now assume that at t_2 it is no longer possible for him to do B. Should he now do A? It is still necessary but no longer part of a sufficient plan and it seems that we must again resort to the maxim 'ought implies can' to stop the conclusion that he should pointlessly perform A. This suggests that it is more accurate to say that at t_1 he should do A if and only if he will do B (though it is also true then that he should perform both A and B). But if so is not the logic of satisfaction based on the idea that one should do that which is both necessary and sufficient for a valid goal?

Let us turn to the second difficulty facing the logic of satisfaction. Imagine that I can achieve G_1 by either A or B, each action being sufficient by itself and neither being necessary. According to the logic of satisfaction it is neither the case that I ought to do A nor that I ought to do B since neither is necessary. It is true that, assuming I have no other way of realizing G_1, I ought to do A or to do B. I thus have a reason to do A because it is *sufficient* though not necessary for doing A or B. But this seems no more than a roundabout way of saying that I have reason to or ought to do that which is sufficient for the realization of a valid goal (G_1 in our case) regardless of whether it is necessary or not.

The logic of satisfactoriness seems free of such objections. It is true that where G_1 will be achieved by doing both A and B but not by either of them separately it follows, by the logic of satisfactoriness, that one ought to perform both A and B and it does not follow that one ought to perform each by itself. One cannot infer 'A ought to be done' from 'A and B ought to be done'. But this is just as it should be. There is no reason to perform A by itself. There is reason to do it only as part of a plan to do both A and B. The logic of satisfactoriness enables us to derive in such circumstances the conclusion that both actions should be performed and that either should be done if the other is going to be done and that is all we are entitled to infer in these circumstances.

The main allegedly counter-intuitive consequence of the logic of satisfactoriness is that it leads to massive overkill: blowing up a house is a way of killing a fly, therefore when killing a fly is justified we should blow up the house. But in so far as killing the fly is concerned there is indeed nothing wrong with blowing up the house. We regard this as absurd only because of the other bad consequences of the action. They make us prefer other methods of getting rid of the fly and in fact they are such as to justify putting up with the fly rather than blowing up the house if there is no other way of getting rid of it. The logic of satisfactoriness is superior to the logic of satisfaction, for practical inference is about how to achieve valid goals, not about taking necessary steps for their realization. But like any other practical logic it has to allow for conflicts of reasons. It is important to realize that problems of overkill affect the logic of satisfaction no less than that of satisfactoriness. One has only to imagine that blowing up the house is—as it may be—the only way of getting rid of a fly or some other minor nuisance.

4. CONFLICTS OF REASON AND NORMATIVE STATEMENTS

Much of the work in deontic logic, useful as it is, is of marginal interest to those concerned with practical reasoning because it is altogether oblivious to the problems presented by conflicts of reasons. It can be regarded as an exploration of the logic of conclusive reasons. On the assumption that we have a conclusive reason to follow a certain goal they explore what other things we have conclusive reason to do. But the main task of the theory of practical reason is to establish what one has (*prima facie*) reason for doing and how to resolve conflicts of reasons and establish that which one should do all things considered. The need to account for conflicts led to talk of *prima facie* reason or ought or duty which caused considerable confusion (see Searle). The basic idea is sound as is the idea of 'ought other things being equal'. Given that reasons can conflict, i.e. that we can have reasons to perform incompatible actions, the notion of a reason must be independent of that of reason's ultimate verdict as to what is to be done in a certain situation. Reason's ultimate verdict is often the result of adjudicating between conflicting considerations pointing to the desirability of different and mutually incompatible courses of action. What then is 'a reason'? It is just one such consideration. It is a fact which by itself is suffici- ent to necessitate a certain course of action, provided no other factors defeat it. Hence if we know no more, that fact is sufficient to determine what we should do. But it is merely a *prima facie* reason in that knowledge of other facts may revise that judgement. Other facts may constitute considera- tions defeating that reason and the practical necessitation of that action.

We sometimes say that a certain premiss P (say; 'John promised to do A') entails that John ought to do A and that another premiss Q (say, 'Doing A will insult John's father') entails that John should refrain from doing A. Since P and Q are consistent and can in fact both be true we are faced with the problem of how to account for the conflict without allowing contradictions to creep in. It is here that much of the work done in deontic logic fails us. It secures itself from contradiction by denying the reality of practical conflict. But several of the essays in the present volume show that this is not inevitable (see particularly Chisholm and also Williams, Harman, and Searle). As a first step we relativize the conclusion: relative to P John ought to do A. Relative to Q he ought to refrain from A. We do use such relativized locutions when we say 'morally you ought to ø' or 'as a teacher you ought not to ø'. Such relativized ought-statements seem to be logically equivalent to reason statements of the kind: 'p is a reason for x to ø' and the conclusion of the inferences examined may be expressed either by a reason or a relativized ought-statement.

It is sometimes the case that though a certain fact is a reason for an action, if we 'add' another fact the resulting more complex fact is not a reason for that action: the complex fact that John made a promise and was later released from it is not a reason for John to do as he promised, though its component fact that John promised is such a reason. When this is the case we could say that the added fact ('John was released from his promise') defeats the reason ('John promised'). There are several kinds of defeating facts. In particular some will be conflicting reasons, i.e. reasons for refraining from the act for which the defeated reason is a reason: 'Doing A will insult John's father' in the example above. Other defeating facts are not themselves reasons (at least not reasons for any incompatible action): John's release from his promise is no reason for him for not doing as he promised or indeed for any action at all. I shall call defeating conditions which are not conflicting reasons cancelling conditions. When one of two conflicting reasons defeats another and is not defeated by it it overrides the other.[5] A reason for a person to perform an action which is not overridden or cancelled is a conclusive reason for that person to perform that action.

We thus get the picture of an inference whose premises include a statement indicating a valid goal (in some loose interpretation of that expression) and are sufficient to entail that a certain action is sufficient to its realization and whose conclusion is a statement that those facts are a reason for that action. When the inference is of this character (assuming it contains no redundant premises) then its premises, if true, state an atomic reason. Sometimes it is impossible to realize all the goals (all parts of the goal) stated by the premises: p entails that p is a reason for ø-ing and q entails that q is a reason for not ø-ing. In that case if p and q entail that p and q is a reason to ø and do not entail that it is a reason for not ø-ing, p is the overriding reason. We need a second type of inference to establish which is the overriding reason (see further below).

We saw that the conclusions of such inferences are logically equivalent to relativized ought-statements: relative to p and q (or so far as p and q go) one ought to ø. Non-relativized or simple ought-statements state what there is an undefeated reason to do. In a way the same is true of relativized ought-statements (i.e. reason statements of the type p is a reason for . . .). The facts to which such a statement, if true, is relative include some which are reasons for the act (i.e. it ought to be done relative to them alone) and others which may include conflicting reasons.[6] The statement entails that the reasons for the act override whatever conflicting reasons are specified in the conditions to which it is relative. A non-relativized ought-statement states that there are reasons for the act which are not defeated.[7] Here we must tread carefully. Consider 'One ought not to deceive'. We use such sentences to make relativized statements, for example morally one ought not to deceive. But others assert it by a non-relativized statement: there is an undefeated reason not to deceive. Do they mean that there is a conclusive reason never to deceive? If so they will be contradicting themselves if they also assert in the same sense that one ought to keep one's promises. Sometimes one cannot do both, and, since a conclusive reason is one which is not cancelled and which overrides all conflicting reasons, it cannot be the case that there is always both a conclusive reason not to deceive and a conclusive reason to keep promises.

It seems that non-relativized ought-statements mean roughly the same as statements that there is a reason which is defeated only by weighty circumstances or more likely (since some promises, for example, are fairly trivial in the eyes of many who endorse such statements) that they are generally undefeated. I shall assume that non-relativized ought-statements mean that there is a reason which is not always defeated: that one ought to keep one's promises means that on every occasion on which one promised to perform an act there is a reason to perform it which is not defeated on all those occasions (though it may be defeated on some). Usually the making of such statements conversationally implies much more, for example, that the reason is of the same character on all those occasions, etc. If this analysis is correct then a non-relativized ought-statement concerning what is to be done on a single occasion entails that there is a conclusive reason for that action on that occasion. A general non-relativized ought-statement, on the other hand, usually means no more than that there is a reason for such action. If one assumes (an analogy with Chisholm) that no general reason can be always defeated and assumes that the ought-statement refers to the full scope of at least one reason then that is all the information it conveys. That the reason is not altogether defeated is logically true.

A non-relativized ought-statement, i.e. a statement of undefeated reasons, is entailed by a statement of a reason, i.e. a relativized ought-statement and a closure statement to the effect that there are not defeating facts of the relevant kind. It is debatable whether there are true non-relativized ought-statements respecting all practical questions. Often the reasons affecting a practical problem may all point to one solution or when conflicting may be comparable so that some override the others (even if we may not know which solution is supported by a conclusive reason). But many other problems are—it is alleged—affected by reasons which are incommensurable so that neither overrides the other and neither defeats the other. One can only state that, for example, moral reasons support one solution whereas prudential ones support another. In such cases it is alleged there is no possible over-all judgement.

It will not be possible to discuss this issue here. It is, however, pertinent to point out that this is the most extreme position on the very difficult problem of the reality and ultimate, i.e. non-reducible, nature of conflicting reasons. At the other extreme is the view that all conflicting reasons are merely different installations of one value (as in many versions of utilitarianism) and thus fully comparable. But there are a variety of views taking various middle positions, namely regarding reasons as generated by different sources, different and independent values or ideals which are nevertheless at least sometimes commensurable though not necessarily through any precisely formulable ranking or any other precise formula but by the exercise of a trained and experienced judgement: several essays, especially those of Williams and Wiggins, bear on these questions, but this volume could not contain a full discussion of it.

5. WHAT FACTS ARE REASONS?

There is no doubt that there are many more and different kinds of practical inferences. I have been trying merely to reflect various views on the nature of reasons and of some elementary kinds of practical inferences. But what kinds of facts are reasons? What kinds of statement can serve as premisses of valid practical inferences? In a sense every fact can be a reason. After all, do we not cite facts such as that it will rain or that the kettle is boiling or that the train is late as reasons? Every fact can be a reason since a reason is a fact stated by a premiss of a sound argument excluding redundant premisses or those stating conflicting reasons (they are reasons too but for a different action). Of the different reasons which make up one complete reason we may distinguish some as operative reasons to be contrasted with the rest which are merely auxiliary. The operative reasons state valid goals. The auxiliary reasons state facts pointing to a way of realizing the goal: (1) G is in my interest; (2) P is sufficient for G; (3) doing A will (or is likely to) bring about that P; it follows that relative to (1), (2), (3) I ought to do A. Here (1) states an operative reason. (2) and (3) state auxiliary reasons. (1) is itself a complete reason: it is a reason for bringing about that G. (2) and (3) are by themselves no reason for any action. This is the mark of operative reasons: they are minimal complete reasons, atomic reasons none of the components of which is a complete reason for any action.

When we ask what kinds of facts are reasons we mean what kinds of facts are operative reasons. The essays by Nagel, Grice, and Foot bear on the problem but it is impossible to do justice in this volume to the vast amount of writing on the subject. Similarly, I shall confine myself to two or three remarks. One fashionable position is to regard as operative reasons for an agent only the facts of his having certain goals, his so-called desires, wants, or pro-attitudes towards certain states of affairs. This view is clearly unacceptable if it means that a person is completely free to adopt any goals he likes. Though ultimately a person may knowingly choose a goal the realization of which involves his exposure to extremes of heat or cold, yet he cannot help having it as a goal, other things being equal, to avoid such extremes. Here the necessitation is contingent. But similarly, a person cannot help but adopt as a goal the avoidance of pain or hunger or suffering, other things being equal. This time the necessitation is logical depending on the nature of these concepts, although it is contingent that humans (though perhaps not that persons) are susceptible to such states.

The important fact is not that such goals are inescapable but that when we act or contemplate action to achieve them we regard not the fact that we have the goal but the fact that makes it an inevitable goal as the reason. In other words, it is that one is hungry or in pain which is the reason, not that one adopted a goal of curing the pain or the hunger. I do not wish to deny that the desire to cure or avoid pain or hunger is often mentioned as a reason. My only point is, first, that as was noted above (see p. 8), the desire to avoid pain or hunger is not something separate from the pain and the hunger which is contingently conjoint with them. It is part of what it is to be in pain or hungry. Secondly, this desire is not the having of a goal in the sense in which the philosophers whose views we are examining use this term. If anything it is the reason because of which (or because of his recognition of which) the person has this goal.

The first point above helps to explain the sense in which all reasons (at least all non-moral reasons) may be said to be of one kind, i.e. desire, and the sense in which there may be many of them around: interests, enjoyment, pleasure, hunger, pain, etc. The second point is more obscure and may be clarified by an analogy with moral considerations where the difference between the reason and the having of the goal is much more obvious. Let us assume that a person made it his goal to do his moral duty on a certain occasion. When asked for his reason he will cite his duty, not his desire to perform it. If a desire to do one's moral duty is not a logically necessary desire then to have it as one's reason for doing one's duty is an act of extreme self-indulgence. Normally to say of a person that he wants to do his (moral) duty is to say that his reason for acting is that this is his duty and not that his reason is that he wants to do his duty. Here we see clearly the distinction between the reason and the having of a goal, i.e. a desire in the broad sense, and I suggested that the same is true of pain or pleasure desires. In all these cases that a person has a goal is a true statement but it does not state a reason (though it entails that he has one).[8]

A person's reasons are of two kinds: primary and derivative. Primary reasons are the agent's interests, needs, and (spontaneous, felt) desires. The derivative ones are those reasons he has, independently of his spontaneous desires, to adopt certain goals because other people have primary reasons to pursue them. This distinction is sometimes identified with the distinction between prudential and moral reasons. But it has been often pointed out that one may have spontaneous desires which are not at all prudential or self-interested. They may be altruistic or encompass the pursuit of some moral or aesthetic ideals, etc. Besides, what spontaneous desires one has is partly constitutive of one's interests—a man whose life is built on the support of some moral causes has virtually identified his prudential interests with certain moral concerns. It may also be that derivative reasons are not all moral, but that is by the way.

The ultimate motivation for the view I have been criticizing, namely that only the fact that a person has goals is reason for him, is the belief that moral and other derivative considerations are reasons only if adopted by the agent and that at least his adoption or non-adoption of moral considerations is not necessitated by reason or nature. The truth or falsity of this claim is the fundamental question of moral epistemology.[9]

[1] This should not be taken to imply that there is no common core to human, animal, and inanimate action.

[2] Stating that reasons are facts does not imply that facts are an ultimate ontological kind. Merely that the analysis of the identity and ontological status of reasons follows that of facts.

[3] Note that I am using 'goals' broadly and 'desire' narrowly to mean a desire which is spontaneous or not based on reason. A desire is both an explanatory and a guiding reason. That a man has certain goals is an explanatory but not as such a guiding reason. The guidance is provided by those facts which justify the adoption of the goals (if any). The distinction between two kinds of reasons should not be interpreted too rigidly. Sometimes we say 'I should ø because I believe that p' (explanatory reason in a guiding context) and sometimes 'I ø-ed because p' (and not 'because I thought that p'—a guiding reason in an explanatory context). We sometimes refer to good or bad reasons to indicate the relation between explanatory and guiding reasons. A good explanatory reason is one to which a guiding reason corresponds. A bad explanatory reason is one to which no guiding reason corresponds. But these expressions have other uses too.

[4] To believe that a fact is a reason for a certain action is to believe in the soundness of an inference from statement of that fact to the conclusion that in so far as that fact is concerned one ought to perform that action.

[5] In my article below and in *Practical Reason and Norms* I have suggested that there are other kinds of defeating conditions but for present purposes I shall disregard them.

[6] Consider: 'The events of last night constitute a reason for A.' These events may include also a reason against A. The statement entails that they are overridden.

[7] Not that they could not be defeated. If different facts were to be the case they may well have defeated those reasons. But when the statement applies to future events it entails that no such facts will in fact exist. One important question is are there any absolute reasons, namely ones which cannot be defeated or at least which cannot be overridden?

[8] The having of the goal is not even the specific explanatory reason. It merely indicates that the action was intentional under that description. It is the pain or one's spontaneous felt desire for an ice-cream or one's belief that a certain act is morally valuable which are the explanatory reasons not the true fact that as a consequence of these one has certain goals.

[9] I am grateful to Rosalind Godlovitz, Peter Hacker, John Mackie, William Newton-Smith, and Mary Tyles for many helpful comments on a draft of this Introduction.

I

PRACTICAL REASON

R. EDGLEY

I t has been a common conviction among philosophers, and still is, that there is an important difference between practical matters and theoretical matters; between answers to such practical questions as 'What is to be done?' and answers to such theoretical questions as 'What is the case?' This distinction has sometimes been thought to be such that though reason can be theoretical there is an important sense in which it cannot be practical. One influential idea might be put vaguely like this: reason is non-substantive in such a way that, unlike theories, actions, being events, are not accessible to it. It is this idea, and the view of the practical-theoretical distinction it is based on, that I want to consider. A recent short way with this idea and its associated view of the practical-theoretical distinction has been to object that it neglects the pervasiveness of the notion of rules, and thus fails to appreciate that theoretical reasoning is governed by rules of inference which, being rules, are themselves practical. I shall take it that this objection, implying that theoretical matters are a species of practical matters, has been adequately criticized by, e.g., D. G. Brown in 'Some Misconceptions of Inference' (*Analysis*, June 1955). My argument will nevertheless have this in common with the objection, that it will contend that the view being considered exaggerates the practical-theoretical distinction and thus misconceives the idea of reason, practical and theoretical.

The way in which I have drawn the distinction between practical and theoretical matters above does not itself imply an exclusive dichotomy between them. For an answer to the practical question, 'So-and-so ought to be done,' could also be represented as an answer to the theoretical question: 'It is the case that so-and-so ought to be done.' That is, this way of drawing the distinction is compatible with the view that practical matters are a species of theoretical matters, and this would clearly not justify the conclusion that if reason is exclusively theoretical it cannot be practical. But there is a standard objection to this move: namely, that answers of the sort 'So-and-so ought to be done' are not answers to the question 'What is the case?' because they are not propositions and cannot be true or false; that is, they are not theoretical.

From *Mind*, 1965, pp. 174–86, 188–91. Reprinted by permission of Basil Blackwell, Publisher.

Some views about what these answers are, if not propositions, are unacceptable because their account of the way in which they are practical and non-theoretical fails to allow for the possibility of accepting an answer but not acting, or deciding to act, in accordance with it. The view that these answers express decisions or intentions is of this sort. The view that they express feelings or attitudes avoids this objection, but few emotivists have produced an argument where it is required, in support of the contention that these practical answers, contrary to appearances, are not propositions.

HUME'S ARGUMENT

Hume is an exception. In the chapters 'Of the influencing motives of the will' and 'Moral distinctions not deriv'd from reason' he brings forward considerations that are important and fundamental enough to provide a basis, if valid, for the account given by him and many other empiricists of the rest of morals, including the more conspicuous and popular doctrine that 'ought' cannot be deduced from 'is'. He argues that reason is essentially theoretical and that practical judgements cannot be also theoretical. 'Reason,' he says, 'is the discovery of truth and falsehood': it is therefore what he calls 'representative', i.e. its products represent or misrepresent other things and are not, like the things represented, 'original existences' in the world of realities. He does not, however, jump to the sceptical conclusion that reason cannot be practical by flatly asserting, contrary to appearances, that practical judgements cannot be propositions, i.e. 'representative'. He takes the more plausible step of treating practical judgements as practical in this sense, that they are connected with action in such a way that if such judgements could be conclusions of reason, so also could actions; and it follows that since actions, having no truth-value, because they are not 'representative' but 'original existences', cannot be conclusions of reason, neither can practical judgements. 'Reason,' says Hume, 'is perfectly inert.'

Hume's argument can be represented as follows. A reason, of whatever sort, is, as a reason, a fact or truth from which something follows. In being a reason, therefore, the fact or truth can be treated as the premiss of an argument, and what the reason is a reason for is what follows from it, the conclusion of the argument, something that must in consequence have a truth-value. It follows that there cannot be a reason for doing anything; for actions cannot be true or false, i.e. they cannot follow, in the appropriate sense, from any truth as a premiss, any consideration that might ordinarily be said to be the reason for the action. But anything that could be a reason for a practical judgement that something ought to be done would necessarily be a reason for doing that thing; and since there cannot be a reason for doing anything, there cannot be a reason for any practical judgement.

Most sceptical arguments about morals, or practical matters generally, entail similar sceptical conclusions about theoretical matters such as mathematics or science. Hume's argument appears to escape this objection, as it was no doubt meant to: his aim at this point is to display reason in practical matters as peculiarly vulnerable to scepticism. But this is an illusion. Typically, it does not succeed in discriminating between practical and other judgements. For it follows from his argument that there can be no reason for believing anything whatsoever, any more than for doing anything. Believing something cannot be true or false, any more than doing something can be true or false. What can be true or false is what is believed, a proposition, in Hume's language something 'representative'. But believing is a psychological state, in Hume's language 'an original existence': 'believe' is a psychological verb. Thus on Hume's argument believing something can be no more rationally justified than doing something.

Hume is in a certain way prepared for this attempted *reductio* by being prepared to accept it, though not of course as a *reductio*. His theory of belief anticipates the necessary distinction between two senses of 'belief', between what is believed and believing it, between what he calls 'the idea' and 'the manner of our conceiving' it, its force or vivacity; and in the Appendix to the *Treatise* he repeatedly refers to belief as a feeling or sentiment, and italicizes the doctrine that 'belief is nothing but a peculiar feeling, different from the simple conception'. Indeed, he does of course present arguments for a general scepticism with regard to reason, and in the chapter in which he does so he claims 'that belief is more properly an act of the sensitive, than of the cogitative part of our natures'. My point is that it is this general scepticism, and not simply scepticism about practical reason, that follows from his argument on morals, from his idea that reason is inert.

THE PRACTICAL-THEORETICAL DISTINCTION, AND REASON

What obscures these more drastic implications of Hume's argument and makes it appear to tell against practical but not theoretical reason is the possibility of drawing the practical-theoretical distinction in two ways. Hume contrasts actions with propositions; but another possibility is to contrast doing with believing. Hume's contrast excludes both doing and believing from what is theoretical. The distinction as I presented it in my first paragraph was analogous to Hume's: the practical question 'What is to be done?' was contrasted with 'What is the case?' and because actions and propositions are such an oddly assorted pair this formulation of the questions imparted to the practical-theoretical distinction an effect of maximum contrast. But doing and believing are rather less oddly assorted, and the question 'What is to be done?' contrasts less bewilderingly with the question 'What is to be believed?'

The fact is that if these philosophical terms 'practical reason' and 'theoretical reason' are translated into more familiar language we find that reference to what Hume would have called 'original existences' is a normal context of the concept of reason; and that the notion of practical reason signified by the common idea of, e.g., a reason for doing something contrasts with a notion of theoretical reason that is signified not by the idea of a reason for the truth of a proposition, as Hume's account would require, but by the idea of, e.g., a reason for believing something. In other words, the phrase 'a reason' occurs typically in harness with a psychological verb, indicating that what the reason justifies is the personal feature designated by the verb: as in 'a reason for believing, thinking, supposing, feeling convinced, maintaining, concluding that . . .'; and also 'reason to believe, think, suppose, feel convinced, maintain, conclude that . . .' Certainly propositions and theories, what a person says, asserts, claims, or believes, are among the sorts of things that can be justifiable, reasonable, rational, and logical. But words of this latter group can also describe personal features designated by psychological verbs: 'it's justifiable, reasonable, rational, logical to believe, think, suppose, feel convinced, conclude, say, assert, claim that . . .' In a certain way these latter locutions give the meaning of the former, but not vice versa: to say that what he believes is reasonable is to say that what he believes it is reasonable to believe. I mean that in the two statements 'What he believes is reasonable' and 'What he believes is true' the expression 'is reasonable' is not a predicate of the proposition he believes in the sense in which the expression 'is true' is a predicate of that proposition. If what he believes is, e.g., that Smith donates to charity, to say 'What he believes is true' is to imply that it is true that Smith donates to charity; but to say 'What he believes is reasonable' is not to imply that it is reasonable that Smith donates to charity. If it means anything at all, the statement 'It is reasonable that Smith donates to charity' means 'It is reasonable that Smith should donate to charity'; and on this interpretation what is said to be reasonable is not the original belief that Smith does donate to charity but the belief that he should, and with it Smith's action itself, his donating to charity, which in Hume's language is another 'original existence'. My point is not, of course, the point that it is sometimes reasonable to believe what turns out to be untrue. It is that the notion of reason insistently couples itself to notions designating 'original existences'.

The sorts of things that can be true or false, then, are in themselves not the sorts of things for which there can be reasons, not the sorts of things that can be reasonable or unreasonable. What then is the connection between something's being true and there being reasons for believing it? It might be thought that the fact that something is true is a sufficient reason for believing it. There is a familiar objection to this idea: namely, that to assert the truth of one's opinion is not to give a reason for holding it, since repeating one's views is no way of justifying them. However, the idea has its point, and what the point is can be seen by considering a different objection to it: though believing that p is believing that p is true, so also hoping or fearing that p is hoping or fearing that p is true, and these items are similar in this respect, that there can be a reason for hoping, fearing, or believing that p which is not evidence for the truth of p, and even when the evidence is that p is false; e.g. a reason for believing that you will succeed might be that believing this makes success more likely or that your confidence keeps your old mother happy. What has to be said, I think, is that these are not theoretical reasons. Reasons of this sort for believing something are connected with that borderline conceptual area where believing becomes something of a practical matter, i.e. where such concepts as trying to convince oneself that . . . and refusing to believe that . . . take over from contemplative concepts like seeing that . . . and realizing that. . . . A reason for believing that p is a theoretical reason when the truth or probable truth of p follows from the reason. This brings out what is acceptable in Hume's doctrine, and the concession qualifies my earlier advocacy of the ordinary notion of a reason for believing something as a familiar part of the philosophical concept of theoretical reason. It also reveals the relation between the two versions I proposed of a theoretical question: as a theoretical question, the question 'What is to be believed?' is limited by the question 'What is the case?' the limiting question implying a contemplative direction to one's interest.

HUME'S MISTAKE

It might be thought that this concession is enough to restore Hume's argument. For I have implied that the premiss of a reasonable argument is a reason for believing the conclusion. I have therefore in effect admitted that arguments are among the sort of things that can be reasonable or unreasonable, and arguments in this logician's sense are not 'original existences' like actions and psychological states. I am willing to admit these last two points; but this is not enough to save Hume's argument. For his case, with its principle that reason is perfectly inert, presupposes that arguments and their conclusions are the only sorts of things that can be reasonable or unreasonable. My contention is that if there can be reasonable arguments there can be reasons for believing things; and that what a reason is a reason for cannot be the conclusion of an argument. Thus the fact that an action, not being true or false, cannot be the conclusion of an argument (i.e. that reason cannot be practical in this sense) does not show that there cannot be reasons for doing things (i.e. that reason cannot be practical in this sense).

Hume's basic mistake is a misconception about the way in which practical reason, if there could be such a thing, would be practical, i.e. connected with action. The connection would be a connection between reason in practical judgements, i.e. judgements of conduct, and reason in conduct itself; so that a prior question is, in what way are practical judgements practical, i.e. connected with action? One thing that could be said would be this, that practical judgements are practical in the sense that they can be conformed to or contravened by actions that do not thereby confirm or falsify them. This being so, it might seem, as it apparently did to Hume, that if reason could be practical, so that practical judgements would be possible conclusions of reasonable arguments, actions conforming to them would also have to be possible conclusions of such arguments. But this is an error. If reason is practical it is so in this way, that for a practical judgement to be the conclusion of a reasonable argument implies not that an action could be a conclusion of that argument but that the premisses of the argument, in being reasons for believing the practical judgement, e.g. for believing that one ought to do a certain thing, are necessarily also reasons for acting in conformity with the judgement, i.e. for doing that thing.

REASONS AND CAUSES

Hume plainly construes the claim that reason can be practical to mean that reason can cause action; and his view that reason is inert is intended as a denial of this. Hume might therefore have thought of reasons for doing things as causes of action, and thus of reasons for believing things as causes of belief. I have in effect agreed with Hume that propositions cannot have causes, but I have argued that the sorts of things for which there can be reasons are not propositions but 'original existences', things that can have causes. I want now, then, to consider the question whether reason is substantive in this way, that a reason for something can be in some sense a cause of it. To do this I shall look at a fairly recent version of the view that reasons are not causes.

This view could be represented as follows. The question 'Why do you believe that p?' can be answered either by an explanation in terms of causes, which shows how the belief originated, or by an attempted justification in terms of reasons, which seeks to support the truth of the belief. These answers are logically independent: the history of chronology of a belief implies nothing about its justifiability or logic, and vice versa. Moreover every belief must have both a history and a logic; for they are concerned each with a different element of the belief. 'Believe' is a psychological verb and the history of a belief is therefore a psychological story; what is believed, a proposition, is a logical entity, having only logical properties and relations, which are non-temporal.

My argument that what a reason justifies is not what can have a truth-value, even when the reason is theoretical, but, e.g., believing something, which is psychological, might be thought to imply that reasons can be causes. For certainly things psychological have causes. But my argument does not imply that the reasons are the causes. There may, for a start, be a reason for believing something though no one in fact believes that thing. 'Believe' is a psychological verb, but in the phrase 'a reason for believing' it is not used to refer to a belief that somebody actually has. This is still true even when somebody has a reason for believing something: to say that somebody has a reason for believing something is not to imply that he or anybody else does in fact believe that thing. But what about the expression 'his reason for believing that p'? To specify somebody's reason for believing that p is of course to imply that he believes that p. But is that reason the cause of his believing that p? Whether it is or not, the view that reasons are not causes might still be protected by the observation that somebody's reason for believing that p is not necessarily a reason, it may be no reason at all, for believing that p; unparadoxically, a reason for believing that p is necessarily a good reason, whereas somebody's reason might be a bad one. In other words, unlike the notion of a cause of something, an explanation, the notion of a reason for believing something, a justification, is normative, not descriptive. This is the core of the view that reasons are not causes.

It might seem to follow, and some philosophers give the impression of thinking, that bad reasons are causes but good reasons are not. This idea gets its support from the following considerations. If Smith is asked 'Why do you believe that tomorrow will be fine?' he may answer this by saying 'My reason is that there was a red sky this evening.' Now it may be false that there was a red sky this evening, and even if it were true that fact may not be a good reason for believing that tomorrow will be fine. But if Smith's reply was honest, it must be true of *him* that he believes that there was a red sky this evening and also that if there is a red sky in the evening the following day will be fine. This is why, if Jones now asks me 'Why does Smith believe that tomorrow will be fine?' and I think that Smith's reason was a bad one, I can reply 'Because he thinks that there was a red sky this evening and also that if there is a red sky in the evening the following day will be fine.' This reply, unlike Smith's, does not attempt to justify Smith's belief, it simply explains it; it does not give reasons for believing that tomorrow will be fine, it says what makes Smith believe this. But it does not follow from all this that bad reasons, being no reasons at all, are causes in some sense in which good reasons cannot be causes. For clearly, my explanation of Smith's belief would have been equally true even if his reason had been a good one: it is simply that this explanation is logically independent of any assessment of his reason as bad or good.

What follows is that Smith's reason, good or bad, is not a cause. His reason is that something is the case, something that has a truth-value, a proposition or putative fact, e.g. that there was a red sky this evening. But this proposition could not have been his reason unless he had believed it, whether it was true or false. When somebody believes something, and for the reason that something is the case, what explains his belief is not that something is the case, not the reason, good or bad, but his believing that it is the case; e.g. Smith believes that tomorrow will be fine because he believes that there was a red sky this evening. Of course, Smith might have answered my question 'Why do you believe that tomorrow will be fine?' by saying 'My reason is that there was, I believe, a red sky this evening.' But this use of the psychological verb 'believe' is parenthetical. To put the matter summarily: a reason for believing that p is the fact that q if the truth or probable truth of p follows from q; and somebody's reason for believing that p is the fact that q if that person believes that p because he believes that q and also that p follows from q.

My claim that these reasons are not causes, however, gives no support to another part of the view under consideration, namely that because reasons are not causes the question 'Why do you believe that p?' must always have two logically independent answers, one concerned with justification and logical matters, the other concerned with psychological origins. The attempted justification 'My reason for believing that tomorrow will be fine is that there was a red sky this evening', even if the reason is a good one, is not logically independent of the explanation 'I believe that tomorrow will be fine because I believe that there was a red sky this evening and also that if there is a red sky in the evening the following day will be fine.' Roughly, the explanation follows from the attempted justification by making the (explicit or implicit) parenthetical verbs descriptive and non-parenthetical. This view, unlike the other, makes it easy to see how our beliefs can originate from a consideration of the reasons that support them, e.g. the evidence for them. It is also compatible with the possibility that though somebody might believe something for a reason, so that his belief can be explained in the manner indicated, his belief nevertheless originated in a non-rational way. One of the confusions of the view under consideration is the idea that explanations are necessarily in terms of origins. But the question 'What led you here?' is not the same as the question 'What keeps you here?' You may have come to the meeting in the hope of hearing a good paper; you may remain out of politeness. Similarly, the question 'How did you first come to believe that p?' is not the same as the question 'Why do you continue to believe that p?' or 'Why do you now believe that p?'. I may have believed that the earth is round ever since I was six years old, and perhaps what made me believe it at first was that I was told it by a schoolteacher who, I later realized, was not a reliable source of information. Though I may never have ceased to believe it, what made me start to believe it may not be what makes me continue to believe it, for before I lost faith in my schoolteacher I may have become acquainted with the evidence, considered and rejected the arguments of the Flat Earth Society, etc. Thus if I am now asked 'Why do you believe that the earth is round?' and I give my reasons, I am also, by implication, giving a descriptive explanation of my belief, though its origins may have been quite different.

What I have argued shows that some familiar philosophical dichotomies, e.g. between reasons and causes, logic and psychology, etc., related as they are to a distinction between 'original existences' and what is 'representative', or between reality and language, are too crude because they neglect the complex position of the concept of belief, and also, perhaps, possible distinctions between logic and reason. What is believed, a proposition, has a logic; believing it is something psychological and has causes; but believing it is also what there can be reasons for, and a person's reasons for believing something connect closely with the causes of his belief.

REASON AND PASSION

Many of these considerations apply, with obvious modifications, to the notion of a reason for doing something. It follows that the question 'Can reason be practical?' has two senses: 'Can there be reasons for doing things?' and 'Can reason cause action?' We can deny that reason can cause action without committing ourselves, like Hume, to denying that there can be reasons for doing things. We cannot, of course, deny that there can be reasons for doing things without denying that reason can cause action; and perhaps it would be charitable to regard Hume's argument not as confusing these two matters but as passing legitimately, though not explicitly, from one to the other.

Whatever the cause, having concluded that reason cannot cause action he argues that a passion is necessary to motivate conduct. It is evident from what I have said that this cannot follow simply on the principle that causes and effects must be 'original existences' and cannot be propositions; for beliefs also are 'original existences', and on that principle alone would be as qualified as passions to cause action. Here too, then, Hume's assumption is that the proper contrast with actions in the practical-theoretical distinction is propositions; and passions, as 'original existences', connect with what is practical rather than with what is theoretical.

One of my aims is to show that the practical-theoretical distinction has been exaggerated by being represented as a distinction between actions and propositions, and that actions and beliefs present a less formidable contrast. I can further this aim, and strengthen the point that beliefs are 'original existences', by indicating briefly some of the extensive possibilities of connections between passions and beliefs of all logical kinds, whether practical or not, i.e. between the passions and what is theoretical. Thus: as with doing something I can want to believe something, I can believe it passionately, I can feel inclined to believe it, I can believe it because I am angry, jealous, depressed, or excited; like conduct, beliefs can be partial or impartial; and though fools may be different from knaves, it does not follow that a person may not, e.g., believe inconsistent things because he is selfish, vain, inconsiderate, cowardly, proud, or kindhearted. It may, then, appear odd that the conflict between reason and passion has figured so much more prominently, and that the possible necessity of passions as causes has been considered so much more seriously, in the philosophy of practical matters than in the philosophy of theoretical matters. If there are grounds, as I think there are, for regarding the passions as more important in the practical than in the theoretical field, one of them at least is the opposite of what some philosophers seem to have thought; it is that to do something because one wants to is not to be the slave of passion but to do it of one's own free will, necessarily for some reason, and often for a good reason. This is certainly not true of believing something. But this is not because beliefs, being propositions, have their being exclusively in the operational area of the reason or intellect, and can be appraised and accounted for only in terms of logic, as true or false, consistent or inconsistent, etc.; a man's moods, feelings, attitudes, character, and moral qualities can have their bearing on them.

LOGICAL PROPERTIES AND RATIONAL PRINCIPLES

I want now to consider whether the practical-theoretical contrast can be diminished from the other side: if beliefs can be appraised and accounted for in moral terms, like actions, can actions be appraised, like beliefs, in terms of logic? As Hume said, actions cannot be true or false, like propositions; but can they not, like beliefs and propositions, be consistent or inconsistent?

If p is true and the truth or probable truth of q follows from p, then the fact that p is a good reason for believing that q. This hypothetical indicates something of the relation between logic and reason: it shows how, to put the point figuratively, truths about logical properties are reflected normatively as requirements imposed upon us by reason. For the antecedent of the hypothetical is concerned entirely with logical matters, propositions and their properties, truth and implication; whereas the consequent is in some sense normative, a principle that can be conformed to or contravened by the psychological states of people, i.e. by their believing something. It is in this way that logical truths are also normative 'laws of thought'. And it is for this reason that some words designating the logical properties of propositions are also words of appraisal applicable to people and their psychological states: e.g. it is inconsistent to believe inconsistent things, and the person who believes inconsistent things can himself be appraised as inconsistent; and inconsistency is contrary to reason.

Principles of logic (and the range of the word 'principles' aptly bears this out) thus have a dual function, and the notion that, e.g., analytic principles are non-substantive can be misunderstood. As truths about the way things are they give us no information: they cannot be falsified, i.e. contravened. As norms about the way things ought to be they cannot be falsified either; but they can be contravened, by our beliefs, statements, and arguments about the way things are. Though I cannot logically, I logically can, believe that p and that p implies q without also believing that q: this is not possible if I am to be logical, but it is logically possible. And if it is psychologically impossible, this is not because the *modus ponens* principle is analytic but because its truth is obvious.

UNIVERSALITY

However plain these things may seem when we are concentrating on theoretical matters, in the area of practical reason, such is the strength of our philosophical prejudices about the distinction between theory and practice, they are easily forgotten. This is evident from some familiar views about the status of what is generally regarded as the most important analytic principle in this area, the principle of universality. This principle may be formulated as follows: if a particular person ought to do a certain thing in a particular situation, he and anyone else in a situation of the same relevant kind ought to do the same kind of thing.

Some philosophers have questioned the importance of this principle on the ground that being analytic and logically necessary it cannot be an object-level principle about actions, a rule of conduct; it must be a second-level rule, e.g. about language. It is therefore formal and non-substantive, and thus not a practical principle; to be practical a principle must be substantive, capable of being conformed to or contravened by what people do. It is a familiar idea that analytic principles are not action-guiding.

Some odd suggestions are sometimes associated with this view, e.g. that since the principle of universality is a rule of language about the word 'ought', someone who appears to contravene the principle must be using the word 'ought' in an unusual way, with an unusual meaning. If this were the case, analytic principles would be non-substantive in the strong sense that they not only could not be falsified but also could not be contravened: no one could ever say or believe inconsistent things. It would be logically impossible, not simply illogical, to believe logically impossible things. This is one way of making people less illogical and irrational, but not, one feels, the most satisfactory way.

What then is the status of the principle of universality? I have argued that the view that it is non-substantive in the sense that it cannot be contravened by our moral beliefs, judgements, principles, and codes is untenable. The question I want to raise now is whether it can be substantive in what might be thought to be a stronger sense, i.e. whether it can be contravened not only by beliefs but also by actions. If the principle is analytic, is it the case that analytic principles are non-substantive in the sense that they are not action-guiding? Can analytic reason be practical?

One thing to notice is that the principle is a principle of theoretical reason in a wider sense than the one already indicated: as with other matters we have considered, it does not discriminate between practical and theoretical matters. Once it is realized that the word 'ought' is not a peculiarly moral word, it is tempting to suppose that universality is a requirement of practical reason in general, moral and otherwise; and certainly it can be formulated as a principle about reasons for doing things. Thus: if the fact that p is a reason for doing some particular thing, any fact of the same relevant kind is equally a reason for doing the same kind of thing. Since a reason for doing something is necessarily a reason for believing that that thing ought to be done, or would be a good thing to do, it follows that the principle is theoretical in this sense, that it holds of reasons for believing that something ought to be done. But it is theoretical in a still wider sense; and, indeed, it applies even more widely than this, wherever the notion of reason itself is applicable: for universality is a requirement of reason in general, not simply of practical reason. It could be said to hold in virtue of the meaning of the word 'reason'. Thus, if the fact that p is a reason for something, any fact of the same relevant kind is equally a reason for the same kind of thing. This is true, whether the reason is a reason for doing something, believing something, hoping, fearing, or wanting something, or what not. In particular, when the reason is a reason for believing or thinking that q, the principle holds whatever the logical status of the proposition q, without discrimination. Represented in this way, the principle of universality is the requirement that every inference must have a principle.

It does not follow that the principle of universality is not closely connected with the meaning of the word *ought*. For this word, like many others selected for special consideration by moral philosophers, is not only not peculiar to moral matters, it is not peculiar to practical matters in general. Consider this variant on an old joke: 'The regiment ought to move off at 8 p.m. The moon ought to rise at 9 p.m.' Though not without qualification, the word 'ought' signifies the pressure of reason in general, theoretical as well as practical.

A *prima facie* case for the contention that though analytic the principle of universality can be contravened by actions is this: actions can be consistent or inconsistent, and inconsistency is the contravention of an analytic principle. But it might be objected: this inconsistency cannot be of the same kind as inconsistency of beliefs. For though believing something cannot be true or false, what is believed can be: and it is because propositions can be inconsistent that beliefs can be inconsistent. It is this relationship of a belief to its object that makes inconsistency logically possible, i.e. it is this that makes it logically possible to believe what is logically impossible. Actions cannot have this kind of relation to propositions or to anything else: there is a difference between believing something and what is believed, but no comparable difference between doing something and what is done. It is not logically possible to do what is logically impossible, i.e. it is not logically possible for actions to be inconsistent. Thus, it might be claimed, though Hume's argument is faulty in detail, it can be modified to allow for believing and doing to represent the theoretical-practical distinction and still prove his point; for the possibility of rational appraisal of belief is derivative from the logical properties of what is believed, i.e. propositions. In Hume's language, believing is 'representative' in a way in which doing is not, and it is because of this that believing things is, and doing things is not, subject to rational appraisal as, e.g., consistent or inconsistent.

However, what Hume meant by 'representative' is not clear. He held, e.g., that passions are like actions in being 'original existences' and not 'representative'; but passions are like beliefs in this respect, that as a distinction can be drawn between believing and what is believed, i.e. between a belief and its object, so also a distinction can be drawn between a passion and its object, e.g. between wanting something and what is wanted, between approval and what is approved of, between fear and what one is afraid of, between hope and what one hopes for. It may be that contrasting propositions with passions is as inept as contrasting propositions with actions. It may be less inept to contrast believing something with wanting or approving of something, and what is believed with what is wanted or approved of. Things approved of are not representative in the sense of being true or false, but logical properties are not confined to things that can be true or false. If arsenic is by definition a poison it would be inconsistent, but logically possible, to approve of giving a patient arsenic but not of giving him poison. In approving of one I am 'logically committed' to approving of the other, i.e. I ought in consistency, that is, to be logical, to approve of both or of neither.

But because no comparable distinction can be drawn between an action and its object, i.e. between doing something and what is done, actions clearly cannot be inconsistent in this way. And it might be thought that if we ask the question 'Of what sort must an "original existence" be for it to be a possible subject of logical appraisal?' the answer is 'The sort of thing that has an object in this sense, so that it can be logically possible to . . . what is logically impossible.' Thus it is logically possible, though inconsistent, to *approve* of giving a patient arsenic but not of giving him poison; and logically possible, though inconsistent, to *decide* to give him arsenic but not to give him poison; but it is clearly not logically possible to *give* him arsenic and not give him poison. However, this is logically impossible because such a thing would not only contravene the analytic principle that arsenic is poison, it would falsify it. The question is whether the principle of universality, though analytic, is a principle of a different sort, namely one that actions could contravene without falsifying. What is proved by the impossibility of giving a patient arsenic without giving him poison is that an action logically cannot be inconsistent with itself, as a belief can be inconsistent with itself. But when a person's belief is inconsistent with itself, or self-contradictory, the inconsistency in what is believed can always be analysed into a conjunction of two propositions, one inconsistent with the other; and this conjunction of two propositions can be represented as a temporal conjunction of two beliefs, i.e. as two beliefs held at the same time, one inconsistent with the other. Clearly, a person's actions cannot be inconsistent in exactly this way, since he cannot do inconsistent things at one and the same time. But no such impossibility is required to contravene the principle of universality. This principle compares two different situations of the same relevant kind, and says that if a particular thing is what ought to be done in one, something of the same relevant kind is what ought to be done in the other. It is logically possible for someone to do different things on occasions of the same relevant kind, and this at least would not falsify the principle of universality.

II

ON PRACTICAL REASONING

G. E. M. ANSCOMBE

'PRACTICAL reasoning', or 'practical syllogism', which means the same thing, was one of Aristotle's best discoveries. But its true character has been obscured. It is commonly supposed to be ordinary reasoning leading to such a conclusion as: 'I ought to do such-and-such.' By 'ordinary reasoning' I mean the only reasoning ordinarily considered in philosophy: reasoning towards the truth of a proposition, which is supposedly shown to be true by the premisses. Thus: 'Everyone with money ought to give to a beggar who asks him; this man asking me for money is a beggar; I have money; so I ought to give this man some.' Here the conclusion is entailed by the premisses. So it is proved by them, unless they are doubtful. Perhaps such premisses never can be certain.

Contemplating the accounts given by modern commentators, one might easily wonder why no one has ever pointed out the mince pie syllogism: the peculiarity of this would be that it was about mince pies, and an example would be 'All mince pies have suet in them—this is a mince pie—therefore etc.' Certainly ethics is of importance to human beings in a way that mince pies are not; but such importance cannot justify us in speaking of a special sort of reasoning. Everyone takes the practical syllogism to be a proof—granted the premisses and saving their inevitable uncertainty or doubtfulness in application—of a conclusion. This is so whether Aristotle's own example has been taken:

> Dry food suits any human
> Such-and-such food is dry
> I am human
> This is a bit of such-and-such food

yielding the conclusion

> This food suits me

or whether, adopting a style of treatment suggested by some modern authors, the first premiss is given in an imperative form. We may note that

From *Intention* (Basil Blackwell, 1957), pp. 57–63, 65, 70–7, 78–9. Reprinted by permission of the publishers.

authors always use the term 'major' and 'minor' of the premisses of practical syllogism: having regard to the definition of these terms, we can see that they have no application to Aristotle's practical syllogism, though they could be adapted to the imperative form if we assimilate 'Do!' to the predicate of a proposition. Consider the following:

Do everything conducive to not having a car crash.
Such-and-such will be conducive to not having a car crash.
Ergo: Do such-and-such.

Both this and the Aristotelian example given before would necessitate the conclusion. Someone professing to accept the opening order and the factual premiss in the imperative example must accept its conclusion, just as someone believing the premisses in the categorical example must accept its conclusion. The first example has the advantage of actually being Aristotle's, apart from the conclusion, but the disadvantage, so far as its being practical is concerned, that though the conclusion is necessitated, nothing seems to follow about doing anything. Many authors have pointed this out, but have usually put it rather vaguely, saying, e.g., that the reasoning does not compel any action; but Aristotle appears to envisage an action as following. The vague accounts that I have mentioned can be given a quite sharp sense. It is obvious that I can decide, on general grounds about colouring and so on, that a certain dress in a shop window would suit me very well, without its following that I can be accused of some kind of inconsistency with what I have decided if I do not thereupon go in and buy it; even if there are no impediments, such as shortage of cash, at all. The syllogism in the imperative form avoids this disadvantage; someone professing to accept the premisses will be inconsistent if, when nothing intervenes to prevent him, he fails to act on the particular order with which the argument ends. But this syllogism suffers from the disadvantage that the first, universal, premiss is an insane one,[1] which no one could accept for a moment if he thought out what it meant. For there are usually a hundred different and incompatible things conducive to not having a car crash; such as, perhaps, driving into the private gateway immediately on your left and abandoning your car there, and driving into the private gateway immediately on your right and abandoning the car there.

The cause of this mischief, though it is not entirely his fault, is Aristotle himself. For he himself distinguished reasoning by subject matter as scientific and practical. 'Demonstrative' reasoning was scientific and concerned what is invariable. As if one could not reason about some particular non-necessary thing that was going to happen except with a view to action! 'John will drive from Chartres to Paris at an average of sixty m.p.h., he starts around five, Paris is sixty miles from Chartres, therefore he will arrive at about six'—this will not be what Aristotle calls a 'demonstration' because, if we ask the question what John will do, that is certainly capable of turning out one way or another. But for all that the reasoning is an argument that something is true. It is not practical reasoning: it has not the form of a calculation what to do, though like any other piece of 'theoretical' argument it could play a part in such a calculation. Thus we may accept from Aristotle that practical reasoning is essentially concerned with 'what is capable of turning out variously', without thinking that this subject matter is enough to make reasoning about it practical. There is a difference of form between reasoning leading to action and reasoning for the truth of a conclusion. Aristotle however liked to stress the similarity between the kinds of reasoning, saying[2] that what 'happens' is the same in both. There are indeed three types of case. There is the theoretical syllogism and also the idle practical syllogism[3] which is just a classroom example. In both of these the conclusion is 'said' by the mind which infers it. And there is the practical syllogism proper. Here the conclusion is an action whose point is shewn by the premises, which are now, so to speak, on active service. When Aristotle says that what happens is the same, he seems to mean that it is always the same psychical mechanism by which a conclusion is elicited. He also displays practical syllogisms so as to make them look as parallel as possible to proof syllogisms.

Let us imitate one of his classroom examples, giving it a plausible modern content:

Vitamin X is good for all men over 60
Pigs' tripes are full of vitamin X
I'm a man over 60
Here's some pigs' tripes.

Aristotle seldom states the conclusion of a practical syllogism, and sometimes speaks of it as an action; so we may suppose the man who has been thinking on these lines to take some of the dish that he sees. But there is of course no objection to inventing a form of words by which he *accompanies* this action, which we may call the conclusion in a verbalized form. We may render it as:

(*a*) So I'll have some
or (*b*) So I'd better have some
or (*c*) So it'd be a good thing for me to have some.

Now certainly no one could be tempted to think of (*a*) as a proposition entailed by the premises. But neither are (*b*) and (*c*), though at first sight they look roughly similar to the kind of conclusion which commentators usually give:

What's here is good for me.

But of course in the sense in which this is entailed by the premisses as they intend it to be, this only means: 'What's here is a type of food that is good for me,' which is far from meaning that I'd better have some. Now the reason why we cannot extract 'I'd better have some' from the premisses is not at all that we *could not* in any case construct premisses which, if assented to, yield this conclusion. For we could, easily. We only need to alter the universal premiss slightly, to:

It is necessary for all men over 60 to eat any food containing Vitamin X that they ever come across

which, with the other premisses would entail the conclusion in the form 'I'd better have some' quite satisfactorily. The only objection is that the premiss is insane, as would have been the corresponding variant on Aristotle's universal premiss:

Every human being needs to eat all the dry food he ever sees.

In short the 'universality' of Aristotle's universal premiss is in the wrong place to yield the conclusion by way of entailment at all.

Only negative general premisses can hope to avoid insanity of this sort. Now these, even if accepted as practical premisses, don't lead to any particular actions (at least, not by themselves or by any formal process) but only to not doing certain things. But what Aristotle meant by practical reasoning certainly included reasoning that led to action, not to omissions. Now a man who goes through such considerations as those about Vitamin X and ends up by taking some of the dish that he sees, saying, e.g., 'So I suppose I'd better have some', can certainly be said to be *reasoning*; on the other hand, it is clear that this is another type of reasoning than reasoning from premisses to a conclusion which they prove. And I think it is even safe to say that (except in, say, doing arithmetic or dancing, i.e. in skills or arts—what Aristotle would call τέχναι) there is no general positive rule of the form 'Always do X' or 'Doing X is always good—required—convenient—, a useful—suitable—etc.—thing' (where the 'X' describes some specific action) which a sane person will accept as a starting-point for reasoning out what to do in a particular case. (Unless, indeed, it is hemmed about by saving clauses like 'if the circumstances don't include something that would make it foolish'.) Thus though general considerations, like 'Vitamin C is good for people' (which of course is a matter of medical fact) may easily occur to someone who is considering what he is going to eat, considerations of the form 'Doing such-and-such quite specific things in such-and-such circumstances is always suitable' are never, if taken strictly, possible at all for a sane person, outside special arts.

But, we may ask, even if we want to follow Aristotle, need we confine the term 'practical reasoning' to pieces of practical reasoning which look very parallel to proof-reasonings? For 'I want a Jersey cow; there are good ones in the Hereford market, so I'll go there' would seem to be practical reasoning too. Or 'If I invite both X and Y, there'll be a strained atmosphere in view of what X has recently said about Y and how Y feels about it—so I'll just ask X.' Or again 'So-and-so was very pleasant last time we met, so I'll pay him a visit.' Now Aristotle would have remarked that it is mere 'desire' in a special sense ($\dot{\epsilon}\pi\iota\theta\nu\mu\dot{\iota}\alpha$) that prompts the action in the last case; the mark of this is that the premiss refers to something merely as pleasant. The point that he is making here is, however, rather alien to us, since we do not make much distinction between one sort of desire and another, and we should say: isn't it desire in some sense—i.e. wanting—that prompts the action in all the cases? And 'all cases', of course, includes ones that have as large an apparatus as one pleases of generalizations about morals, or medicine, or cookery, or methods of study, or methods of getting votes or securing law and order, together with the identification of cases.

This is so, of course, and is a point insisted on by Aristotle himself: the $\dot{\alpha}\rho\chi\dot{\eta}$ (starting-point) is $\tau\dot{o}$ $\dot{o}\rho\epsilon\kappa\tau\dot{o}\nu$ (the thing wanted). For example, the fact that current school geometry text books all give a faulty proof of the theorem about the base angles of an isosceles triangle will not lead a teacher to discard them or to make a point of disabusing his class, if he does not want to impart *only* correct geometrical proofs. He will say that it doesn't matter; the Euclidean proof, Pons Asinorum, is too difficult; in any case Euclid starts (he may say) with the unjustifed assumption that a certain pair of circles will cut; and are you going to suggest worries about the axiom of parallels to school children and try to teach them non-Euclidean geometry? and much else of the sort. All this obscures the essential point, which is that, rightly or wrongly, he does not want to impart *only* correct geometrical reasoning. It then becomes relevant to ask what he does want to do. Let us suppose that he is reasonably frank and says he wants to keep his job, occupy his time in 'teaching', and earn his salary.

But it is misleading to put 'I want' into a premiss if we are giving a formal account of practical reasoning. To understand this, we need to realize that not everything that I have described as coming in the range of 'reasons for acting' can have a place as a premiss in a practical syllogism.

E.g. 'He killed my father, so I shall kill him' is not a form of reasoning at all; nor is 'I admire him so much, I shall sign the petition he is sponsoring.' The difference is that there is no calculation in these. The conjunction 'so' is not necessarily a mark of calculation.

It may be said: 'if "he was very pleasant : . . so I shall pay him a visit" can be called reasoning, why not "I admire . . . so I shall sign"?' The answer is that the former is not a piece of reasoning or calculation either, if what it suggests is, e.g., that I am making a return for his pleasantness, have this reason for the kind act of paying a visit; but if the suggestion is: 'So it will probably be pleasant to see him again, so I shall pay him a visit,' then it is; and of course it is only under this aspect that 'desire' in the restricted sense ($\varepsilon\pi\iota\theta\upsilon\mu\iota\alpha$) is said to prompt the action. And similarly: 'I admire . . . and the best way to express this will be to sign, so I shall sign . . .' is a case of calculating, and if that is the thought we can once again speak of practical reasoning. Of course 'he was pleasant . . . How can I make a return? . . . I will visit him' can occur and so this case assume the form of a calculation. Here a return, *under that description*, becomes the object of wish; but what is the meaning of 'a return'? The primitive, spontaneous, form lies behind the formation of the concept 'return', which *once formed* can be made the object of wish; but in the primitive, spontaneous, case the form is 'he was nice to me—I will visit him'; and similarly with revenge, though once the concept 'revenge' exists it can be made the object, as with Hamlet. We must always remember that an object is not what what is aimed at *is*; the description *under which* it is aimed at is that under which it is *called* the object.

Then 'I want this, so I'll do it' is not a form of practical reasoning either. The role of 'wanting' in the practical syllogism is quite different from that of a premiss. It is that whatever is described in the proposition that is the starting-point of the argument must be wanted in order for the reasoning to lead to any action. Then the form 'I want a Jersey cow, they have good ones in the Hereford market, so I'll go there' was formally misconceived: the practical reasoning should just be given in the form 'They have Jersey cows in the Hereford market, so I'll go there.' Similarly 'Dry food' (whatever Aristotle meant by that; it sounds an odd dietary theory) 'suits anyone etc., so I'll have some of this' is a piece of reasoning which will go on only in someone who wants to eat suitable food. That is to say, it will at any rate terminate in the conclusion only for someone who wants to eat suitable food. Someone free of any such wish might indeed calculate or reason up to the conclusion, but leave that out, or change it to—'So eating this would be a good idea (if I wanted to eat suitable food).' Roughly speaking we can say that the reasoning leading up to an action would enable us to infer what the man so reasoning wanted—e.g. that he probably wanted to see, buy, or steal a Jersey cow.

There is a contrast between the two propositions 'They have some good Jerseys in the Hereford market' and 'Dry food suits any man', supposing that they both occur as practical premisses, i.e. that the man who uses the one sets off for Hereford, and the man who uses the other takes a bit of the dish that he sees, believing it to be a bit of some kind of dry food. In the first case, there can arise the question 'What do you want a Jersey cow for?' but the question 'What do you want suitable food for?' means, if anything, 'Do give up thinking about food as suitable or otherwise'—as said, e.g., by someone who prefers people merely to enjoy their food or considers the man hypochondriac.

Are there any further restrictions, besides the ones we have mentioned, on possible objects of wanting, when the idea of the thing that is (in fact) wanted is expressed in the first premiss of a practical syllogism? There are, we may say, no further absolute restrictions, but there are some relative ones. For, as I have remarked, if 'There are good Jerseys in the Hereford market' is used as a premiss, then it can be asked 'What do you want a Jersey for?' Let the answer be: 'A Jersey would suit my needs well'—and it is in fact this or a form of this that Aristotle would accept as first premiss: the reasoning in his chosen form would run: '(1) Any farmer with a farm like mine could do with a cow of such-and-such qualities (2) e.g. a Jersey.' Now there is no room for a *further* question 'What do you want "what you could do with" for?' That is to say, the premiss now given has characterized the thing wanted as desirable.

But is not anything wantable, or at least any perhaps attainable thing? It will be instructive to anyone who thinks this to approach someone and say: 'I want a saucer of mud' or 'I want a twig of mountain ash.' He is likely to be asked what for; to which let him reply that he does not want it *for* anything, he just wants it. It is likely that the other will then perceive that a philosophical example is all that is in question, and will pursue the matter no further; but supposing that he did not realize this, and yet did not dismiss our man as a dull babbling loon, would he not try to find out in what aspect the object desired is desirable? Does it serve as a symbol? Is there something delightful about it? Does the man want to have something to call his own, and no more? Now if the reply is: 'Philosophers have taught that anything can be an object of desire; so there can be no need for me to characterize these objects as somehow desirable; it merely so happens that I want them,' then this is fair nonsense.

But cannot a man *try to get* anything gettable? He can certainly go after objects that he sees, fetch them, and keep them near him; perhaps he then vigorously protects them from removal. But then, this is already beginning to make sense: these are his possessions, he wanted to own them; he may be idiotic, but his 'wanting' is recognizable as such. So *he* can say perhaps 'I want a saucer of mud.' Now saying 'I want' is often a way to be given something; so when out of the blue someone says 'I want a pin' and denies wanting it *for* anything, let us suppose we give it him and see what he does with it. He takes it, let us say, he smiles and says 'Thank you. My want is gratified'—but what does he do with the pin? If he puts it down and forgets about it, in what sense was it true to say that he wanted a pin? He used these words, the effect of which was that he was given one; but what reason have we to say he wanted a pin rather than: to see if we would take the trouble to give him one?

It is not a mere matter of what is usual in the way of wants and what is not. It is not at all clear what it meant to say: this man simply wanted a pin. Of course, if he is careful always to carry the pin in his hand thereafter, or at least for a time, we may perhaps say: it seems he really wanted that pin. Then, perhaps, the answer to 'What do you want it for?' may be 'to carry it about with me', as a man may want a stick. But here again there is further characterization: 'I don't feel comfortable without it; it is pleasant to have one' and so on. To say 'I *merely* want this' without any characterization is to deprive the word of sense; if he insists on 'having' the thing, we want to know what 'having' amounts to.

Then Aristotle's terms: 'should', 'suits', 'pleasant' are characterizations of what they apply to as desirable. Such a characterization has the consequence that no further questions 'what for?' relating to the characteristic so occurring in a premiss require any answer. We have seen that at least sometimes a description of an object wanted is subject to such a question, i.e. such a question about the description does require an answer. This, then, will by why Aristotle's forms of the practical syllogism give us such first premisses.

Aristotle gives us a further practical syllogism when he remarks 'a man may know that light meats are digestible and wholesome but not know which meats are light'.[4] Here the description 'digestible and wholesome' might seem not to be a pure desirability-characterization. But since wholesome means good for the health, and health is by definition the *good* general state of the physical organism, the characterization is adequate for a proper first premiss and does not need to be eked out by, say, 'health is a human good' (a tautology).

Let us now consider an actual case where a desirability-characterization gives a final answer to the series of 'What for?' questions that arise about an action. In the present state of philosophy, it seems necessary to choose an example which is not obscured by the fact that moral approbation on the part of the writer or reader is called into play; for such approbation is in fact irrelevant to the logical features of practical reasoning; but if it is evoked, it may seem to play a significant part. The Nazis, being pretty well universally execrated, seem to provide us with suitable material. Let us suppose some Nazis caught in a trap in which they are sure to be killed. They have a compound full of Jewish children near them. One of them selects a site and starts setting up a mortar. Why this site?—Any site with such-and-such characteristics will do, and this has them. Why set up the mortar?—It is the best way of killing off the Jewish children. Why kill off the Jewish children?—It befits a Nazi, if he must die, to spend his last hour exterminating Jews. (I am a Nazi, this is my last hour, here are some Jews.) Here we have arrived at a desirability-characterization which makes an end of the questions 'What for?'

Aristotle would seem to have held that every action done by a rational agent was capable of having its grounds set forth up to a premiss containing a desirability-characterization; and as we have seen, there is a reasonable ground for this view, wherever there is a calculation of means to ends, or of ways of doing what one wants to do. Of course 'fun' is a desirability-characterization too, or 'pleasant': 'Such-and-such a kind of thing is pleasant' is one of the possible first premisses. But cannot pleasure be taken in *anything*? It all seems to depend on how the agent feels about it! But *can* it be taken in anything? Imagine saying 'I want a pin' and when asked why, saying 'For fun'; or 'Because of the pleasure of it.' One would be asked to give an account making it at least dimly plausible that there was a pleasure here. Hobbes [5] believed, perhaps wrongly, that there could be no such thing as pleasure in mere cruelty, simply in another's suffering; but he was not *so* wrong as we are likely to think. He was wrong in suggesting that cruelty had to have an end, but it does have to have a point. To depict this pleasure, people evoke notions of power, or perhaps of getting one's own back on the world, or perhaps of sexual excitement. No one needs to surround the pleasures of food and drink with such explanations.

Aristotle's specifications for the action of a rational agent do not cover the case of 'I just did, for no particular reason.' But where this answer is genuine, there is no calculation, and therefore no intermediate premisses (like 'Any site with such-and-such characteristics will be a suitable one for setting up my mortar,' and 'This is the best way to kill off the children') about which to press the question 'What for?' So we may note, as we have done, that this sort of action 'for no particular reason' exists, and that here of course there is no desirability-characterization, but that does not show that the demand for a desirability-characterization, wherever there is a purpose at all, is wrong.

With 'It befits a Nazi, if he must die, to spend his last hour exterminating Jews' we have then reached a terminus in enquiring into that particular order of reasons to which Aristotle gave the name 'practical'. Or again: we have reached the prime starting-point and can look no further. (The question 'Why be a Nazi?' is not a continuation of *this* series; it addresses itself to one of the particular premisses.) Any premiss, if it really works as a first premiss in a bit of 'practical reasoning', contains a description of something wanted; but with the intermediary premisses, the question 'What do you want that for?' arises—until at last we reach the desirability-characterization, about which 'What do you want that for?' does not arise, or if it is asked has not the same point, as we saw in the 'suitable food' example.

But in saying this, I do not at all mean to suggest that there is no such thing as taking exception to, or arguing against, the first premiss, or its being made the first premiss. Nor am I thinking of moral dissent from it; I prefer to leave that out of account. But there are other ways of taking exception to, or dissenting from, it. The first is to hold the premiss false; as a dietician might hold false Aristotle's views on dry food. It does indeed befit a Nazi to exterminate Jews, the objector may say, but there is a Nazi sacrament of dying which is what really befits a Nazi if he is going to die, and has time for it. Or again the objector may deny that it befits a Nazi as such to exterminate Jews at all. However, both these denials would be incorrect, so we may pass quickly on to other forms of demurrer. All of these admit the truth of the proposition, and all but one oppose the desire of what it mentions, namely to do what befits a Nazi in the hour of death. The one that does not oppose it says: 'Yes, that befits a Nazi, but so equally does such-and-such: why not do something falling under *this* description instead, namely . . .' Another says: 'To be sure but at this moment I lose all interest in doing what befits a Nazi.' And yet another says 'While that does indeed befit a Nazi, it is not quite necessary for him to do it. Nazism does not always require a man to strain to the utmost, it is not as inhuman as that: no, it is quite compatible with being a good Nazi to give yourself over to soft and tender thoughts of your home, your family, and your friends, to sing our songs and to drink the healths of those we love.' If any of these considerations work on him, the particular practical syllogism of our original Nazi fails, though not on account of any falsehood in the premiss, even according to him, nor on account of any fault in his practical calculation.

A (formal) ethical argument against the Nazi might perhaps oppose the notion of 'What a *man* ought to do'[6] to the Nazi's original premiss; setting up a position from which it followed incidentally that it did not befit a man to be a Nazi since a man ought not to do what befits a Nazi. Of course it is merely academic to imagine this; if the man with the moral objection were clever he would adopt one of the three last-mentioned methods of opposing the hero, of which the first one would very likely be the best. But the following (vague) question is often asked in one form or another: if desirability-characterizations are required in the end for purposive action, then must not the ones which relate to human good as such (in contrast with the good of film stars or shopkeepers) be in some obscure way compulsive, if believed? So someone who gets these right *must* be good; or at least (logically) *must* take a course within a certain permitted range or be ashamed. Some such idea too lies at the back of the notion that the practical syllogism it ethical.

'Evil be thou my good' is often thought to be senseless in some way. Now all that concerns us here is that 'What's the good of it?' is something that can be asked until a desirability-characterization has been reached and made intelligible. If then the answer to this question at some stage is 'The good of it is that it's bad,' this need not be unintelligible; one can go on to say 'And what is the good of its being bad?' to which the answer might be condemnation of good as impotent, slavish, and inglorious. Then the good of making evil my good is my intact libery in the unsubmissiveness of my will. *Bonum est multiplex*: good is multiform, and all that is required for our concept of 'wanting' is that a man should see what he wants under the aspect of some good. A collection of bits of bone three inches long, if it is a man's object, is something we want to hear the praise of before we can understand it as an object; it would be affectation to say 'One can want anything and I *happen* to want this,' and in fact a collector does not talk like that; no one talks like that except in irritation and to make an end of tedious questioning. But when a man aims at health or pleasure, then the enquiry 'What's the good of it?' is not a sensible one. As for reasons against a man's making one of them his principal aim; and whether there are orders of human goods, e.g., whether some are greater than others, and whether if this is so a man need ever prefer the greater to the less,[7] and on pain of what; this question would belong to ethics, if there is such a science. All that I am concerned to argue here is that the fact that *some* desirability-characterization is required does not have the least tendency to show that *any* is endowed with some kind of necessity in relation to wanting. But it may still be true that the man who says 'Evil be thou my good' in the way that we described is committing errors of thought; this question belongs to ethics.

The conceptual connection between 'wanting' (in the sense which we have isolated, for of course we are not speaking of the 'I want' of a child who screams for something) and 'good' can be compared to the conceptual connection between 'judgement' and 'truth'. Truth is the object of judgement, and good the object of wanting; it does not follow from this either that everything judged must be true, or that everything wanted must be good. But there is a certain contrast between these pairs of concepts too. For you cannot explain truth without introducing as its subject intellect, or judgement, or propositions, in some relation of which to the things known or judged truth consists; 'truth' is ascribed to what has the relation, not to the things. With 'good' and 'wanting' it is the other way round; as we have seen, an account of 'wanting' introduces good as its object, and goodness of one sort or another is ascribed primarily to the objects, not to the wanting: one wants a *good kettle*, but has a *true idea* of a kettle (as opposed to wanting a kettle well, or having an idea of a true kettle). Goodness is ascribed to wanting in virtue of the goodness (not the actualization) of what is wanted; whereas truth is ascribed immediately to judgements, and in virtue of what actually *is* the case. But again, the notion of 'good' that has to be introduced in an account of wanting is not that of what is really good but of what the agent conceives to be good; what the agent wants would have to be characterizable as good by him, if we may suppose him not to be impeded by inarticulateness. Whereas when we are explaining truth as a predicate of judgements, propositions, or thoughts, we have to speak of a relation to what is really so, not just of what seems so to the judging mind. But on the other hand again, the good (perhaps falsely) conceived by the agent to characterize the thing must *really* be one of the many forms of good.

It will have become clear that the practical syllogism as such is not an ethical topic. It will be of interest to an ethicist, perhaps, if he takes the rather unconvincing line that a good man is by definition just one who aims wisely at good ends. I call this unconvincing because human goodness suggests virtues among other things, and one does not think of choosing means to ends as obviously the whole of courage, temperance, honesty, and so on. So what can the practical syllogism have to do with ethics? It can only come into ethical studies if a correct philosophical psychology is requisite for a philosophical system of ethics: a view which I believe I should maintain if I thought of trying to construct such a system; but which I believe is not generally current. I am not saying that there cannot be any such thing as moral general premises such as 'People have a duty of paying their employees promptly,' or Huckleberry Finn's conviction, which he failed to make his premiss: 'White boys ought to give runaway slaves up'; obviously there can, but it is clear that such general premisses will only occur as premisses of practical reasoning in people who want to do their duty.[8] The point is very obvious, but has been obscured by the conception of the practical syllogism as of its nature ethical, and thus as a proof about what one ought to do, which somehow naturally culminates in action.

Of course 'I ought to do this, so I'll do it' is not a piece of practical reasoning any more than 'This is nice, so I'll have some' is. The mark of practical reasoning is that the thing wanted is *at a distance* from the immediate action, and the immediate action is calculated as the way of getting or doing or securing the thing wanted. Now it may be at a distance in various ways. For example, 'resting' is merely a wider description of what I am perhaps doing in lying on my bed; and acts done to fulfil moral laws will generally be related to positive precepts in this way; whereas getting in the good government is remote in time from the act of pumping, and the replenishment of the house water-supply, while very little distant in time, is at some spatial distance from the act of pumping.

[1] No author, of course, has proposed this syllogism. I am indebted for the idea of it, however, to a passage in Mr. R. M. Hare's book, *The Language of Morals*, p. 35.

[2] *De Motu Animalium VII*.

[3] *Ethica Nicomachea*, 1147[a] 27–8.

[4] *Ethica Nicomachea*, 1141[b] 18.

[5] *Leviathan*, Part I, Chap. VI.

[6] But is it not perfectly possible to say: 'At this moment I lose all interest in doing what befits a man'? If Aristotle thought otherwise, he was surely wrong. I suspect that he thought a man could not lack this interest except under the influence of inordinate passion or though 'boorishness' (ἀγροικία), i.e. insensibility.

[7] Following Hume, though without his animus, I of course deny that this preference can be as such 'required by reason', in any sense.

[8] It is worth remarking that the concepts of 'duty' and 'obligation', and what is now called the 'moral' sense of 'ought', are survivals from a *law* conception of ethics. The modern sense of 'moral' is itself a late derivative from these survivals. None of these notions occur in Aristotle. The idea that actions which are necessary if one is to conform to justice and the other virtues are requirements of divine law was found among the Stoics, and became generally current through Christianity, whose ethical notions come from the Torah.

III

ON SO-CALLED PRACTICAL INFERENCE

G. H. VON WRIGHT

1. SINCE the publication of Anscombe's *Intention* (1957) practical inference
has been a live topic in philosophy. There can be little doubt that the topic
is important. I would claim, for example, that practical inference as a
schema of explanation plays a comparable role in the human sciences to
that of nomological deductive explanation in the natural sciences. To vin-
dicate this claim is difficult, however. This is so, for one thing, because the
logical nature of practical reasoning is much more obscure than that of
deductive and other forms of 'theoretical' argument.

The division of inferences ('syllogisms') into theoretical and practical
stems from Aristotle. The most exciting thing which Aristotle has to say
about the topic is that a practical inference leads up to or ends in action,
that its conclusion is an action.[1] About the premisses he is not very clear.
The example he gives of the major premiss often mentions something
generic which is good or ought to be done, e.g. that dry food suits every
man or that sweet things ought to be tasted.[2] The minor premiss mentions
some particular thing which 'falls under' the generic label, e.g. that this
particular dish is dry or this particular lump of white stuff is sweet. In these
examples the conclusion would be that the person who argues proceeds to
eat the stuff.

According to Anscombe the first premiss of a practical inference mentions something wanted.[3] This characterization, it seems, does not fit
Aristotle's version of practical inference very well. It fits better another
type of inference. This is an inference in which the first premiss mentions
an end of action and the second premiss some means to this end. The
'practical' conclusion which results from the premisses would consist in
using the means to secure the end.

Aristotelian practical inferences, one could say, subsume a particular
thing or action under some general principle or rule about what is good for
us or is our duty. The study of reasoning of this kind is relevant to the
question—central not least to Plato's and Aristotle's thinking—how knowing the good is related to being good and to right action.

From *Acta Sociologica*, Vol. 15, No. 1, pp. 39–53. Reprinted by permission of
Universitetsforlaget, Publishers to the Norwegian Universities.

The second type of practical inference is not concerned so much with right conduct as with purposive behaviour and intentional action generally. Its study is relevant above all to the problems of explaining and understanding conduct—both of individuals and of groups of men.

Of both types of practical inference it is right to say, with Anscombe, that their study has been much neglected. But perhaps not as thoroughly neglected as she seems to have thought. In his *Logic*, Hegel construed purposive action as an inference, leading from the subjective setting of an end through insight into the objective connections of natural facts to the objectivation of the end in action.[4] (This is a very summary description of a complex and perhaps not very clear idea.) And in his lectures on the philosophy of history Hegel applied the same schema to the historical process as a realization, through the actions of individual and collective agents, of the 'aims' immanent in the absolute mind. The Hegelian conceptualization of action as inference also left an impact on Marx and Marxist thinking.[5]

In this paper I shall discuss only practical inference which views actions as the use of means to attain ends.

2. Let it be assumed that the premisses of a practical argument, when conducted in the first person, are:

I want to attain the end *E* (e.g. make this hut habitable).
Unless I do action *A* (e.g. heat the hut) I shall not attain *E*.

It may very well be the case that, if I have this end in view in combination with that opinion of the means to its realization, then I shall actually proceed to act in the appropriate way. But what sort of *connection* would this signify between want and thought on the one hand and action on the other? Can I say that wanting and opining *make* me act? If so, would this be a form of causal efficacy? Or would it be more like a logical compulsion?

Before we proceed to answering these questions we must consider the following 'objection' to the first person premiss as stated above. Cannot a person at the same time want to attain several ends? And can it not then happen that some of his ends (wants) are mutually incompatible? For example, that in order to attain one of the ends, he thinks he must forbear doing something which he thinks he must do in order to attain another end of his? Then there are two practical arguments for him. He may act in accordance with the premisses of one of them. But could he then, in any sense, be said to have been compelled to act in the way he acted?

Suppose we change the word 'want' in the first premiss to 'intent'. One does not normally speak of intending to attain ends. Some further change in the first premiss will therefore be required here.

One speaks of pursuing ends. Pursuit of ends is intentional action. The phrases 'pursue an end intentionally' and 'pursue an end' I shall regard as synonymous. To speak of intending to pursue an end points to the future. It is like saying that one is planning or has resolved to go after something later on. But an agent in pursuit of an end can rightly be said to intend to make the end-state, i.e. the state which obtains when the end is attained, materialized or come true.

It may now be suggested that, if one pursues an end E, then one cannot, for conceptual reasons, at the same time pursue another end E, the pursuit of which one considers (causally or logically) incompatible with pursuit of E. I shall accept this as a valid point about 'the logic of intention'.

It seems obvious that 'I pursue the end E' is a logically stronger statement than 'I want to attain the end E'. The first entails the second, but not vice versa. A plausible way of coping with the difficulty caused by possibly conflicting ends would therefore be to replace the first premiss in the practical argument under consideration by

I intend to make it true that E (e.g. that this hut is habitable)

and the second premiss by

Unless I do A, I shall not achieve this.

Is there a conclusion which can be said to follow logically from the two premisses thus reformulated?

I think there is one for which this claim can be made. It is the conclusion:

I will do A.

This is what we call a *declaration of intention*. An inference is normally thought to be between true or false propositions. But it is doubtful whether a declaration of intention could qualify as a proposition. The logical nature of the argument therefore is obscure.

In order to see things in a clearer light, let us shift the argument from the first person to the third person. What we then get is, in the first place:

X intends to make it true that E
Unless he does A, he will not achieve this
Therefore X will do A.

Here all three components of the inference are clearly propositions. The conclusion is a prediction about a certain agent's conduct.

It is quite clear, however, that this argument *is not* logically conclusive. There are several reasons, why this is so. For one thing, both premisses may be true but X himself need not know or think that the second is true, i.e. he need not realize that he will not attain his end unless he does *A*. And then there is, of course, no guarantee whatsoever that he will do *A*. (I shall not here take up for separate discussion the possibility that *X* is not aware (conscious) of his intention and whether this would affect the conclusiveness of the inference.)

We might now try to make the argument approach conclusiveness by expanding the second premiss to something like

X thinks that unless he does *A*, he will not bring about that *E* comes true.

It should be noted that the same expansion may be said to be implicit in the premiss in the first person. For, if I argue to myself 'Unless I do *A*, I shall not achieve this or that,' then I also subscribe to the *truth* of the statement. Perhaps I do not claim to *know* it to be true, but at least I believe it or consider it highly probable.

In the case of the premiss in the third person, however, its expansion is not merely to make explicit a concealed presupposition. It adds something substantial to the statement. We shift from a statement about 'objective facts' to a statement about a person's 'epistemic attitudes'.

It may be suggested that in order to make the argument in the first and the third person run completely parallel we must not only add the above epistemic clause to the second premiss of the argument in the third person, but also change the conclusion of the argument in the first person to

I shall do *A*.

When cast in this form the conclusion is a prediction about my own future behaviour. This would turn the first person argument into a special case of the third person argument. Such a 'reifying' move is possible, but it misses what is specifically 'first person' about the first person argument.

3. There is, however, also another course to be tried in order to make the argument in the third person conclusive. We leave the premisses as they (originally) stand and change the conclusion to:

Therefore *X* has to (must) do *A*.

Whether this conclusion follows logically from the premisses depends upon hów one interprets the meaning of 'has to' or 'must' here. The following seems tó me a reasonable view to take: A must-do statement (in the third person) is elliptic. It says that an action is a necessary condition for the attainment of some end which is left unspecified in the statement. On this view the statement '*X* must do *A*' would be short for '*X* is in pursuit of some end of action of his which he will not attain unless he does *A*'. And *this* follows logically from the premisses (by application of the principle $fa \rightarrow$ $(Ex)fx$ and assuming that an agent's intending to make a state of affairs come true entails that this state is an, intermediate or ultimate, end of his action).

Consider this variation of the argument:

X intends to make it true that E
Unless Y does A, he (i.e. X) will not achieve this
Therefore Y must do A.

Shall we call this a valid argument? The answer again depends upon our understanding of the 'must' here. The argument is conclusive, if 'Y must do A' is short for '*Someone* is in pursuit of an end of action which he will not attain unless Y does A.' Is this a feasible interpretation? Perhaps must-statements are sometimes thus understood. But why not then take an even more 'liberal' attitude and say that sometimes 'Y must do A' means simply 'Unless Y does A, something or other will not happen (be the case)'? Here the necessity of action need not be related to any end at all, nor to any-body's intentions.

Consider finally the following variant:

X intends to make it true that E
Unless Y does A, he (i.e. X) will not achieve this
Therefore he must make Y do A.

But must he? Assume that we (or X himself) know that he cannot make Y do A, that nothing he does will move Y to this. Then we should perhaps say that X must give up pursuing E as an end. And if pressed about the meaning of this last 'must' we might say: X must do this, or else he will suffer frustration. But maybe X is so keen on his end that giving it up in-volves a still bigger frustration for him. Then we might conclude that X *must learn* how to make Y do A (which may or may not involve teaching Y how to do A). And this conclusion would follow, logically, if we change the second premiss to 'unless X learns how to make Y do A, he will not make it true that E'. We are back at the first pattern.

Generally speaking: If there is something which an agent cannot do and which is such that, unless he does it, he will not attain a certain end of his, then he must *learn* how to do it or else he will not attain this end. Learning how to do something can be a practical necessity in much the same sense as is doing something. Furthermore, that somebody else does something can be necessary (causally or logically), if an agent is to attain his ends in much the same sense in which it may be necessary for this that something should happen. These last two are comparable cases. I propose, however, that the term *practical necessity* be reserved for the first pair of cases. Practical necessity is the necessity of doing something under which an agent is, if he is to attain some end *of his own*.

An agent thus is under a practical necessity of doing everything which it is necessary that he should do, if he is to attain the ends he pursues. But can an agent intend to do anything (make it true that E, for example) without being able (generically) to do this?[6] Does intention presuppose ability—pursuit of ends ability to obtain them? I would answer as follows:

One can intend to do only such things which one either one can do or realizes that one cannot do but intends to learn to do and thinks one can learn to do.[7] (This is not a psychological observation about intending, but a rule about the logical grammar of the concept.)

Sometimes an agent thinks he can do something which, in fact, he cannot generically do. By trying to do this thing but failing to accomplish it he may come to realize his inability—and, if the action was a practical necessity for him, the practical necessity of acquiring the ability. But it may also happen that when the agent realizes his inability to do the required thing, he 'changes his mind', i.e. gives up the pursuit of his original end.

4. Let us again shift back to the first person case. Consider this inference:

I intend to make it true that E
Unless I do A, I shall not achieve this
Therefore I must do A.

Can I be mistaken about my own intentions, think that I intend to do something which, in fact, I do not intend to do? Without prejudging an answer to this question, let us just lay it aside.

The second premiss can surely, 'objectively speaking', be false. Then the conclusion too will normally be false. (It will be false, unless I also pursue some end which is different from E and for the attainment of which the doing of A is required.)

When the second premiss is false, it may still be the case that I (mistakenly) *think* it true. And then I will also think of the conclusion as true, i.e. I will think of the doing of A as a practical necessity incumbent upon me. Thus arguing from the two premisses above makes the conclusion *valid for me*, even though the second premiss may be false and therewith the conclusion false too. This is a peculiarity of a practical inference in the first person.

If the second premiss of a practical inference in the first person is true, then the agent who conducts the argument will *rightly* consider himself to be under the practical necessity of acting which is stated in the conclusion. If it is false, however, he (normally) will *mistakenly* consider himself to be so. The practical necessities under which an agent (rightly or mistakenly) considers himself to be we may call his *subjective* practical necessities. And we can distinguish them from the *objective* practical necessities under which he is, as a matter of objective truth. There can be a discrepancy between the groups, either because the first one does not embrace all the members of the second, or because it contains members which are not members of the second. Each source of discrepancy is a source of frustration for an agent in pursuit of ends.

5. We now leave the 'must do' case. The arguments henceforth to be discussed are:

I intend to make it true that *E*
Unless I do *A*, I shall not achieve this
Therefore I will do *A*.

Third person case:

X intends to make it true that *E*
He thinks that unless he does *A*, he will not achieve this
Therefore he will do *A*.

The conclusion of the first person inference, we said, is a declaration of intention. This intention may not have been formed until we realized the practical necessities involved in our aiming at a certain end. So its formation may come later, after the first intention was already formed. We can speak of a *primary* and a *secondary* intention here.

The connection between the two intentions is, moreover, a kind of logically necessary connection. The second (epistemic) premiss can be said to 'mediate' between the primary intention of the first premiss and the secondary intention of the conclusion. One can also speak of a transfer or *transmission of intention*. The 'will' to attain an end is being transmitted to (use of) the means deemed necessary for its attainment.

This principle of 'transmission of intention from ends to means' is basically identical, it seems, with a principle which Kant thought analytically (logically) true and which he expressed in the following words: 'Who wills the end, wills (so far as reason has decisive influence on his actions) also the means which are indispensably necessary and in his power.'[8]

I said there was 'a kind of' logical connection here. For, although I think it obvious that the conclusion of our first person argument follows logically from the premisses, this 'following' has a peculiar nature: A declaration of intention is not a true or false proposition. Whether an argument which is actually conducted from premisses of the kind under consideration will terminate in a declaration of intention is, in a certain sense, contingent and not logically necessary. Perhaps such arguments as often as not terminate in a *change* of intention on the agent's part. Realizing what is necessary for him to do and perhaps feeling a strong aversion against doing this, he changes his mind and gives up pursuit of the original good (cf. above p. 49). And even if the agent does not change his primary intention, he need not *declare* his secondary intention, not even to himself, 'in thought'. He can nevertheless be said to *have* it and, moreover, to have it necessarily. If he declares his intention, he only 'reveals' to the world, or admits to himself, something about himself which is already there.

So what is logically necessary is something which holds between true and false propositions and which is best expressed in the form of a third person inference of the following type:

X intends to make it true that E
He thinks that, unless he does A, he will not achieve this
Therefore X *intends to do A*.

This argument, however, moves wholly on the level of intentions and epistemic attitudes. *It* does not, it seems, link intention with action. Or does it, after all? We shall return to this question presently (in Section 7).

6. Even after we have added the epistemic clause 'X thinks that' to its second premiss the argument in the third person, ending in a prediction, remains inconclusive. This is due to the existence of a time gap, separating the premisses from the conclusion. The premisses may be true, but the agent has not yet performed the action. This leaves open the truth-value of the conclusion.

Assume that the premisses are true at a certain time. Normally, they will then remain true for some time. Unless X does A *within this time span*, we shall have to say that the prediction failed to come true. For, if X does A, but only after the end of the time span, his action is irrelevant to the argument. So is it also, if after the lapse of this time he does *not* do A.

It can happen that we wait for the prediction to come true and, having waited for some time, begin to doubt whether the premisses still obtain. Suppose we find that they do no longer obtain. Does it follow that the conclusion was invalidly drawn from the premisses? Not necessarily. For assume that what X intends to achieve is the result of a 'long time project' and that the doing of A has to be done at a late stage of it, or that the doing of A can be postponed to a late stage. There is in any case *a latest time* when A will have to be done. Suppose now the agent 'gives up' his project before this time arrives. Then it could still be true that, had he not given it up, he would have done A before the time was up.

So in order to show that the conclusion 'he will do A' was falsely drawn from the premisses, we should have to show that the agent failed to do A at *the latest time* when he thought the time was up for him to do it and the premisses were still valid. This observation makes it possible for us to eliminate considerations relating to the time gap from considerations relating to the logical conclusiveness of the inference schema here. The problem can be reduced to a question about a given moment in time, we shall call it 'now', and the argument reformulated as follows:

X intends (now) to make it true that E
He thinks that unless he does A now, he will not achieve this
Therefore he will do A now.

The mere fact therefore that in ever so many cases an agent will never do what he considers himself under a practical necessity of doing, if he is to attain some end of his, is by itself quite irrelevant to our problem. For in many of those cases the agent had changed his mind before the time was up in which he had to do the thing he never did.

Is the statement that an agent *will* do a certain thing *now* a 'prediction'? The answer depends upon what we think of the 'now'. Is 'now' the present *instant*? Very often we conceive of the 'now' as having duration, extension in time; sometimes we mean by it today or even this year. So what is 'now' supposed to mean in the argument we are discussing here? Not necessarily an instant in time, but rather a *temporal location* of some duration. Of this 'location', however, the following must hold true: We cannot slice it up into an earlier part of which it is true that the agent did not even *begin* to do A then and a later part of which it is true that he then did A. The 'now' of which we are here speaking covers what may be called the *spacious present* of the performance of an action. Most actions take some time to perform. Only when the action is one which can be performed at an instant ('in an inkling') does the specious present of its performance, the 'now', shrink to a point. (Whether there are such actions, I do not know.)

Under the above conception of the 'now', *will do A now* 'reduces' to *does A now*. One could also say that 'will do' has no proper application to the 'now'-case—and that the conclusion to match the two premisses must be reformulated 'Therefore he does A now.' In any case, the conclusion is no longer a prediction. It is a description of what an agent does, is engaged in doing, now.[9] ('He will accomplish the doing of A now' would be a prediction which is compatible with the present tense description 'he does A now'.) So, in non-linguistic terms, the conclusion is an action. This is exactly what Aristotle said it should be.

But what remains open to debate is, whether this conclusion *follows*, i.e. whether an agent's present intentions and awareness of what he has to do right now in order to make them effective will of logical necessity lead, 'compel', 'prompt' him to action.

7. From what was said before about 'transmission of intention' we should from the two premises

X intends to make it true that E
He thinks that, unless he does A now, he will not achieve this

be able to conclude:

Therefore X intends to do A now.

The problematic conclusion was

Therefore X does A now.

Our next task will be to compare the two conclusions. If an agent does A, is it then also true to say that he intends to do A?

Sometimes a man is said to have done various things which he never intended but which happened to be consequences of his action. (He may even have foreseen that they were going to happen.) Perhaps one could call this 'accidental doing' and distinguish it from 'intentional doing'. Here we understand by 'doing' only intentional doing. Thus the practical argument would be invalidated. if it could be shown that on some occasion its (above) premises were true and that the agent did A, though only accidentally, by mistake or as an unintended consequence of his acting.

So our question must be given this more precise formulation: Does it follow that an agent intends to do A, if he intentionally does A?

It is important to distinguish between intentional doing and intention(s) to do. 'Intend to do' normally refers to the future. If 'now' designates the specious present of the action, then under this normal use 'intend to do now' is a self-contradictory phrase of a sort. (Not to be confused with 'intend now to do' which is logically in order.) 'Intend to do', like 'will do', has no proper application to the 'now'-case. But what happens then to a persisting intention to do, when the moment of action is there? A suggestion would be that it 'matures' and emerges on the behavioural level as intentional action.

Shall we say then that the two conclusions which we are comparing are identical? Shall we say that when the transmission of intention argument is applied to the present moment, then the conclusion which emerges is that X does A now?

The answer to the first question is, I think, affirmative. To answering the second affirmatively there is an objection, however. This objection may appear so grave that, in fact, it shows that action cannot possibly follow logically from premises about intentions and epistemic attitudes.

8. Something happens which *prevents* X from doing A. He stumbles or has a stroke or someone seizes him and keeps him immobile.

If intention is for the future and the preventive occurs before the agent makes the intention effective, he will normally either change his intention or evaluate the practical requirements of the situation differently. This case therefore does not affect the problem of the validity of the inference schema which we are discussing.

If the preventive interference occurs within the specious present of the action but after the agent has commenced acting (set himself to act, embarked upon the road to the end), then we usually describe the case by saying that he *tried* but failed to accomplish the thing. Failure to accomplish can also be due to a change of intention within the specious present of the action. Then we say that the agent began or tried, but gave up. Failure can finally be due to the agent's not knowing, how to accomplish the thing. This can be called failure of ability. The agent had misjudged his powers. He intended to make it true that E. He realized that doing A was a practical necessity for this. He thought he could do A. But he was mistaken. Learning how to do A, or at least perfecting his ability, was a prior practical necessity for him (cf. above p. 48). Since he did not understand this, he proceeded to do things in the wrong order, so to speak. He set himself to do A but found that he could not accomplish it. This is another case of trying but failing.

It is a common feature of all these cases of failure to do A that the agent *embarks* on the action and that the failure is one of *accomplishing* the action. Embarking on an action involves some physical effort and therefore some behaviour or conduct aiming at the (completed) action. If the agent's embarking on the action is, moreover, a logical necessity under the premisses, we could still say that Aristotle was substantially right in thinking that a practical argument terminates in (some) action.

But we have also to consider the case, at least as a theoretcial possibility, that the preventive interference occurs exactly at the same time as the specious present for the action begins. Then the agent cannot be said to have embarked upon the action. There was no time for doing this. At most we could then say that he *would* have embarked upon it, had he not been prevented.

If we understand 'prevented' to mean either prevented right at the beginning of the action or prevented in the course of an attempt to perform it, we can state the conclusion which finally emerges from our considerations of the form of a practical inference as follows:

Therefore X does A now, unless he is prevented or else cannot accomplish the action.

9. In order to show that an agent *does* a certain thing *A*, it is not enough to show that *A*, the result of the action, happens as a causal consequence of some movements in the agent's body (raising of arms, twisting of hands, etc.). We must also show that what took place was *intentional*, i.e. was a case of an agent's *doing A* as distinct from merely bringing it about without intending it.

To establish that the agent's causing *A* to come about is a case of his doing *A* is not to establish, in addition to the happening of *A*, a different event which so to speak occurs 'inside the agent'. It is to *understand* (the meaning of) the agent's conduct, i.e. to see that by certain changes in his body or changes causally connected with changes in his body the agent is *aiming* at this result. If he aims at it without achieving it, we shall have to say that the agent tried but failed—either because of insufficient ability or because he was prevented.

Now we can see more clearly, I think, wherein the claim to logical validity of the practical inference consists. Given the premisses

X now intends to make it true that *E*
He thinks that, unless he does *A* now, he will not achieve this

and excluding, hypothetically or on the basis of investigations, that he is prevented, then his actual conduct, whatever it may 'look like', either is an act of doing *A* or aims, though unsuccessfully, at being this. Any description of his behaviour which is logically inconsistent with this is also logically inconsistent with the premisses. Accepting the premisses thus forces on us this understanding of his conduct—unless for some reason we think that a preventive interference occurred right at the beginning of his action.

10. What *uses* has the type of argument which I here call practical inference?

One can distinguish between a *retrospective* and a *prospective* use.

When the argument is used retrospectively we start from the conclusion and so to speak reconstruct a set of premisses to match it. Then the 'conclusion' normally is the established or hypothetically assumed proposition that an agent has done a certain thing, performed an action *A*. (But it can also be the proposition that he set himself to do a certain thing which he failed to accomplish, either because he changed his mind, or was prevented, or did not possess the needed ability. Here I shall consider only the 'normal' case.)

An agent did *A*. *Why* did he do it? We *explain* his action by placing it in the 'teleological perspective' of his aiming at some end and his epistemic attitude to the requirements of the situation, i.e. his judging the action a practical necessity under this end. This is a prototype case of what is usually called *teleological explanation*.

I did *A*. Someone challenges me: Why did I do this? I may *justify* my conduct by reference to what I was after and that I thought my doing of *A* a practical necessity for me. (This, however, is not the only sense in which a man is said to 'justify' his actions.)

When the argument is used prospectively we set out from the premises and 'extract' from them a conclusion. In the first person case the argument ends in a *declaration* (formation) of *intention* to do a certain thing. I *commit* myself to doing it. Such use of the argument takes place particularly in situations where I *ponder* what I have to do in order to attain some already set aim of mine.

In the third person case the prospective (forwardlooking) argument produces a *prediction*. Since so and so is the agent's aim and he evidently considers the doing of *A* necessary for its attainment, he will (probably) do *A*.

Is there, in addition to the retrospective and prospective uses of practical inference also, something which might be called an 'instantaneous' use of it? Is there explanation of action only on the basis of what is *now* the case— and is there intentional action which is *simultaneous* with the construction of a justification for it?

I think the answer to these questions is no. When practical inference functions as an argument it either looks to the past for the motivations or to the future for an action. So in any use of the argument there is a time gap involved between premises and conclusion and with this gap there is also a rift in the logical connection between the intention and epistemic attitude on the one hand and the action on the other hand.

When therefore, in Section 6, we closed this time gap, we thereby also obliterated the character of an argument or an inference from the propositional connections which we were investigating. What happened to our 'practical inference' was in the end (Section 9) that we turned it into a set of conditions under which the conduct of an agent has to be interpreted or understood in a certain way, viz. as the doing of *A* or as aiming at this result. The premises of the practical inference became the description of a teleological perspective in which conduct is being understood as intentional.

What then will be our final position on the question of conclusiveness of practical arguments?

When the argument is used retrospectively to explain or, in the first person, to justify action, the clause 'unless prevented or else cannot accomplish the action' does not appear in it. That the agent did or tried to do *A* is not called into question and is, moreover, something that was logically bound to happen, assuming that the teleological frame, the intention and the epistemic attitude which the premises attribute to him, lasted up to the moment of action. For, granting the truth of this assumption, the premises then set the conditions for *interpreting* what happened.

When the argument is used prospectively in the first person, the clause 'unless prevented or else cannot accomplish the action' likewise is no part of the argument. Therefore we have no logical guarantee here concerning that which the agent will in fact do. But this is not what the argument purports to give either. Its binding nature stems from the fact that its conclusion declares the intention which an agent is logically bound to have within the teleological frame which in the premises he acknowledges for his prospective action.

Only when the argument is used prospectively in the third person, is the unless-clause a part of it. We know that if this clause is satisfied and if the teleological frame attributed to the agent in the premises remains stable up to the moment of action, then conduct of the predicted character is logically bound to follow. (Since this is how the situation will then have to be understood by us.) But whether the clause will be satisfied and whether the teleological frame will remain stable, we cannot know in advance. It is therefore contingent, whether the prediction will be fulfilled or not.

POSTSCRIPT ON UNDERSTANDING

The 'logical core' of the propositional connections which I have been discussing in this essay can be called a schema of interpretation or of understanding conduct as being intentional (action). This schena is what a practical inference 'becomes' when it is applied to the moment of action, the 'now'-case—and ceases to be an inference. I tried to show how the validity of this schema is relevant to the validity of the inference.

This schema also has an independent use, namely for purposes of *understanding* what an agent is doing—as distinct from the (third person) uses of inference which is to *explain* why an agent did what he did or to *predict* what he is going to do. But here a warning is in place.

On no account must it be thought that the understanding of behaviour as action is always based on an interpretation of an agent's conduct in the light of some intentions and cognitions which we attribute to him. To think thus would be to distort the logic of the situation seriously. It would, moreover, be a similar distortion to the one of which philosophers make themselves guilty, when they say that any statement about physical objects is the result of interpreting certain sense-data.

In the normal cases we say off-hand of the way we see people behave that they perform such and such actions—raise their arms, walk or run, open key-locks or hand things over to one another. Many of these actions we ourselves know how to perform; those, and others which *we* cannot do, have a familiar 'look' or 'physiognomy' which we recognize. We are further acquainted with innumerable ends for the sake of which these actions may be performed (when not 'done for their own sake'). Therefore we need not first seek for the agent's end of action in order to be able to tell *what* he is doing. Only when we are curious, *why* he is doing what we already think we know he is doing, do we look for a specific object of intention with him. (Explanation of action follows *after* understanding behaviour as action.)

These are the normal cases. But there are others. There are first of all the abortive cases, when an agent fails to accomplish the action. Even then we can usually say what, in fact, he did. He, for example, grabbed a handle and pulled, twisted his hand, etc., and in doing these things he was trying, though unsuccessfully, to do a certain thing which one normally does by doing just those things (and perhaps something else besides). In what he *did* we see at once what he was *aiming* at—and therefore we say that he *tried* to do so and so. On the whole only when failure to accomplish is due to insufficient know-how, or to quite false conceptions of how to achieve the result (of the action), may it be necessary to 'interpret' what we witness in the light of hypothetical aims and cognitions of the agent. We then say some such thing as: 'Evidently he is trying to open the safe but has no idea of how to do it.'

Secondly, there are cases when we are unfamiliar with the (kind of) action and therefore do not understand *what* the agent is doing. Perhaps he performs some strange ceremony. Even then we can usually describe various things which he is doing in the course of doing this strange thing. We, e.g., see *him move* his legs and arms in certain ways and not only see *his legs and arms move*. When we nevertheless say we do not understand what he is doing, this is because we feel reluctant to say that what he primarily intends to do is to make those movements with his limbs but suspect that the object of his primary intention is something which is done *by* moving legs and arms in a certain way. (Perhaps he is saluting or dancing.) We must learn what the new action 'looks' like, become acquainted with its 'physiognomy' before we can understand what a man is doing, who behaves in this way. We can learn this by being told what the agent is doing, sometimes by just being told the *name* of the action. (I can learn to recognize when a man is saluting without having any idea why people salute.)

So not even in the cases of unfamiliar actions is a practical inference always or normally needed to understand what is being done. Only in some, rather exceptional, situations will the construction of a practical argument be helpful here. We see a person go through some movements, the significance of which we do not understand 'in themselves'—but we have a strong hunch that he evidently intends to do a certain thing in behaving thus, e.g. that he is saluting somebody in the street. (But then we must also know, not just the name of the action, but also something about the occasions on which it is appropriate to perform it.) 'So this is how these people salute,' is our guess. Here a practical inference can be said to guide our understanding.

Sometimes we mistake behaviour for action when in fact it is not. A person's arm goes up and I say I see him raise his arm. Then I learn that what I witnessed was a physiological experiment and that the person's neural system was being stimulated in a way which made his arm go up. (Perhaps the experimenter had even told him not to raise his arm 'himself'.) Then I must withdraw the claim, implicit in what first I said, that the person raised his arm. I can redescribe what I saw in a way which does not carry that claim with it by saying that I saw his arm rise. When thus I modify my orignal description, it is tempting to speak, *post hoc*, of a false interpretation of what I saw. We say: I interpreted what I *really saw*, viz. his arm rise, as a case of seeing him raise his arm—but this was premature. This is like the case, when we withdraw a physical object statement and replace it by a sense-data statement, because it turned out that the object we saw was only illusory—say a column very skilfully drawn on the wall. In both cases, however, is it misleading to say that we interpreted what we saw in the wrong way. For we did not *interpret* what we saw at all.

I can understand something as an action and be mistaken in thus understanding it. I can see something as a physical object and be mistaken in thus seeing it. But this is not to say that what I really *saw* was, e.g., his arm rising and not him raising his arm—or a painting on the wall and not a column. Understanding is compatible with misunderstanding, one could say. Only when we are on our guard against misunderstanding or confined about the nature of the case, do we *interpret* what we immediately witness. And if what we witness are the movements of some living beings, the interpretation normally consists in the construction of a practical inference to match the case.

---

[1] *De Motu Animalium* 701ª 12–14.
[2] *Ethica Nicomachea* 1147ª 6–7 and 1147ª 28–30.
[3] *Intention*, Sect. 35.
[4] *Wissenschaft der Logik*, Bk. II, Sect. iii, Ch. 2 B.
[5] As shown by Juha Manninen in 'Praktisen päättelyn mukaisista ajatusmalleista Hegelillä ja Marxilla' ('On Practical Inference Models in Hegel and Marx'), *Psykologia 5*, 1970.

[6] That an agent is (generically) able to do something shall mean that on most occasions, when there is an opportunity for doing this thing and he sets himself to do it, he will also accomplish it. He has the necessary 'know how'. This he may, but need not, possess as a result of learning.

[7] My position here differs slightly from the one which I took in *Explanation and Understanding*. There (pp. 101–3) I suggested that an intention to do something necessarily involves an opinion on the agent's part that he can do the thing.

[8] *The Moral Law*, transl. by H. J. Paton, pp. 84–5.

[9] If instead of 'now' we had put in a reference to an arbitrary moment of time 'at t' in our inference schema, the conclusion 'He will do A at t' or 'He does A at t' can be a prediction relative to the station in time where *we* happen to be. But this is irrelevant. What matters is that the conclusion is not a prediction *relative to the premisses*—in this case that the agent, at t, intends something and considers the doing at that very moment of some action necessary.

IV

PRACTICAL REASONING AND
RATIONAL APPETITE

A. J. P. KENNY

I T is beyond doubt that in addition to theoretical reasoning there is practical reasoning. We work out, with the aid of logic, not only what is the case but also what we ought to do. In practical reasoning as in theoretical we pass from premises to conclusion. The premises, perhaps, set out our desires or our duties; they set out also the facts of the case and the possibilities open; the conclusions are actions or plans of action. But what are the rules by which we pass from premises to conclusion? What are the criteria for validity in practical inference? It is by no means easy to say.

Consider the following simple piece of practical reasoning:

I'm to be in London at 4.15
If I catch the 2.30 I'll be in London at 4.15
So I'll catch the 2.30.[1]

Reasonings of this form—which we might call the *modus ponens* of practical reasoning—are as ubiquitous (and as unlikely to be stated in artificial articulateness) as their counterparts in normal theoretical *modus ponens*. Clearly in some sense we use a different logic, or use logic in a different way, when we reason practically and when we reason theoretically. For in the ordinary logic used in theoretical reasoning '*q*. If *p* then *q*. So *p*' is not a valid argument form, but the fallacy of affirming the consequent.

Practical reasoning and imperative inference appear to be connected. Following Hare, Stenius, and ultimately Frege, we have already distinguished in sentences between a *phrastic* (which contains the descriptive content of the sentence) and a mark of mood—assertoric or imperative—which Hare now calls a *tropic*. An imperative sentence and the corresponding assertoric sentence have the same phrastic, but a different tropic. So does the corresponding expression of intention which might conclude a piece of practical reasoning.

From *Will, Freedom and Power* (Basil Blackwell, 1975), pp. 70, 73–6, 78–92, 93–5. Reprinted by permission of the publishers.

Earlier,[2] we classed expressions of intention and commands together as fiats. This suggests that what we need is a logic of fiats. Plans and projects are examples of fiats. Practical reasoning, therefore, by which we work out plans, and imperative inference, in which we pass from one directive to another, can both be regarded as exemplifying a single pattern of inference which leads from fiat to fiat.

Once we extend the apparatus of formal logic to sentences in moods other than the indicative, we have to consider the relationship between the symbols of logic (in particular the logical constants and quantifiers) and the sign of mood or tropic. In particular we have to consider the order in which these symbols are to be attached to phrastics in order to make well-formed formulae of imperative logic. Consider a sentence such as 'Open the door or open the window.' Is this to be symbolized as '𝔉Apq' or as 'A𝔉p𝔉q'? That is to say, is a disjunctive command to be considered as the result of adding an imperative tropic to a disjunctive phrastic, or as the result of an operation by the disjunctive operator on two sentences each consisting of phrastic plus tropic? A similar question arises for conjunction, and a connected, but more complicated, one for implication.

Hare in the *Language of Morals* assumes that logical constants, when they occur in imperative or assertoric sentences, can occur only within the tropic, so that every sentence begins with a tropic and contains never more than a single tropic.[3] To me, too, this now seems the appropriate rule to adopt.

Other writers, however, think otherwise, and there was a time when I did so too. 'In "if *p* then *q*", I wrote, the variables take the place, not of sentence-radicals [= phrastics], but of something which on the face of it itself has a mood. "If the pubs are open, be sure to have a drink" is quite different from "if the pubs are open, you are sure to be having a drink".'[4] This example does not prove what I then wanted it to prove: because of course the difference between the two sentences can be represented as a difference between ℭCpq and 𝔉Cpq as well as a difference between Cℭpℭp and Cℭp𝔉q.[5] But stronger reasons than the one I gave have been put forward for allowing tropics to occur within logical constants, and these we must now consider.

The first is drawn from the existence of conditional commands. If tropics are not allowed to occur within the scope of logical constants, then it seems that all conditional commands must be capable of translation into commands to bring about the truth of a material implication in the manner which I just suggested. But it does not seem that this is always possible. In the case of bets, there is certainly a difference between a conditional bet and a bet on the truth of a material conditional. If I bet you £5 that if *p* then q, then I win my money if not p; but if I say 'If p, then I bet you £5 that q', then if not p the bet is off and neither of us wins. Is there not a parallel difference in the case of commands? There is the command 'Bring it about that Cpq' which is obeyed by bringing it about that not-p; and there is the conditional command 'If p, bring it about that q'—a command which, if p is not the case, is simply void. The difference, it might be said, could be well brought out by imagining the command that q to be given in sealed orders, only to be opened in the event that p.[6]

There is, I think, a genuine difference here; but it does not call for the admission of the imperative neustic within the phrastic, but rather for a further application of the distinction between fiats and directives. Directives, it will be remembered, are commands and requests: fiats which are issued for execution by the person to whom they are uttered. If we make explicit this reference to agency, then we get two different phrastics:

(1) seeing-to-it by you that if p, then q
(2) if p, seeing-to-it by you that q.

By applying the imperative tropic to these two phrastics, we get the two different commands ('D' for 'seeing-to-it-by-you')

(3) $\Im DCpq$
(4) $\Im CpDq$.

These are different commands, as may be seen if we reflect that a man might be in position to carry out the one but not the other. Suppose, for instance, he has no control over q, and has control over p which he can only exercise if commanded to do so. Then he cannot obey (4), for if p happens he is powerless to prevent q; but he can obey (3), for he can ensure the truth of Cpq by falsifying p, on the authority of the command he has been given.

But the difference between these two commands derives from the different phrastics, and not from any difference in the placing of the imperative tropics. This may be seen by noticing the difference in the assertoric between

(5) $\mathfrak{E}DCpq$
(6) $\mathfrak{E}CpDq$.

It is sufficient to make the second, but not the first, of these is true if not p should occur through no fault of yours.

The main positive reason for keeping tropics out of phrastics is the enormous gain in simplicity. If the logical constants can occur outside tropics, they need wholly redefining. They are defined by their truth-values, but if they are to conjoin not only statements but commands then definition will no longer be adequate. Moreover, if tropics are kept outside phrastics, there is no need to have special formation rules for tropics; the rule is simply that tropics may be added to any well-formed phrastic. On the other hand, if we allow the logical constants to construct molecular sentences out of atomic sentences in different moods, then we shall have to work out rules for the moods of the resulting sentences given the moods of the component sentences, just as we have rules for working out the truth-values of complex sentences for possible combinations of truth-values for their simple components. In some cases this does not seem difficult. A conditional whose antecedent and consequent are both assertoric is clearly itself assertoric; so we will have $C\mathfrak{C}\mathfrak{C} = \mathfrak{C}$. A conditional whose antecedent is assertoric and whose consequent is imperative seems to be a command; so we have $C\mathfrak{C}\mathfrak{F} = \mathfrak{F}$; but what are we to say of $C\mathfrak{F}\mathfrak{C}$? It is hard to think of anything which would be an instance of this. 'If you are going to be such a wet blanket, go home' ($C\mathfrak{C}\mathfrak{F}$) is all right; but 'If go home, you are going to be such a wet blanket' seems ill formed. So too with sentences of the form '$C\mathfrak{F}\mathfrak{C}$'. 'If go away come back soon' is ill formed; it sounds, in fact, like pidgin for 'If you go away come back soon' which is $C\mathfrak{C}\mathfrak{F}$.

If simplicity were all that was in question, it might be argued that this did not matter. Truth-tables, it is often said, supply truth-values to complex sentences where ordinary language does not (e.g. conditionals with false antecedents). Similarly, here logic will supply moods to sentences which in ordinary language do not have moods, and declare well-formed sentences which in ordinary language sound bizarre. So long as the rules coincide with ordinary language in the cases where ordinary language has rules, this will not matter.

But this is not enough. The effect of the suggested rules for operating with tropics is such as to wreck even the simplest laws governing the use of the logical constants. For instance, contraposition. The rule that from Cpq we can infer $CNqNp$ holds for the assertoric mood and for the imperative mood. But what of the alleged mixed moods? $C\mathfrak{C}p\mathfrak{F}q$ is perfectly all right; and it is apparently an imperative. But $CN\mathfrak{F}q\mathfrak{C}p$ is not an imperative; it is simply ill formed.

Again, Cpq is by definition, in many systems, and by tautology in all systems, equivalent to $ANpq$. But whereas if $\mathfrak{F}p$ and $\mathfrak{F}q$ are well-formed imperatives, $A\mathfrak{F}p\mathfrak{F}q$ sounds well enough, it is not the case that where $AN\mathfrak{F}p\mathfrak{F}q$ is well formed, $C\mathfrak{F}p\mathfrak{F}q$ is well formed. And what are we to say of sentences formed by the conjunction of assertions and imperatives? Is $K\mathfrak{F}p\mathfrak{F}q$ an assertion or an imperative? If an assertion, what are its truth conditions? If an imperative, what are its satisfaction conditions?

From all this we can see that the thesis of the *Language of Morals* is the best solution to the problem of the formation rules for the logic of practical inference. What, then, of the transformation rules? These must surely depend on the value to be presumed in practical reasoning: on the practical analogue of truth.

Practical reasoning, I have said, can very well be looked at as a process of passing from one fiat to another according to rules, just as theoretical reasoning consists in passing from one assertoric sentence to another according to rules. The point of the rules for theoretical reasoning is to ensure that one never passes from true assertions to false assertions. What then is the practical analogue?

Fiats contain descriptions of possible states of affairs whose actualization satisfies the desires expressed by them. Among fiats, we have noted, are plans and projects. We can distinguish, among plans and projects, between those which are executed and those which are not executed. But when we are discussing the merits of plans, one thing we are looking for is a plan which will be *satisfactory*. Now of course a plan may be unsatisfactory precisely because it will be difficult to execute: but being executed and being satisfactory are in fact two quite different things. Commonly, in discussing plans, we presuppose our ability to implement them, and try to work out which, of the various plans we might implement, is most satisfactory—i.e. which will best serve our purposes and gratify our desires. We might be inclined to say: what is satisfactory is not the plan, but the state of affairs projected by the plan. Certainly, it is true that a state of affairs may be satisfactory or unsatisfactory; but it would be absurd to say that a plan was not satisfactory simply on the grounds that it was only a plan and not yet executed. For much of practical reasoning consists in the search for a satisfactory plan to execute; if a plan were never satisfactory unless executed, planning would be impossible. For we would have to do everything in our power before we could decide which of the things in our power was the best thing to do; and by then it would be too late.

Obviously satisfactoriness is a relative notion. Execution and non-execution, like truth and falsehood, are absolute notions; an assertion is either true or false, a command is either executed or not. But a plan is not just either satisfactory or not satisfactory: it may be satisfactory to some persons and not to others, satisfactory for some purposes and not for others.

Let us suppose that we desire a certain state of affairs for its own sake, and not as a means to any further end. Then the fiat which expresses this desire will, obviously, be a fiat whose satisfaction will satisfy the desire. Let us call such a *goal-fiat*, and say that it expresses a *purpose*. We are free to settle our purposes; but it does not depend on us which plans are compatible with, or effective of, the achievement of our purposes. Independently of us, certain states of affairs and certain plans are unsatisfactory to certain purposes; viz. those which are incompatible with the desired state of affairs. Independently also of us, any plan whose realization involves the actualization of the desired state of affairs will be satisfactory for that purpose. We cannot guarantee that it will be satisfactory to us (for it may conflict with other purposes of ours) still less that it will be satisfactory to all other persons.

Reflection on theses considerations led me to suggest, some years ago,[7] that the logic operative in practical reasoning was the logic of *satisfactoriness*. This was to consist of the rules which ensure that in practical reasoning we never pass from a fiat which is satisfactory for a particular purpose to a fiat which is unsatisfactory for that purpose. These rules are satisfactoriness-preserving just as rules for assertoric inference are truth-preserving. Trivially, every fiat is satisfactory relative to the purpose expressed by itself.

It is not difficult to construct such a logic of satisfactoriness. First, we must distinguish between *satisfactoriness* and *satisfaction*. A fiat $\mathfrak{F}p$ is satisfied just in case the corresponding assertion $\mathfrak{C}p$ is true. Clearly, a logic of satisfaction would be an exact and uninteresting parallel of assertoric logic: whenever we can infer $\mathfrak{C}q$ from $\mathfrak{C}p$ we can infer the satisfaction of $\mathfrak{F}q$ from the satisfaction of $\mathfrak{F}p$. The relation of the logic of satisfactoriness to the logic of satisfaction is this.[8] Let A and B both be fiats. B may be inferred from A in the logic of satisfaction if necessarily whenever A is satisfied then B is satisfied. B may be inferred from A in the logic of satisfactoriness if necessarily when A is satisfactory to a certain set of wants then B is satisfactory to that set of wants. Rules of inference in the logic of satisfaction are satisfaction-preserving: i.e. they are designed to prevent one passing from a satisfied fiat to an unsatisfied fiat. (They are in fact precisely analogous to the truth-preserving rules of assertoric inference which are designed to prevent one passing from a true premiss to a false conclusion.) Rules of inference in the logic of satisfactoriness are satisfactoriness-preserving: i.e. they are designed to prevent one passing from a satisfactory fiat (plan) to an unsatisfactory fiat. Now a plan is satisfactory relative to a certain set of wants, if and only if whenever the plan is satisfied every member of that set of wishes is satisfied. If it can be proved that if A is satisfied B is satisfied, then it follows that if B is satisfactory A is satisfactory. Again, if it is the case that if A is satisfactory B is satisfactory, then it follows that if B is satisfied A is satisfied. 'Satisfactory' in the last two sentences, of course, means 'satisfactory relative to a given set of wishes or goals'. It follows from all this that the logic of satisfactoriness is the mirror image of the logic of satisfacton. That is to say, whenever the logic of satisfaction permits the inference from A to B, the logic of satisfactoriness permits the inference from B to A.

It is impossible to base the logic of satisfactoriness on satisfactoriness-tables, because satisfactoriness, unlike truth, is a relative notion. But because of the mirror-image relationship between the logics of satisfaction and satisfactoriness it is possible to test the validity of inferences in the logic of satisfactoriness by appeal to truth-tables and quantificational truths. Suppose that we wish to know whether 𝔉P can be derived from 𝔉Q in the propositional calculus of satisfactoriness: i.e. whether, if 𝔉Q is satisfactory, 𝔉P is satisfactory also. The answer is that the inference is valid if *C*PQ is tautologous. For instance, you wish to know whether 𝔉*Kpq* can be inferred from 𝔉*Apq*. To test whether it can, you write *CKpq Apq* and test for tautology in the usual manner.

The reason for this is obvious. If *C*PQ is tautologous, then if 𝔈P is true, 𝔈Q is true; so if 𝔉P is satisfied, 𝔉Q is satisfied; so if 𝔉Q is satisfactory, 𝔉P is satisfactory. (For if 𝔉Q is satisfactory, then if 𝔉Q is satisfied all the members of G are satisfied; if 𝔉P is satisfied, 𝔉Q is satisfied; so if 𝔉P is satisfied, all the members of G are satisfied; so 𝔉P is satisfactory.) So too with the predicate calculus of satisfactoriness: if *C*PQ is a quantificational truth, then 𝔉P can be inferred from 𝔉Q. In general: if *C*QP is a logical law, then 𝔉P yields 𝔉Q in the logic of satisfactoriness.

The logic of satisfactoriness offers a means of solving some of the puzzles which disturbed us. The inference from 'Post the letter' to 'Post the letter or burn the letter' is not valid in this logic, and this conforms with our intuitive expectations. So too, the inference from 'Vote for the Labour candidate' to 'Vote for someone' is invalid. On the other hand, the inference from 'Post the letter or burn the letter' to 'Burn the letter', which is invalid in the logic of satisfaction, is valid in this logic; and the validity of this is recognized by anyone who realizes that he can obey the order 'post the letter or burn the letter' by burning the letter. So too, the logic of satisfactoriness contains an explicit law justifying the inference from 'Vote for someone' to 'Vote for the Labour candidate' which would be tacitly adopted by anyone who obeyed the first order by voting Labour.

The logic of satisfactoriness has certain features which *prima facie* appear paradoxical. For instance, in this logic the inference 'Kill the conspirators; Brutus is a conspirator; so kill Brutus' is invalid. But this result, properly understood, is perfectly correct: the order 'Kill the conspirators' has not been fully obeyed by someone who obeys the order 'Kill Brutus' unless Brutus is the only conspirator, which the premises do not entitle us to conclude. Again, in the logic of satisfactoriness there is an inference from $\mathfrak{F}p$ to $\mathfrak{F}Kpq$, since assertorically $\mathfrak{F}Kpq$ entails $\mathfrak{F}p$. But surely one cannot infer 'open the door and smash the window' from 'open the door'! In answer, we may agree first that the *command* 'open the door and smash the window' can't be inferred from the *command* 'open the door': the logic of satisfactoriness concerns fiats, not directives. From the command 'open the door' one can, however, infer the fiat '$\mathfrak{F}$ (opening of the door and smashing of the window)'; someone who did execute such a plan would indeed obey the original command and satisfy the desire which that command might vent. By executing the command in such a manner, the agent would no doubt annoy the commander; but this would be because he would be acting against the commander's tacit desire that the window should not be broken. If this tacit desire were made explicit, the fiat expressing the commander's state of mind would be of the form $\mathfrak{F}KpNq$; from which there is no inference in the logic of satisfactoriness to $\mathfrak{F}Kpq$. Thus the paradox here is only apparent.

In the logic of satisfactoriness, we can pass from $\mathfrak{F}q$ to $\mathfrak{F}KpCpq$. In other words, the analogue of affirming the consequent is not a fallacy in the logic of satisfactoriness. This gives us a clue how to deal with Aristotle's example, 'He is to be heated; if I rub him he will be heated; so I'll rub him,' which was invalid in his own logic. Similarly, the inference from $\mathfrak{F}\exists x \phi x$ to $\mathfrak{F}\phi a$ is valid in the logic of satisfactoriness; and this suggests a way to deal with the cloak syllogism.[9]

But though the logic of satisfactoriness provides a solution for a number of familiar paradoxes, many people have been repelled by the paradoxes which it is thought to generate in its turn. In fact the application of the logic of satisfactoriness leads to no genuinely paradoxical conclusions, and it is undoubtedly sound in the sense that the application of its rules will preserve from premiss to conclusion the designated value of satisfactoriness. The alleged paradoxical inferences are all instances of overkill, whether metaphorical or literal. But if we object to the line of reasoning 'The newborn claimant to the Kingship of Israel is to be killed; the newborn claimant to the Kingship of Israel is an infant in Bethlehem; so all the infants in Bethlehem are to be killed' it is not Herod's *logic* that we are faulting.[10]

This much, however, must be conceded to the critics of the logic of satisfactoriness, that it is misleading to call it 'the logic of practical reasoning'. I once argued its claim to that name in the following way:

The logic of satisfactoriness, and not the logic of satisfaction, is the principal logic of imperatives. This is because the purpose of practical reasoning is to get done what we want; just as the purpose of theoretical reasoning is to discover truth. The preservation of satisfactoriness, therefore, has in practical inference that place which the preservation of truth has in theoretical inference. Those rules will most deserve the name 'rules of practical inference' which will ensure that in reasoning about what to do we never pass from a plan which will satisfy our desires to a plan which will not satisfy them. And these rules are the rules of the logic of satisfactoriness (art. cit., p. 73).

There are, I now think, two things which are misleading about this. The first is that in speaking of a 'logic of imperatives' and of a 'logic of practical reasoning' one may be thought to be suggesting that in issuing imperatives and in reasoning out our plans we are making use of a set of logical truths different from those which are formalized in the familiar propositional and predicate calculus and the modal systems built on them. And this is certainly not so: one and the same set of logical truths is exploited in both assertoric and practical reasoning. And so if logics are individuated by the set of logical truths which they formalize, there is not a logic of commands which differs from the logic of statements, nor a logic of practical reasoning which differs from the logic of theoretical reasoning.

However, it is possible to think of logic as primarily the study of patterns of inference rather than the formalization of logical truths. Historically, both approaches have been made dominant in the work of different authors. The traditional 'Aristotelian' logic concentrates almost exclusively on valid patterns of inference, and had little to say about logical truths. Wittgenstein's *Tractatus*, by attempting to reduce all propositions to truth-functions of logically unrelated elementary propositions, and by offering truth-tables to display the relationships between different truth-functions, made the notion of logical truth dominant and attempted to render rules of inference superfluous. Most contemporary logical systems employ both logical truths and rules of inference: in axiomatic systems such as Frege's the logical truths which are the axioms and theorems are dominant, and rules of inference within the system are applied only to logical truths; in natural deduction systems such as Gentzen's it is the rules of inference which are basic; they are applied to non-logical propositions and the logical truths are yielded only as the results of particular applications of the rules.

In assertoric logic, to every valid inference schema there corresponds a logically true conditional statement, and to every logically true conditional statement there corresponds a valid inference schema; so that it may seem to be a matter merely of combinatorial elegance, not of philosophical importance which approach is taken. But of course when we turn to study the logic of imperatives or fiats, the matter is quite different. For here, it seems, we can take only the rules-of-inference approach. For commands, requests, and wishes, not having truth-values at all, *a fortiori* cannot be logical truths.

But even in the assertoric case there is an ambiguity in speaking of 'logical truth'. A logically true assertion is not the same thing as a logically true proposition. 'Truth' as applied to propositions must be distinguished from 'Truth' as applied to assertions. This point was brought out very clearly by Erik Stenius in his book *Wittgenstein's Tractatus*. Stenius distinguishes between *descriptive* truth and *modal* truth. Descriptive truth and descriptive falsehood are properties of phrastics or sentence-radicals: a phrastic has descriptive truth if there is in reality a state of affairs answering to it. Modal truth is a property only of sentences in a particular *mood*, namely the assertoric. If—with a degree of oversimplification, as Stenius admits—we take the indicative mood as the mood of assertion, then an assertion is a move in a language-game whose principle is:

(A) Produce a sentence in the indicative mood only if the sentence-radical is a true description.

The word 'true' in this rule refers to the concept of truth as applied to sentence-radicals; the concept of 'truth' as applied to assertions is a different one and can thus be defined in terms of it without circularity. Stenius observes:

> The concept of truth appearing in the moral rule 'Always speak the truth' is the modal truth. The moral rule says that you must always play the language-game of the indicative mood correctly, not that you must always produce true sentence-radicals. Only the existence of rule (A) makes it possible to deceive people by breaking it.

It is not difficult to produce the corresponding rule for the imperative:

(B) Produce a sentence in the imperative mood only if the sentence-radical is to be made true.[11]

The notion of descriptive truth thus enters into an account of the imperative as well as of the indicative mood. But clearly descriptive truth is separable both from assertoric truth and from the correct use of imperatives. An assertion of a conditional, If *p* then *q*, may be a true assertion even though both the phrastics, *p* and *q*, are false—descriptively false, that is, for being unasserted they have no assertoric truth-value, are neither true nor false assertions. The felicitous utterance of an imperative, on the other hand, actually presupposes that the sentence-radical it involves is descriptively false; for only if it is false can it be made true. And clearly the notion of assertoric truth applies neither to the phrastic of the command nor to the command as a whole.

Now when we speak of logical truth what we are principally concerned with is descriptive or propositional truth, not assertoric truth. Of course, someone who asserts a proposition which is a logical truth—a description which is true in virtue of its logical form—will *eo ipso* make a logically true assertion. But the truth which logic is ultimately concerned with is the descriptive truth of propositions which are themselves neutral with regard to the various speech-acts which may employ them as phrastics or sentence-radicals. In this sense there are not two logics, one assertoric and one imperative: there is one logic, which is itself neither assertoric nor imperative, but propositional and which is used in different ways in commands and statements, in practical and in theoretical reasoning.

We can thus see what is correct and what is incorrect in talking about 'the logic of practical reasoning'. The other thing which was misleading in my earlier remarks about the logic of satisfactoriness is this. I said that the purpose of practical reasoning was to get done what we want, while the purpose of theoretical reasoning is to discover truth. This, I think, is correct, but it does not follow from that by itself that the logic of satisfactoriness is the practical analogue of theoretical formal logic. Because in getting done what we want we have to make use of the logic of satisfaction as well as the logic of satisfactoriness; and in the discovery of truth we make use not only of deductive logic but of 'inductive logic' as well. So that what we have to examine is not simply the relationship between two terms, theoretical and practical logic, but between four terms, theoretical deductive and theoretical inductive logic, and the practical logic of satisfaction and satisfactoriness.

This was very clearly brought out in Professor Hare's paper, 'Practical Inferences' (pp. 59–73 of his book of that name). When we have to fulfil commands and intentions, Hare explained, we have to reason from them to the necessary and sufficient conditions for fulfilling them. The Aristotelian examples of practical reasonings, he says, are some of them reasonings to necessary conditions (as in 'Everyone is to march, so I'm to march'), and some of them reasonings to sufficient conditions (as in 'I must have a covering, so I must have a cloak'), and Aristotle did not pay sufficient attention to the difference between these two. The logic of satisfaction and the logic of satisfactoriness, Hare maintains, correspond respectively to reasoning to necessary conditions and reasoning to sufficient conditions. These do not amount to a new 'imperative logic'; for reasoning to sufficient conditions no less than reasoning to necessary conditions occurs in the assertoric as well as the imperative case.

The logic of necessary and sufficient conditions is a well-worn application of ordinary logic; and so it is not necessary to claim that Kenny's logic of satisfactoriness, when redescribed as a logic of sufficient conditions, introduces any element peculiar to imperatives or practical inferences. It might be the case (though, as we shall see, it is not) that in practical reasoning we always inferred suficient conditions, and in theoretical reasoning never. In actual fact, the most that can be said is that reasoning to sufficient conditions is somewhat commoner (because more commonly useful) in practical thought than in theoretical (loc. cit., p. 68).

We reason to necessary conditions in practical contexts, for example, when we are seeking to obey a negative prohibition; and we reason to sufficient conditions in theoretical contexts, for instance, when we are seeking an explanation, whether in scientific contexts of theory building or in ordinary life as when we reason thus: 'Harry is late; but the 10.45 being late is something that would make Harry late; so (perhaps) the 10.45 is late.' Inferences to explanation, Hare shows, are isomorphic to inferences in the logic of satisfactoriness.

The considerations which Hare adduces show that the mirror-image relationship between theoretical and practical reasoning is more complicated than at first appears. In theoretical argument it is reasoning to necessary conditions—deductive theoretical logic—which is *conclusive*, in the sense of ensuring that the conclusion has the value which the reasoning aims at, namely truth; only deductive inference makes it certain that if the premises are true the conclusion is also. Inference to the best explanation, or inductive logic, as a host of philosophers of science have insisted, is never conclusive in the sense of showing that it is logically impossible for the premises to be true and the conclusion false. On the other hand, in practical inference it is only the logic of satisfactoriness which is *conclusive*, in the sense of ensuring that the conclusion has the value that the reasoning aims at, namely the satisfaction of the reasoner's wants. The logic of satisfaction—reasoning to necessary conditions for satisfaction—is never conclusive in the sense of ensuring the arrival of what is wanted. Having carried out a piece of practical reasoning to necessary conditions, and put the conclusion into action, the reasoner cannot then rest secure in the confidence that what he has done will bring about the state of affairs he wants: there may be *more* that he has to do in order to achieve his goals. In particular, to take Hare's example, one never comes to the end of satisfying a negative prohibition. In real life, both practical and theoretical inference is a mixture of both kinds of reasoning;[12] but the relationship of the elements so mixed differs in the two cases.

The upshot of Hare's discussion of reasoning to sufficient and necessary conditions is that the thesis of the mirror-image relationship between theoretical and practical reasoning needs complication rather than recantation. He offers also, however, a more searching criticism of the theory based on the notions of assent and consistency.

According to the logic of satisfactoriness, I can deduce the command 'Shut the door' from the command 'Shut the door or shut the window.' But in the case of ordinary valid logical inferences he who assents to the premisses is *compelled* not to dissent from the conclusion, on pain of logical inconsistency. It might be suggested that with the present inference this rule does not hold. I can without any inconsistency agree to shut the door or shut the window, and then refuse to shut the the door provided that I shut the window.

It can, as Hare agrees, be replied to this that to assent, in the logic of satisfactoriness, is to find what is assented to satisfactory for a given purpose. But this reply seems to strain the meaning of 'assent': to assent to a command—to say 'Yes' to something like 'Shut the door'—is surely to agree to obey it; to assent to a plan—to say 'Yes' to something like 'Let's have a picnic'—is to agree to execute it. And surely someone may without any inconsistency assent to a fiat in that sense without assenting to another fiat which is derivable from it in the logic of satisfactoriness: to use another of Hare's examples one may assent to 'Book me a room in the best hotel in town' and fail to assent to 'Book me all the rooms in all the hotels in town.'

Consideration of this example brings out a point which we encountered earlier, that the logic of commands is more complicated than the logic of fiats in general. In particular, if we are to discuss the notion of assent to a command, we have to give different accounts of commander's assent (e.g. what commands he would regard as validly drawn transmissions of his commands down a chain of command) and commandee's assent (e.g. what other commands he is committed to accepting in virtue of having accepted a given command). This is a difficult topic which it is fortunately not necessary to pursue in attempting to give an account of practical reasoning: the difficulty which Hare points out suffices to show that the logic of satisfactoriness needs very drastic supplementation if it is to be regarded as the logic of commands.

However, Hare's objection does not seem to me to be equally damaging to the proposal to assign a central place to the logic of satisfactoriness in the case of practical reasoning, and reasoning about fiats in general. For if someone had expressed his current wants adequately in a goal-fiat, then there *is* something inconsistent in his refusing to welcome a fiat which is derivable from it in the logic of satisfactoriness. If my *only* want is to have the door open, why should I object if someone opens the door and smashes the window? Of course, there is something insane in the idea of having only a single want of that kind; and the reason I would object in the case in point is that I don't want the window smashed. But if that is among my wants, then it should be included in the goal-fiat from which the practical reasoning starts. If I dislike a conclusion to which a piece of practical reasoning leads, then it shows that I have inadequately specified ...y goals; and if I am to be consistent I must revise my goals, review the list of purposes which constitute my goal-fiat.

This feature of practical reasoning has led some people to the belief that the logic of satisfactoriness is really only an enthymematic version of the logic of satisfaction: a piece of practical reasoning in the logic of satisfactoriness is really a piece of reasoning in the logic of satisfaction with some of its premisses suppressed. Consider the example given earlier.

I am to be in London at 4.15
If I catch the 2.30 I'll be in London at 4.15
So I'll catch the 2.30.

This is valid, it is suggested, only because it is enthymematic, with an unstated premiss reflecting the fact that I don't want to be in London any earlier than I have to be. If such a premiss is made explicit, then there will be a reasoning to necessary conditions, which will bring out that if I'm to be in London as close to 4.15 as possible but no later, I must take the 2.30.[13]

What such examples show is not that reasoning in the logic of satisfactoriness is enthymematic, but that it is defeasible. The reasoning is not enthymematic, for no extra premisses needed to be added to ensure that the use of reasoning will lead from satisfactory premisses only to a satisfactory conclusion. But the reasoning is defeasible because if we add further satisfactory premisses we cannot be sure that the conclusion will remain satisfactory. Theoretical deductive reasoning is not defeasible in the sense that the addition of a premiss cannot invalidate a previously valid inference: if a conclusion follows from a given set of premisses it can be drawn from any larger set containing those premisses no matter how many are added to the set. With practical reasoning in the logic of satisfactoriness this is not so. Though catching the 2.30 may be a reasonable conclusion from the premisses first set out, it ceases to be reasonable if we add the premisses that the 2.30 is always crowded to bursting point, and that it would be a good thing to work on the train.

The defeasibility of practical reasoning comes about because of satisfactoriness being—like explanation—a relative notion: something is not satisfactory *simpliciter*, but satisfactory relative to a given set of wants; just as something is not an explanation *simpliciter*, but an explanation of a given set of data. The only way to avoid defeasibility in practical reasoning would be to insist that the premiss setting out the goal should be not only correct but also complete; that *all* the wants to be satisfied by one's action should be fully specified. If we could do this, then there would be no danger of some further premiss being added—some further want turning up—which would negative the satisfactoriness of the action described in the solution.

Both Aristotle and St. Thomas sometimes write as if they thought that the first premiss of a piece of practical reasoning must be a universal plan of life of this kind, specifying an all-embracing good. Indeed, the type of premiss they had in mind was something not only universal, but also objective. They regarded the value to be transmitted by practical reasoning as not being satisfactoriness, but rather goodness: and goodness, in their view, was not something relative to the wants of a given individual, but something objectively discernible. For them, rules of practical reasoning would be rules designed to ensure that if the state of affairs described in the premiss which sets out the goal of the practical reasoning is good, and if the form of reasoning is valid, then the state of affairs described in the conclusion is good. Goodness in practical reasoning would then be the analogue of truth in theoretical reasoning. Moreover, just as there were self-evident truths which played a special part in the use of theoretical reason, there were, on the Aristotelian view, self-desirable goods which had the cardinal role in practical reasoning.

Such a line of thought is very alien to contemporary philosophical fashion. To attempt a serious evaluation of it would call for an extended treatise. But whether or not the objectivity of the designated value refutes the Aristotelian theory of practical reasoning, the universality of the postulated major premisses seems to me to establish the theory's inadequacy.

The notion of a premiss which is complete enough to prevent defeasibility while specific enough to entail a practical conclusion is surely chimerical. Only in restricted contexts can we even approach completeness in the specification of practical premisses: we insist, for instance, that the listing of contra-indications on a marketed drug should be not only accurate but, within limits, complete. But even if we could specify a whole plan of life in the Aristotelian manner this would only prevent defeasibility in the logic of satisfactoriness, it would not prevent the defeasibility of any Aristotelian 'logic of goodness'. It would not prevent a situation in which an action which one argument may show to be a good action may be shown by a further argument to be a bad action. This is something which Aquinas himself often insisted upon. He took this as showing, however, not that practical reasoning was defeasible, in the sense that an argument from certain premisses to the goodness of a state of affairs represented in a conclusion might by means of the addition of further premisses be rendered invalid or brought to cease to hold, but rather as showing a difference between goodness and truth. It is a presupposition of truth-functional logic that any proposition which has the value 'true' does not also have the value 'false'; but it is not the case that a proposal for action which has the value 'good' may not also have the value 'bad'. On the Thomist view an argument which shows to be bad a conclusion which another argument showed to be good need not in any way contradict that argument: it merely establishes that the proposal contained in the conclusion has both good and bad aspects. Moreover, an argument which shows something to be a good thing to do in no way shows that something incompatible with the conclusion it reaches may not also be a good thing to do.

This feature of practical reasoning was repeatedly stressed by Aquinas. It provided, he believed, the sense in which practical reasoning does not necessitate its conclusions; and he saw the contingency of the conclusions of practical reason as being the fundamental ground of the freedom of the human will.

The contrast just mentioned between truth and goodness seems to me to show that if there could be a logic of objective goodness as envisaged in the Thomist tradition it would bear no simple relation to the assertoric logic of truth. It would need, for instance, to be a three-valued system in order to allow for the possibility of actions being a mixture of good and evil without falling into plain inconsistency. I shall not hazard any conjecture about the form it might take.

The logic of satisfactoriness, however, does not prevent the special difficulties such a project raises: and provided that it is allowed to remain defeasible it seems neither chimerical nor unfamiliar. In the logic of satisfactoriness the analogy of the Thomist contingency of goodness is precisely the feature of defeasibility.

The logic of satisfactoriness is no more than a part of practical reasoning. We have already observed that it needs to be supplemented with a logic of the description of action before it can become genuinely practical; and that in order to become an imperative logic it needs to incorporate features to take account of the difference between fiats and directives. Moreover, it fails to represent adequately something which is intuitively of great importance in practical reasoning: the weighing up of the pros and cons of a particularly course of action. Where an agent's goals are consistently realizable, then the consideration of the advantages and disadvantages of particular actions can be seen as the search for a conclusion-fiat derivable from a goal-fiat which will incorporate all the ends which provide the standards of advantageousness and disadvantageousness for the case in point. But there is no guarantee that the ends are capable of joint attainment, and in such a case what is needed is not a refinement of the

Aristotelian end-means reasoning, but something more like contemporary decision theory.

[1] 'I'm to be ' in the premiss is not meant to express any obligation; the premiss is intended as a colloquial equivalent to 'Fiat (my being in London at 4.15)'.

[2] [In Ch. 3 which is now reprinted here—Ed.]

[3] 'In their ordinary uses the common logical connectives "if", "and", and "or", like the sign of negation, are best treated as part of the phrastics of sentences.' 21.

[4] *Action, Emotion and Will*, 228.

[5] Here and elsewhere I use the Polish notation for the truth-functional connectives, writing 'Kpq' for 'p and q', 'Apq' for 'p or q', 'Cpq' for 'if p then q' and 'Epq' for 'p if and only if (iff) q'.

[6] Cf. M. Dummett, 'Truth', 57.

[7] In an article 'Practical Inference' (*Analysis*, 1966) on which part of this chapter is based.

[8] In what follows the 'propositional variables' p, q, r are to be taken to range over unasserted phrastics; P, Q, R, are metalogical variables to represent expressions built up out of p, q, r, etc., and logical constants; A, B, are metalogical variables to represent expressions built up from the type of expression represented by P, Q, R, plus either an assertoric or imperative tropic.

[9] Aristotle's cloak syllogiam in fact contains mixed premisses, one imperative setting out a goal, and one assertoric setting out the facts of the case. A possible rule for such inferences is this. Remove the assertoric tropics from the assertoric premisses: conjoin their phrastics with the phrastics of the imperative conclusions and assign an imperative tropic to this conjunction. Then the inference is valid in imperative logic if an assertion corresponding to the goal-fiat can be derived in assertoric logic from the conjunction of the other premisses and the conclusion (e.g. '𝔍p 𝔍Cap; so 𝔍q' is valid in practical reasoning because '$KCqpq$' entails 'p'). The rationale of this is twofold. (1) In order to begin practical reasoning one must accept the facts as they are (e.g. one cannot reason practically about Communist China without accepting its existence) and this corresponds to replacing the assertion with the corresponding fiat. (2) The means chosen must be sufficient for the goal to be reached; and this will be so when the conclusion conjoined with the other premisses entails, in theoretical logic, the goal-premiss's assertoric equivalent. But the complications introduced by mixed premisses make it difficult to formalize Aristotle s examples just as they stand.

[10] Thus Alf Ross's criticism of the logic of satisfactoriness (*Directives and Norms*, 176) misses the point. Professor Anscombe, who agrees in rejecting Ross's complaint ('Von Wright on Practical Inference . . .'), says that the inference from 𝔍p to 𝔍(Kpq) is acceptable only when effecting two things is *a way* of effecting one of them, so that the second fiat would be a description of a single action: it would be futile, having effected that p, to go on later to effect that q in satisfaction of the original wish that p. Her point shows that the logic of satisfactoriness concerns merely the relations between states of affairs qua want-satisfactions: in order to be applied to the *bringing about* of states of affairs—and thus to become a genuinely practical logic, rather than a wish-fulfilment logic ensnaring Midases and useful only to fairy godmothers—it needs supplementing with logic of the description of actions. Von Wright in a number of papers (most recently 'Handlungslogik' in *Normenlogik*, ed. Lenk) has outlined such a logic: in a form, however, which enshrines the implausible axiom that one brings it about that p and q if and only if one brings it about that p and one brings it about that q.

[11] Stenius's own rule is 'Make the sentence radical true'—obviously a rule directed to the listener, not the speaker. This seems to be an incorrect formulation of the rule; it would have the consequence that disobedience to a command was always an abuse of language, parallel to a lie.

[12] I used to think that the logic of satisfactoriness alone was sufficient for practical reasoning and that cases of 'reasoning to necessary conditions' could be dealt with as cases of reasoning, in the logic of satisfactoriness, to conditions which were both sufficient and necessary. But, as Professor Anscombe has pointed out to me, this won't deal with such inferences as 'I'll never get to the station tomorrow unless I pack this case tonight; so I will pack it tonight.'

[13] I owe this suggestion to Professor F. Stoutland. He argues that unless the example given is enthymematic, we would have to admit the validity of the parallel reasoning.

If I am to be in London six months hence
If I catch today's 2.30 I'll be in London six months hence
So I'll catch today's 2.30.

But of course, for the reasons given, there is nothing paradoxical in accepting this reasoning as valid.

V

PRIMA FACIE OBLIGATIONS[1]

JOHN SEARLE

I

THE first thing to notice about the notion of a *prima facie* obligation is that it is not a term in ordinary discourse, moral or otherwise, but is a technical term introduced by philosophers in discussing problems of moral philosophy. As such, one might hope to find some fairly clear explanation of the notion, but the discussions I have seen of this notion are extremely confused. Some, though by no means all, of the confusion is due to Ross, who first introduced the distinction between *prima facie* duties (and obligations) and some other kind of duties (and obligations).[2] I shall not spend much space on Ross's account, because it does not seem to me that it can be made consistent internally. But when any new technical term is introduced in philosophy without explicit definition, there are at least two questions one must ask of it; Ross answered these questions and his answers have influenced his successors. The two questions are, what motivates the introduction of the term in the first place, and what other terms is it opposed to? Ross's answer to the first question is reasonably clear:

> If, as almost all moralists except Kant are agreed, and as most plain men think, it is sometimes right to tell a lie or break a promise, it must be maintained that there is a difference between *prima facie* duty and actual or absolute duty. When we think ourselves justified in breaking, and indeed morally obliged to break, a promise in order to relieve someone's distress, we do not for a moment cease to recognize a *prima facie* duty to keep our promise, and this leads us to feel, not indeed shame or repentance, but certainly compunction, for behaving as we do; we recognize further, that it is our duty to make up somehow to the promise for the breaking of the promise.[3]

The picture that Ross has is this: In real life situations one often has conflicting duties, obligations, etc. For example, I may have an obligation to Smith to attend his party (because, let us say, I promised to come) and also an obligation to stay and help Jones (because, let us say, he is bleeding to death and crying for my help). In such a case I am justified in breaking the promise. In such a case the obligation to keep the promise, says Ross, is

'Prima Facie Obligations' (© 1978 by John R. Searle). Printed by permission of the author (not previously published).

only a *prima facie* obligation. For future reference let us call situations of this sort, where there is a conflict of reasons of a generally 'moral' kind *conflict situations*, and this particular example *the conflict situation*. The notion of *prima facie* duty or obligation in Ross's account is introduced to characterize certain features of conflict situations.

But Ross's answer to the second question is much less clear. He begins[4] by opposing *prima facie* duty to 'duty *sans phrase*' or 'duty proper'. Later, in the passage quoted above he opposes *prima facie* duty to 'actual or absolute duty'. This multiplicity of opposing terms is inherited by his followers. Thus Hintikka[5] opposes *prima facie* obligations to 'actual', 'absolute', and 'overall' obligations, treating all of these as equivalent, at least for purposes of making the contrast. But this multiplicity of contrasting terms ought to arouse our suspicions. They are by no means equivalent, and there are in fact at least two quite different distinctions lurking in the notion of a *prima facie* obligation, and these in turn provide two different and inconsistent descriptions of the conflict situation.

The first distinction: *prima facie* vs. actual obligations: According to one version of the notion of *prima facie* obligations, which we might call Ross's official view, to say that

1. *X* has a *prima facie* obligation to do *A*

does not entail

2. *X* has an obligation to do *A*,

because it is consistent with

3. *X* does not really have any obligation at all to do *A*, he only *seems* to have that obligation.

On this account *prima facie* obligations are contrasted with actual or real ones and the correct way to describe the conflict situation is to say that

4. I have no obligation at all to keep my promise. I do indeed *seem* to have an obligation, because promise-keeping, as Ross says, has a 'tendency to be our duty', but when all the facts are known it turns out that I have an obligation to help Jones, but none whatever to go to Smith's party.

I shall later argue that this is a false description of the conflict situation. It is, however, the one which Ross explicitly endorses and which his theory commits him to holding. An immediate difficulty with it is that on this view the promise in the conflict situation ends up counting for nothing. It is exactly as if I had never made a promise at all. Ross is uncomfortable with this result, because it is hard to make it consistent with his original remarks about conflict situations quoted above. If there is no real or actual obligation at all, then what is it exactly that I 'do not for a moment cease to recognize'? And why should I feel any 'compunction' or 'make up' anything to the promisee if I have no real or actual obligation to him? Ross's remarks about tendencies are clearly not sufficient to obviate this inconsistency. To say, as he does, that promise-keeping has a 'tendency' to be our duty is like saying glass windows have a tendency to break when struck. If I strike this window and it does not break, it is just as unbroken as if I had never struck it at all. Similarly if all that promises do is generate tendencies to be duties, then the fact that in this case I have no duty at all to keep the promise renders the conflict situation exactly as if I had never made a promise in the first place, for in this case the 'tendency' is inoperative. But this view is unacceptable because it makes it mysterious and inexplicable that I should have any 'compunction' about breaking the promise and that I should have 'a duty to make up to the promisee for the breaking of the promise'. If the promise does not create any actual obligations but only seems to (*'prima facie'*) then I should be able to ignore it altogether once all the facts are known. This difficulty with Ross's conception of *prima facie* obligations leads to a second conception of *prima facie* obligations which is implicit in Ross and explicit in other authors such as Hintikka.

The second distinction: *prima facie* vs. absolute obligations: According to this second version of the notion of *prima facie* obligations which Ross denies that he holds, but which I believe some features of his account presuppose, to say that

    1. *X* has a *prima facie* obligation to do *A*

does indeed entail

    2. *X* has an obligation to do *A*

but only because

    5. *Prima facie* obligations are a species or kind of obligations. They are inherently subject to being overruled or overridden by other obligations (and other reasons for acting in conflict situations). An obligation that overrides them is called an absolute obligation. Relative to a given situation, a *prima facie* obligation can become an absolute obligation if it overrides all other obligations.

Ross explicitly denies that he thinks of *prima facie* obligations as a kind of obligation,[6] but unless we suppose that in some sense *prima facie* obligations are a kind of obligation it is very hard to make sense of this account. For example he actually provides a list of the principal types of *prima facie* duties;[7] also, he provides an analogy between the way different *prima facie* obligations produce a resultant obligation and the way different forces operating on a body produce a resultant velocity.[8] Unless we think of *prima facie* obligations as a kind of actual obligations, like actual forces operating on a body, there is no point to the analogy. But, most importantly, his description of conflict situations, with all his talk of our 'compunctions' etc. for promises broken, makes no sense unless we ascribe some actual status to the *prima facie* obligations, that is, unless we think of them as a kind of obligation. Ross apart, I am here primarily concerned to argue that there are in fact two different contrasts contained in the notion of *prima facie* obligations. Whether or not Ross held the second, other philosophers, e.g. Hintikka, certainly have.

According to the second contrast the proper way to describe the conflict situation is:

6. In the conflict situation there actually are two inconsistent obligations. However, one is of a lower status than the other. It is only a *prima facie* obligation and it is overruled by the other which is an absolute obligation. The *prima facie* obligation, however, does not cease to exist, it is simply of a member of a class of obligations, the *prima facie* class, which are less compelling than the absolute class.

II

The foregoing is an attempt to bring some sort of order into the discussion about and those discussions which use the notion of *prima facie* obligations.

Its result, however, is that there are two quite distinct notions and they are not consistent, that is, if 'obligation' is supposed to be univocal, then the two contrasts provide inconsistent descriptions of the conflict situation, for on the first version there is no obligation at all to keep the promise and on the second version there is. Is there any way out of this inconsistency, and more generally is there any merit in these distinctions and their attendant terminology? I think the views embodied in both contrasts are mistaken—though there is more truth in the second than in the first—and we would do well in philosophy to abandon the terminology of *prima facie* obligations and duties as it embodies confusions.

What is the correct way to describe the status of the obligations in conflict situations? The first point to emphasize is that most moral conflicts in real life are cases where there are genuinely valid reasons for doing one thing and at the same time reasons for not doing that thing but doing something inconsistent with it. In the case of conflicting obligations of the sort that we described above one is under an obligation to do one thing (go to the party) and at the same time one is under an obligation to do something inconsistent with it (stay and help the bleeding Jones). That is, using

7. (Op&Oq)& -poss(p&q).

In extreme cases I may have an obligation to do one thing and another independent obligation not to do that very same thing:

8. Op&O-p.

I would argue that where the possibility in question in 7 is logical possibility, that is, where *q* entails -*p*, 8 follows from 7. But whether or not that is a correct view of entailed obligations, both 7 and 8 describe the form of common conflict situations in real life: one has two obligations which are such that it is impossible to fulfil both. The states of affairs described by 7 and 8 are not only logically possible, they are what the study of moral conflict, logically speaking, is all about. In some systems of deontic logic it is denied that 7 and 8 are logically possible; the reason for this is that it is awkward to construct a semantic model for a deontic calculus which allows 7 and 8, but that should not be surprising since the notion of a genuine moral conflict is a notion of a situation where there is no possible world which satisfies all one's obligations.

Many philosophers—and not just Ross—have tried to deny that 7 and 8 correctly represent the structure of conflict situations, but there is no way that these denials can account for certain obvious features of moral conflicts, as we shall shortly see. Now, because 7 and 8 give the logical structure of conflict situations it is important to note that the negation of Op is not O-p, but rather -Op; that is the negation of '*X* is under an obligation to do *A*' is 'It is not the case that *X* is under an obligation to do *A*' and not '*X* is under an obligation not to do *A*' since one can be under independent obligations both to do and not to do *A*.

Now when one is in a situation of the sort represented by 7 and 8, one cannot act so as to satisfy both obligations. One obligation has to *override* another if one is to satisfy either. Often in real life it will be obvious how to resolve the conflict, and in the example we gave above the obligation to attend the party is quite trivial relative to the obligation to help Jones. But in the hard cases one may simply not be able to decide what to do on rational grounds alone. Reflection on the relative weights of our obligations (and commitments and duties and other sorts of reasons) may not be sufficient to provide a rational answer to 'What ought we to do, all things considered?'

This account of the conflict situation will provide a basis for seeing what is wrong with the two previous accounts. On the first account, 7 and 8 do not really represent conflict situations, because one of the obligations does not really exist at all, it is only '*prima facie*' and not real and hence there really is no such obligation. There are so many things wrong with this account that one hardly knows where to begin to criticize it, but here are three obvious objections to it. First, if taken seriously, it has the consequence of denying the obvious fact about human experience, that there really are moral conflicts. According to it one element in the conflict is not really there at all. Second, it becomes impossible on this account to describe the situation in which one obligation overrides another. In order for one obligation to override another, or to be more important than another, or to take precedence over another, the other has to be there in the first place, otherwise there is nothing to override. It is a paradoxical feature of this account that it denies the crucial feature of conflict situations— conflicting obligations where one overrides another—which gave rise to the doctrine in the first place. Third, the thesis denies such obvious conceptual truths as that promises create obligations. What its adherents are forced to claim is that promises create *prima facie* obligations, but on this version all that can mean is that promises *seem* to create obligations or, on Ross's version, they *tend* to create obligations, but in cases where the obligations they seem or tend to create are overridden by other obligations they do not create any obligations at all. It is, I think, not surprising that no adherent of this view has ever given an adequate analysis of promising. I conclude that the first version of *prima facie* obligations must be abandoned. It is simply a mistake to conclude from the features of the conflict situation that the obligation to keep the promise does not exist, that it is not a real obligation.

But what about the second version? It at least has the merit of granting that conflicting obligations can actually exist and continue to exist even when one overrides another. Furthermore, it has the merit of recognizing the distinction between a weaker and a stronger obligation in cases like the conflict situation; but such cases hardly give any grip to the view that there are two distinct classes of obligations, *prima facie* and absolute, because what is absolute in one situation may be *prima facie* in another. For example, my obligation to help Jones may be overridden by my obligation to prevent an explosion which will otherwise destroy the whole city. That is, if the *prima facie* versus absolute distinction is construed in terms of relative moral strengths then whether or not an obligation was *prima facie* or absolute would depend on the particular conflict situation under consideration, and we would not be able to specify two separate classes of obligations independently of specifying different conflict situations. To make this point clear we need to distinguish between particular statements of obligation such as

9. Brown is under an obligation to do *A* because he promised to do *A* and general statements of obligation such as

10. All promises create obligations.

The question we are now asking is: can we make any sense of the distinction between *prima facie* and absolute obligations construed as species of obligations where '*prima facie*' and 'absolute' are supposed to be prefixed to 'obligation(s))' in sentences of the kind exemplified by 9 and 10? In the particular cases, such as 9, we will not be able to get two independent classes of obligations because, if the criterion is overridingness, then the obligation in 9 may be absolute relative to one conflict situation and *prima facie* relative to another. If on the other hand we think of the *prima facie* absolute distinction as applying to general statements of obligation such as 10, then we would get the result that all obligations (or at least all minus one) are *prima facie*. This is because any obligation is subject to being overridden by special considerations in particular circumstances. That is, given the reasonable assumptions that any two general obligations can conflict in particular (actual or possible) conflict situations and that over- ridingness is a transitive relation, then there could mathematically speaking be at most one absolute general obligation, because there could be at most one obligation such that it overrides all others and no others override it. In neither case, the particular or the general, do we get a useful classification of obligations into two kinds, *prima facie* and absolute. Furthermore, actual conflict situations can be readily and accurately described without introducing this muddled terminology. The correct account of the way obligations relate to conflict situations is the following. Obligations (and similarly with duties, responsibilities, commitments, etc.) provide reasons for acting. Obligations for various purposes may be divided into/ categorized as legal, financial, social, moral, parental, etc., and the classes are not in general exclusive. Often in particular situations our obligations are in conflict with each other and with moral as well as other sorts of reasons for acting. Sometimes it will be clear how to resolve the conflict, but sometimes it will not.

The terminology of '*prima facie* obligations' has survived in philosophy not in spite of but because of its ambiguity. Many philosophers are inclined to say that in conflict situations, the weaker obligations do not exist at all. But the obvious falsity of this position is an embarrassment, and the em- barrassment is masked by saying it is only a '*prima facie* obligation'.

Is there any sense at all to the distinction between *prima facie* obligation and something else, whatever it might be? As so often in philosophy, there is a genuine and valid distinction to be marked even though the terminology is a source of confusion. Consider the differences and similarities between the members of the following list

(a) Jones has an obligation to do A
(b) Jones has a duty to do A
(c) It would be a good thing if Jones did A
(d) Jones ought, other things being equal, to do A
(e) Jones ought to do A
(f) All things considered, Jones ought to do A.

No two members of this list are synonymous though they are obviously related in certain ways. Deontic logic has been a source of confusion here because various non-synonymous members of this list have been offered as readings for the deontic operator O, sometimes even in the same article. Now the correct insight that underlies the muddled jargon of *prima facie* is simply this: Because (a) entails (d) but not (f), the assertion of (a) is consistent with the denial of (f) and indeed with

(g) All things considered, Jones ought not to do A.

In characteristic conflict situations, statements of the form (a) and (g) are both true. That is what is meant by saying that the obligation to do A is overridden by some more important consideration. The truth, then, that underlies the *prima facie* jargon is that in conflict situations one can both have an actual (real, valid, honest-to-john) obligation and yet one ought not, all things considered, to do what one is under an obligation to do. The reason people have felt uncomfortable about this is that it sounds odd to say (a) simpliciter in cases where (g) is true, and this has led to the twin mistakes of supposing that (a) is not an actual but only a *prima facie* obligation, or of supposing that it is a member of a special species of low grade obligations (*prima facie* vs. absolute). But the reason for the oddness of saying a simpliciter derives from the principles of conversation and not from the semantics of 'obligation'. On the principle that one should give the maximum amount of relevant information, it would be misleading to say (a) simpliciter if one knew that (g) was true. Because (a) entails (d), that is, because obligations give reasons for action and 'ought' expresses reasons for action, one's saying (a) can be an indirect way of saying (e) or even (f). One can indirectly tell someone that he ought to do something by telling him that he has a reason for doing it. But to use Grice's term, that is a matter of implicature and not of entailment. (a) does not entail (f) and it is not inconsistent with (g). So there is a third distinction underlying the traditional terminology, and it is indeed a valid distinction, between what one has an obligation to do and what one ought to do all things considered. But this distinction is marked quite clearly in ordinary language and does not require the introduction of the term *prima facie* to mark it.

But how would one formalize any such a distinction as this? The answer I think is quite obvious. If one is to have a symbolism that accounts for some of the distinctions in the list (a)–(f) and is able to account for conflict situations, one will need (at least) two deontic operators to express the distinctions between (a) and (b) on the one hand and (f) on the other. Let us introduce $O_1, O_2, \ldots O_n$ for the different obligations and duties that may be asserted to exist in statements of form (a) and (b). Let us use O^* for the deontic notion in (f). Then the conjunction of (a), (b), and (g) would be symbolized

11. $O_1p \& O_2p \& O^*\text{-}p$

And the conjunction of (a) and

(h) Jones has an obligation not to do A.

would be symbolized

12. $O_1p \& O_2\text{-}p$

and these remove even the appearance of a logical inconsistency in the description of the conflict situation, because neither

13. $O_1p \supset \text{-}O_2\text{-}p$

nor

14. $O_1p \supset \text{-}O^*\text{-}p$

are valid, unlike

15. $O^*p \supset \text{-}p$

which is valid. 13 denies falsely that there can be inconsistent obligations, and 14 denies falsely that what one is under an obligation to do can be inconsistent with what one ought to do, all things considered. 15 asserts truly that if one ought to do some particular thing, all things considered, then it is not the case that, all things considered, one ought not to do that very thing.

The results of our investigation so far may be summarized as follows: There are three possible ways to construe the alleged distinction between *prima facie* and some other kinds of obligation, as the distinction is supposed to apply to conflict situations:

The first is the distinction between what are really obligations and what only seem to be obligations but are not in fact. This provides a mistaken description of the conflict situation.

The second is the distinction between two kinds or species of obligations, and this also provides a mistaken description.

The third is not a distinction of kinds of obligations, but a distinction between different kinds of deontic statements. It is a distinction between statements asserting the existence of obligations, duties, and other such reasons for acting and statements asserting what one ought to do, all things considered. This third distinction enables us to give a correct description of the conflict situation; because it enables us to describe the fact that one may have inconsistent obligations and the fact that what one ought to do all things considered may be inconsistent with one or more of one's obligations, without either denying the existence of any of one's obligations or dividing them up into categories of absolute and *prima facie*.

---

[1] This is a fragment of a larger (unpublished) paper in which I discuss various problems of deontic logic and some of the criticisms made of my earlier derivation of 'ought' from 'is'. I believe this fragment can stand on its own.

[2] W. D. Ross, *The Right and the Good*, Oxford, 1930.

[3] Ibid., p. 28.

[4] Ibid., p. 19.

[5] Jaakko Hintikka, 'Deontic Logic and its Philosophical Morals', in *Models for Modalities*, D. Reidel Co., Dordrecht, 1969.

[6] Op. cit., p. 20.

[7] Ibid., pp. 21 ff.

[8] Ibid., pp. 28–9.

VI

ETHICAL CONSISTENCY

B. A. O. WILLIAMS

I SHALL not attempt any discussion of ethical consistency in general. I shall consider one question that is near the centre of that topic: the nature of moral conflict. I shall bring out some characteristics of moral conflict that have bearing, as I think, on logical or philosophical questions about the structure of moral thought and language. I shall centre my remarks about moral conflict on certain comparisons between this sort of conflict, conflicts of beliefs, and conflicts of desires; I shall start, in fact, by considering the latter two sorts of conflict, that of beliefs very briefly, that of desires at rather greater length, since it is both more pertinent and more complicated.

Some of what I have to say may seem too psychological. In one respect, I make no apology for this; in another, I do. I do not, in as much as I think that a neglect of moral psychology and in particular of the role of emotion in morality has distorted and made unrealistic a good deal of recent discussion; having disposed of emotivism as a theory of the moral judgement, philosophers have perhaps tended to put the emotions on one side as at most contingent, and therefore philosophically uninteresting, concomitants to other things which are regarded as alone essential. This must surely be wrong: to me, at least, the question of what emotions a man feels in various circumstances seems to have a good deal to do, for instance, with whether he is an admirable human being or not. I do apologise, however, for employing in the following discussion considerations about emotion (in particular, *regret*) in a way which is certainly less clear than I should like.

1. It is possible for a man to hold inconsistent beliefs, in the strong sense that the statements which would adequately express his beliefs involve a logical contradiction. This possibility, however, I shall not be concerned with, my interest being rather in the different case of a man who holds two beliefs which are not inconsistent in this sense, but which for some empirical reason cannot both be true. Such beliefs I shall call 'conflicting'. Thus a

From *Problems of the Self* (Cambridge University Press, 1973), pp. 166–86. Reprinted by permission of the author and the publishers.

man might believe that a certain person was a Minister who took office in October 1964 and also that that person was a member of the Conservative Party. This case will be different from that of inconsistent beliefs, of course, only if the man is ignorant of the further information which reveals the two beliefs as conflicting, viz. that no such Minister is a Conservative. If he is then given this information, and believes it, then either he becomes conscious of the conflict between his original beliefs[1] or, if he retains all three beliefs (for instance, because he has not 'put them together'), then he is in the situation of having actually inconsistent beliefs. This shows a necessary condition of beliefs conflicting: that if a pair of beliefs conflict, then (a) they are consistent and (b) there is a true factual belief which, if added to the original pair, will produce a set that is inconsistent.

2. What is normally called conflict of *desires* has, in many central cases, a feature analogous to what I have been calling conflict of beliefs: that the clash between the desires arises from some contingent matter of fact. This is a matter of fact that makes it impossible for both the desires to be satisfied; but we can consistently imagine a state of affairs in which they could both be satisfied. The contingent root of the conflict may, indeed, be disguised by a use of language that suggests logical impossibility of the desires being jointly satisfied; thus a man who was thirsty and lazy, who was seated comfortably, and whose drinks were elsewhere, might perhaps represent his difficulty to himself as his both wanting to remain seated and wanting to get up. But to put it this way is for him to hide the roots of his difficulty under the difficulty itself; the second element in the conflict has been so described as to reveal the obstacle to the first, and not its own real object. The sudden appearance of help, or the discovery of drinks within arm's reach, would make all plain.

While many cases of conflict of desires are of this contingent character, it would be artificial or worse to try to force all cases into this mould, and to demand for every situation of conflict an answer to the question 'What conceivable change in the contingent facts of the world would make it possible for both desires to be satisfied?' Some cases involving difficulties with space and time, for instance, are likely to prove recalcitrant: can one isolate the relevant contingency in the situation of an Australian torn between spending Christmas in Christmassy surroundings in Austria, and spending it back home in the familiar Christmas heat of his birthplace?

A more fundamental difficulty arises with conflicts of desire and aversion towards one and the same object. Such conflicts can be represented as conflicts of two desires: in the most general case, the desire to have and the desire not to have the object, where 'have' is a variable expression which gets a determinate content from the context and from the nature of the object in question.[2] There are indeed other cases in which an aversion to x does not merely take the form of a desire *not to have* x (to avoid it, reject it, to be elsewhere, etc.), but rather the form of a desire that x *should not exist*—in particular, a desire to destroy it. These latter cases are certainly different from the former (aversion here involves advancing rather than retreating), but I shall leave these, and concentrate on the former type. Conflicts of desire and aversion in this sense differ from the conflicts mentioned earlier, in that the most direct characterization of the desires—'I want to have x' and 'I want not to have x'—do not admit an imaginable contingent change which would allow both the desires to be satisfied, the descriptions of the situations that would satisfy the two desires being logically incompatible. However, there is in many cases something else that can be imagined which is just as good: the removal from the object of the disadvantageous features which are the ground of the aversion or (as I shall call aversions which are merely desires *not to have*) negative desire. This imaginable change would eliminate the conflict, not indeed by satisfying, but by eliminating, the negative desire.

This might be thought to be cheating, since any conflict of desires can be imagined away by imagining away one of the desires. There is a distinction, however, in that the situation imagined without the negative desire involves no loss of utility: no greater utility can be attached to a situation in which a purely negative desire is satisfied, than to one in which the grounds of it were never present at all. This does not apply to desires in general (and probably not to the more active, destructive, type of aversion distinguished before). Admittedly, there has been a vexed problem in this region from antiquity on, but (to take the extreme case) it does seem implausible to claim that there is no difference of utility to be found between the lives of two men, one of whom has no desires at all, the other many desires, all of which are satisfied.

Thus it seems that for many cases of conflict of desire and aversion towards one object, the basis of the conflict is still, though in a slightly different way, contingent, the contingency consisting in the co-existence of the desirable and the undesirable features of the object. Not all cases, however, will yield to this treatment, since there may be various difficulties in representing the desirable and undesirable features as only contingently co-existing. The limiting case in this direction is that in which the two sets of features are identical (the case of ambivalence)—though this will almost certainly involve the other, destructive, form of aversion.

This schematic discussion of conflicts between desires is meant to apply only to non-moral desires; that is to say, to cases where the answer to the question 'why do you want x?' does not involve expressing any moral attitude. If this limitation is removed, and moral desires are considered, a much larger class of non-contingently based conflicts comes into view, since it is evidently the case that a moral desire and a non-moral desire which are in conflict may be directed towards exactly the same features of the situation.[3] Leaving moral desires out of it, however, I think we find that a very large range of conflicts of desires have what I have called a contingent basis. Our desires that conflict are standardly like beliefs that conflict, not like beliefs that are inconsistent; as with conflicting beliefs it is the world, not logic, that makes it impossible for them both to be true, so with most conflicting desires, it is the world, not logic, that makes it impossible for them both to be satisfied.

3. There are a number of interesting contrasts between situations of conflict with beliefs and with desires; I shall consider two.

(*a*) If I discover that two of my beliefs conflict, at least one of them, by that very fact, will tend to be weakened; but the discovery that two desires conflict has no tendency, in itself, to weaken either of them. This is for the following reason: while satisfaction is related to desire to some extent as truth is related to belief, the discovery that two desires cannot both be satisfied is not related to those desires as the discovery that two beliefs cannot both be true is related to those beliefs. To believe that *p* is to believe that *p* is true, so the discovery that two of my beliefs cannot both be true is itself a step on the way to my not holding at least one of them; whereas the desire that I should have such-and-such, and the belief that I will have it, are obviously not so related.

(*b*) Suppose the conflict ends in a decision, and, in the case of desire, action; in the simplest case, I decide that one of the conflicting beliefs is true and not the other, or I satisfy one of the desires and not the other. The rejected belief cannot substantially survive this point, because to decide that a belief is untrue *is* to abandon, i.e. no longer to have, that belief. (Of course, there are qualifications to be made here: it is possible to say 'I know that it is untrue, but I can't help still believing it.' But it is essential to the concept of belief that such cases are secondary, even peculiar.) A rejected desire, however, can, if not survive the point of decision, at least reappear on the other side of it in one or another guise. It may reappear, for instance, as a general desire for something of the same sort as the object rejected in the decision; or as a desire for another particular object of the same sort; or—and this is the case that will concern us most—if there are no substitutes, the opportunity for satisfying that desire having irrevocably gone, it may reappear in the form of a *regret* for what was missed.

It may be said that the rejection of a belief may also involve regret. This is indeed true, and in more than one way: if I have to abandon a belief, I may regret this either because it was a belief of mine (as when a scientist or a historian loses a pet theory), or—quite differently—because it would have been more agreeable if the world had been as, when I had the belief, I thought it was (as when a father is finally forced to abandon the belief that his son survived the sinking of the ship). Thus there are various regrets possible for the loss of beliefs. But this is not enough to reinstate a parallelism between beliefs and desires in this respect. For the regret that can attach to an abandoned belief is never sufficiently explained just by the fact that the man did have the belief; to explain this sort of regret, one has to introduce something else—and this is, precisely, a desire, a desire for the belief to be true. That a man regrets the falsification of his belief that p shows not just that he believed that p, but that he wanted to believe that p: where 'wanting to believe that p' can have different sorts of application, corresponding to the sorts of regret already distinguished. That a man regrets not having been able to satisfy a desire is sufficiently explained by the fact that he had that desire.

4. I now turn to moral conflict. I shall discuss this in terms of *ought*, not because *ought* necessarily figures in the expression of every moral conflict, which is certainly not true, but because it presents the most puzzling problems. By 'moral conflict' I mean only cases in which there is a conflict between two moral judgements that a man is disposed to make relevant to deciding what to do; that is to say, I shall be considering what has traditionally, though misleadingly, been called 'conflict of obligations', and not, for instance, conflicts between a moral judgement and a non-moral desire, though these, too, could naturally enough be called 'moral conflicts'. I shall further omit any discussion of the possibility (if it exists) that a man should hold moral principles or general moral views which are intrinsically inconsistent with one another, in the sense that there could be no conceivable world in which anyone could act in accordance with both of them; as might be the case, for instance, with a man who thought both that he ought not to go in for any blood-sport (as such) and that he ought to go in for foxhunting (as such). I doubt whether there are any interesting questions that are peculiar to this possibility. I shall confine myself, then, to cases in which the moral conflict has a contingent basis, to use a phrase that has already occurred in the discussion of conflicts of desires.

Some real analogy, moreover, with those situations emerges if one considers two basic forms that the moral conflict can take. One is that in which it seems that I ought to do each of two things, but I cannot do both. The other is that in which something which (it seems) I ought to do in respect of certain of its features also has other features in respect of which (it seems) I ought not to do it. This latter bears an analogy to the case of desire and aversion directed towards the same object. These descriptions are of course abstract and rather artificial; it may be awkward to express in many cases the grounds of the *ought* or *ought not* in terms of features of the thing I ought or ought not to do, as suggested in the general description. I only hope that the simplification achieved by this compensates for the distortions.

The two situations, then, come to this: in the first, it seems that I ought to do *a* and that I ought to do *b*, but I cannot do both *a* and *b*; in the second, it seems that I ought to do *c* and that I ought not to do *c*. To many ethical theorists it has seemed that actually to accept these seeming conclusions would involve some sort of logical inconsistency. For Ross, it was of course such situations that called for the concept of *prima facie* obligations: two of these are present in each of these situations, of which at most one in each case can constitute an actual obligation. On Hare's views, such situations call (in some logical sense) for a revision or qualification of at least one of the moral principles that give rise, in their application, to the conflicting *ought*'s. It is the view, common to these and to other theorists, that there is a logical inconsistency of some sort involved here, that is the ultimate topic of this paper.

5. I want to postpone, however, the more formal sorts of consideration for a while, and try to bring out one or two features of what these situations are, or can be, like. The way I shall do this is to extend further the comparison I sketched earlier, between conflicts of beliefs and conflicts of desires. If we think of it in these terms, I think it emerges that there are certain important respects in which these moral conflicts are more like conflicts of desires than they are like conflicts of beliefs.

(*a*) The discovery that my factual beliefs conflict *eo ipso* tends to weaken one or more of the beliefs; not so, with desires; not so, I think, with one's conflicting convictions about what one ought to do. This comes out in the fact that conflicts of *oughts*, like conflicts of desires, can readily have the character of a struggle, whereas conflicts of beliefs scarcely can, unless the man not only believes these things, but wants to believe them. It is of course true that there are situations in which, either because of some practical concern connected with the beliefs, or from an intellectual curiosity, one may get deeply involved with a conflict of beliefs, and something rather like a struggle may result: possibly including the feature, not uncommon in the moral cases, that the more one concentrates on the dilemma, the more pressing the claims of each side become. But there is still a difference, which can be put like this: in the belief case my concern to get things straight is a concern both to find the right belief (whichever it may be) and to be disembarrassed of the false belief (whichever it may be), whereas in the moral case my concern is not in the same way to find the right item and be rid of the other. I may wish that the facts had been otherwise, or that I had never got into the situation; I may even, in a certain frame of mind, wish that I did not have the moral views I have. But granted that it is all as it is, I do not think in terms of banishing error. I think, if constructively at all, in terms of acting for the best, and this is a frame of mind that *acknowledges* the presence of both the two *oughts*.

(b) If I eventually choose for one side of the conflict rather than the other, this is a possible ground of regret—as with desires, although the regret, naturally, is a different sort of regret. As with desires, if the occasion is irreparably past, there may be room for nothing but regret. But it is also possible (again like desires) that the moral impulse that had to be abandoned in the choice may find a new object, and I may try, for instance, to 'make it up' to people involved for the claim that was neglected. These states of mind do not depend, it seems to me, on whether I am convinced that in the choice I made I acted for the best; I can be convinced of this, yet have these regrets, ineffectual or possibly effective, for what I did not do.

It may be said that if I am convinced that I acted for the best; if, further, the question is not the different one of self-reproach for having got into the conflict-situation in the first place; then it is merely irrational to have any regrets. The weight of this comment depends on what it is supposed to imply. Taken most naturally, it implies that these reactions are a bad thing, which a fully admirable moral agent (taken, presumably, to be rational) would not display. In this sense, the comment seems to me to be just false. Such reactions do not appear to me to be necessarily a bad thing, nor an agent who displays them *pro tanto* less admirable than one who does not. But I do not have to rest much on my thinking that this is so; only on the claim that it is not inconsistent with the nature of morality to think that this is so. This modest claim seems to me undeniable. The notion of an admirable moral agent cannot be all that remote from that of a decent human being, and decent human beings are disposed in some situations of conflict to have the sort of reactions I am talking about.

Some light, though necessarily a very angled one, is shed on this point by the most extreme cases of moral conflict, tragic cases. One peculiarity of these is that the notion of 'acting for the best' may very well lose its content. Agamemnon at Aulis may have said 'May it be well,'[4] but he is neither convinced nor convincing. The agonies that a man will experience after acting in full consciousness of such a situation are not to be traced to a persistent doubt that he may not have chosen the better thing; but, for instance, to a clear conviction that he has not done the better thing because there was no better thing to be done. It may, on the other hand, even be the case that, by some not utterly irrational criteria of 'the better thing', he is convinced that he did the better thing: rational men no doubt pointed out to Agamemnon his responsibilities as a commander, the many people involved, the considerations of honour, and so forth. If he accepted all this,

and acted accordingly: it would seem a glib moralist who said, as some sort
of criticism, that he must be irrational to lie awake at night, having killed
his daughter. And he lies awake, not because of a doubt, but because of a
certainty. Some may say that the mythology of Agamemnon and his choice
is nothing to us, because we do not move in a world in which irrational
gods order men to kill their own children. But there is no need of irrational
gods, to give rise to tragic situations.

Perhaps, however, it might be conceded that men may have regrets in
these situations; it might even be conceded that a fully admirable moral
agent would, on occasion, have such regrets; nevertheless (it may be said)
this is not to be connected directly with the structure of the moral conflict.
The man may have regrets because he has had to do something distressing
or appalling or which in some way goes against the grain, but this is not the
same as having regrets because he thinks that he has done something that
he ought not to have done, or not done something that he ought to have
done—and it is only the latter that can be relevant to the interpretation of
the moral conflict. This point might be put, in terms which I hope will be
recognizable, by saying that regrets may be experienced in terms of purely
natural motivations, and these are not to be confused, whether by the
theorist or by a rational moral agent, with *moral* motivations, i.e. motivations that spring from thinking that a certain course of action is one that
one ought to take.

There are three things I should like to say about this point. First, if it
does concede that a fully admirable moral agent might be expected to
experience such regrets on occasion, then it concedes that the notion of
such an agent involves his having certain natural motivations as well as
moral ones. This concession is surely correct, but it is unclear that it is
allowed for in many ethical theories. Apart from this, however, there are
two other points that go further. The sharp distinction that this argument
demands between these natural and moral motivations is unrealistic. Are
we really to think that if a man (*a*) thinks that he ought not to cause
needless suffering and (*b*) is distressed by the fact or prospect of his causing
needless suffering, then (*a*) and (*b*) are just two separate facts about him?
Surely (*b*) can be one expression of (*a*), and (*a*) one root of (*b*)? And there
are other possible connections between (*a*) and (*b*) besides these. If such
connections are admitted, then it may well appear absurdly unrealistic to
try to prise apart a man's feeling regrets about what he has done and his
thinking that what he has done is something that he ought not to have
done, or constituted a failure to do what he ought to have done. This is
not, of course, to say that it is impossible for moral thoughts of this type,
and emotional reactions or motivations of this type, to occur without each

other; this is clearly possible. But it does not follow from this that if a man does both have moral thoughts about a course of action and certain feelings of these types related to it, then these items have to be clearly and distinctly separable one from another. If a man in general thinks that he ought not to do a certain thing, and is distressed by the thought of doing that thing; then if he does it, and is distressed at what he has done, this distress will probably have the shape of his thinking that, in doing that thing, he has done something that he ought not to have done.

The second point of criticism here is that even if the sharp distinction between natural and moral motivations were granted, it would not, in the matter of regrets, cover all the cases. It will have even the appearance of explaining the cases only where the man can be thought to have a ground of regret or distress independently of his moral opinions about the situation. Thus if he has caused pain, in the course of acting (as he sincerely supposes) for the best, it might be said that any regret or distress he feels about having caused the pain is independent of his views of whether, in doing this, he did something that he ought not to have done: he is just naturally distressed by the thought of having caused pain. I have already said that I find this account unrealistic, even for such cases. But there are other cases in which it could not possibly be sustained. A man may, for instance, feel regret because he has broken a promise in the course of acting (as he sincerely supposes) for the best; and his regret at having broken the promise must surely arise *via* a moral thought. Here we seem just to get back to the claim that such regret in such circumstances would be irrational, and to the previous answer that if this claim is intended pejoratively, it will not stand up. A tendency to feel regrets, particularly creative regrets, at having broken a promise even in the course of acting for the best might well be considered a reassuring sign that an agent took his promises seriously. At this point, the objector might say that he still thinks the regrets irrational, but that he does not intend 'irrational' pejoratively: we must rather admit that an admirable moral agent is one who on occasion is irrational. This, of course, is a new position: it may well be correct.

6. It seems to me a fundamental criticism of many ethical theories that their accounts of moral conflict and its resolution do not do justice to the facts of regret and related considerations: basically because they eliminate from the scene the *ought* that is not acted upon. A structure appropriate to conflicts of belief is projected on to the moral case; one by which the conflict is basically adventitious, and a resolution of it disembarrasses one of a mistaken view which for a while confused the situation. Such an approach must be inherent in purely cognitive accounts of the matter; since it is just a question of which of the conflicting *ought* statements is true, and

they cannot both be true, to decide correctly for one of them must be to be rid of error with respect to the other—an occasion, if for any feelings, then for such feelings as relief (at escaping mistake), self-congratulation (for having got the right answer), or possibly self-criticism (for having so nearly been misled). Ross—whom unfairly I shall mention without discussing in detail—makes a valiant attempt to get nearer to the facts than this, with his doctrine that the *prima facie* obligations are not just *seeming* obligations, but more in the nature of a claim, which can generate residual obligations if not fulfilled.[5] But it remains obscure how all this is supposed to be so within the general structure of his theory; a claim, on these views, must surely be a claim for consideration as the only thing that matters, a duty, and if a course of action has failed to make good this claim in a situation of conflict, how can it maintain in that situation some residual influence on my moral thought?

A related inadequacy on this issue emerges also, I think, in certain prescriptivist theories. Hare, for instance, holds that when I encounter a situation of conflict, what I have to do is modify one or both of the moral principles that I hold, which, in conjunction with the facts of the case, generated the conflict. The view has at least the merit of not representing the conflict as entirely adventitious, a mere misfortune that befalls my moral faculties. But the picture that it offers still seems inadequate to one's view of the situation *ex post facto*. It explains the origin of the conflict as my having come to the situation insufficiently prepared, as it were, because I had too simple a set of moral principles; and it pictures me as emerging from the situation better prepared, since I have now modified them—I can face a recurrence of the same situation without qualms, since next time it will not present me with a conflict. This is inadequate on two counts. First, the only focus that it provides for retrospective regret is that I arrived unprepared, and not that I did not do the thing rejected in the eventual choice. Second, there must surely be something wrong with the consequence that, granted I do not go back on the choice I make on this occasion, no similar situation later can possibly present me with a conflict. This may be a not unsuitable description of *some* cases, since one thing I may learn from such experiences is that some moral principle or view that I held was too naïve or *simpliste*. But even among lessons, this is not the only one that may be learned. I may rather learn that I ought not to get into situations of this kind—and this lesson seems to imply very much the opposite of the previous one, since my reason for avoiding such situations in the future is that I have learned that in them both *ought* do apply. In extreme cases, again, it may be that there is no lesson to be learned at all, at least of this practical kind.

7. So far I have been largely looking at moral conflict in itself; but this last point has brought us to the question of avoiding moral conflict, and this is something that I should like to discuss a little further. It involves, once more, but in a different aspect, the relations between conflict and rationality. Here the comparison with beliefs and desires is once more relevant. In the case of beliefs, we have already seen how it follows from the nature of beliefs that a conflict presents a problem, since conflicting beliefs cannot both be true, and the aim of beliefs is to be true. A rational man in this respect is one who (no doubt among other things) so conducts himself that this aim is likely to be realized. In the case of desires, again, there is something in the nature of desires that explains why a conflict essentially presents a problem: desires, obviously enough, aim at satisfaction, and conflicting desires cannot both be satisfied. Corresponding to this there will be a notion of practical rationality, by which a man will be rational who (no doubt among other things) takes thought to prevent the frustration of his desires. There are, however, two sides to such a policy: there is a question, not only of how he satisfies the desires he has, but of what desires he has. There is such a thing as abandoning or discouraging a desire which in conjunction with others leads to frustration, and this a rational man will sometimes do. This aspect of practical rationality can be exaggerated, as in certain moralities (some well known in antiquity) which avoid frustration of desire by reducing desire to a minimum: this can lead to the result that, in pursuit of a coherent life, a man misses out on the more elementary requirement of having a life at all. That this is the type of criticism appropriate to this activity is important: it illustrates the sense in which a man's policy for organizing his desires is *pro tanto* up to him, even though some ways a man may take of doing this constitute a disservice to himself, or may be seen as, in some rather deeper way, unadmirable.

There are partial parallels to these points in the sphere of belief. I said just now that a rational man in this sphere was (at least) one who pursued as effectively as possible truth in his beliefs. This condition, in the limit, could be satisfied by a man whose sole aim was to avoid falsity in his beliefs, and this aim he might pursue by avoiding, so far as possible, belief: by cultivating scepticism, or ignorance (in the sense of never having heard of various issues), and of the second of these, at least, one appropriate criticism might be similar to one in the case of desires, a suggestion of self-impoverishment. There are many other considerations relevant here, of course; but a central point for our present purpose does stand, that from the fact that given truths or a given subject-matter exist, it does not follow that a given man ought to have beliefs about them: though it does follow that, if he is to have beliefs about them, there are some beliefs rather than others that he ought to have.

In relation to these points, I think that morality emerges as different from both belief and desire. It is not an option in the moral case that possible conflict should be avoided by way of scepticism, ignorance, or the pursuit of *ataraxia*—in general, by indifference. The notion of a moral claim is of something that I may not ignore: hence it is not up to me to give myself a life free from conflict by withdrawing my interest from such claims.

It is important here to distinguish two different questions, one moral and one logical. On the one hand, there is the question whether extensive moral indifference is morally deplorable, and this is clearly a moral question, and indeed one on which two views are possible: *pas trôp de zèle* could be a moral maxim. That attitude, however, does not involve saying that there are moral claims, but it is often sensible to ignore them; it rather says that there are fewer moral claims than people tend to suppose. Disagreement with this attitude will be moral disagreement, and will involve, among other things, affirming some of the moral claims which the attitude denies. The logical question, on the other hand, is whether the relation of moral indifference and moral conflict is the same as that of desire-indifference and desire-conflict, or, again, belief-indifference and belief-conflict. The answer is clearly 'no'. After experience of these latter sorts of conflict, a man may try to cultivate the appropriate form of indifference while deny-ing nothing about the nature of those conflicts as, at the time, he took them to be. He knows them to have been conflicts in believing the truth or pursuing what he wanted, and, knowing this, he tries to cut down his commitment to believing or desiring things. This may be sad or even dotty, but it is not actually inconsistent. A man who retreats from moral conflict to moral indifference, however, cannot at the same time admit that those conflicts were what, at the time, he took them to be, viz, conflicts of moral claims, since to admit that there exist moral claims in situations of that sort is incompatible with moral indifference towards those situations.

The avoidance of moral conflict, then, emerges in two ways as something for which one is not merely free to devise a policy. A moral observer cannot regard another agent as free to restructure his moral outlook so as to withdraw moral involvement from the situations that produce conflict; and the agent himself cannot try such a policy, either, so long as he regards the conflicts he has experienced as conflicts with a genuine moral basis. Putting this together with other points that I have tried to make earlier in this paper, I reach the conclusion that a moral conflict shares with a con-flict of desires, but not with a conflict of beliefs, the feature that to end it in decision is not necessarily to eliminate one of the conflicting items: the item that was not acted upon may, for instance, persist as regret, which may (though it does not always) receive some constructive expression. Moral conflicts do not share with conflicts of desire (nor yet with conflicts of belief) the feature that there is a general freedom to adopt a policy to try to eliminate their occurrence.

It may well be, then, that moral conflicts are in two different senses ineliminable. In a particular case, it may be that neither of the *oughts* is eliminable. Further, the tendency of such conflicts to occur may itself be ineliminable, since, first, the agent cannot feel himself free to reconstruct his moral thought in a policy to eliminate them; and, second, while there are *some* cases in which the situation was his own fault, and the correct conclusion for him to draw was that he ought not to get into situations of that type, it cannot be believed that all genuine conflict situations are of that type.

Moral conflicts are neither systematically avoidable, nor all soluble without remainder.

8. If we accept these conclusions, what consequences follow for the logic of moral thought? How, in particular, is moral conflict related to logical inconsistency? What I have to say is less satisfactory than I should like; but I hope that it may help a little.

We are concerned with conflicts that have a contingent basis, with conflict *via* the facts. We distinguished earlier two types of case: that in which it seems that I ought to do *a* and that I ought to do *b*, but I cannot do both; and that in which it seems that I ought to do *c* in respect of some considerations, and ought not to do *c* in respect of others. To elicit something that looks like logical inconsistency here obviously requires in the first sort of case extra premisses, while extra premisses are at least not obviously required in the second case. In the second case, the two conclusions 'I ought to do *c*' and 'I ought not to do *c*' already wear the form of logical inconsistency. In the first case, the pair 'I ought to do *a*' and 'I ought to do *b*' do not wear it at all. This is not surprising, since the conflict arises not from these two alone, but from these together with the statement that I cannot do both *a* and *b*. How do these three together acquire the form of logical inconsistency? The most natural account is that which invokes two further premisses or rules: that *ought* implies *can*, and that 'I ought to do *a*' and 'I ought to do *b*' together imply 'I ought to do *a* and *b*' (which I shall call the *agglomeration principle*). Using these, the conflict can be represented in the following form:

   (i) I ought to do *a*
  (ii) I ought to do *b*
 (iii) I cannot do *a* and *b*.

From   (i) and (ii), by agglomeration
  (iv) I ought to do *a* and *b*;
from (iii) by '*ought* implies *can*' used contrapositively,
  (v) It is not the case that I ought to do *a* and *b*.

This produces a contradiction: and since one limb of it (v), has been proved by a valid inference from an undisputed premiss, we accept this limb, and then use the agglomeration principle contrapositively to unseat one or other of (i) and (ii).

This formulation does not, of course, produce an inconsistency of the *ought–ought not* type, but of the *ought–not ought* type, i.e. a genuine *contradiction*. It might be suggested, however, that there is a way in which we could, and perhaps should, reduce cases of this first type to the *ought–ought not* kind, i.e. to the pattern of the second type of case. We might say that 'I ought to do *b*', together with the empirical statement that doing *a* excludes doing *b*, jointly yield the conclusion that I ought to do something which, if I do *a*, I shall not do; hence that I ought to refrain from doing *a*; hence that I ought not to do *a*. This, with the original statement that I ought to do *a*, produces the *ought–ought not* form of inconsistency. A similar inference can also be used, of course, to establish that I ought not to do *b*, a conclusion which can be similarly joined to the original statement that I ought to do *b*. To explore this suggestion thoroughly would involve an extensive journey on the troubled waters of deontic logic; but I think that there are two considerations that suggest that it is not to be preferred to the formulation that I advanced earlier. The first is that the principle on which it rests looks less than compelling in purely logical terms: it involves the substitution of extensional equivalences in a modal context, and while this might possibly fare better with *ought* than it does elsewhere, it would be rash to embrace it straight off. Second, it suffers from much the same defect as was noticed much earlier with a parallel situation with conflicts of desires: it conceals the real roots of the conflict. The formulation with '*ought* implies *can*' does not do this, and offers a more realistic picture of how the situation is.

Indeed, so far from trying to assimilate the first type of case to the second, I am now going to suggest that it will be better to assimilate the second to the first, as now interpreted. For while 'I ought to do *c*' and 'I ought not to do *c*' do indeed wear the form of logical inconsistency, the blank occurrence of this form itself depends to some extent on our having left out the real roots of the conflict—the considerations or aspects that lead to the conflicting judgements. Because of this, it conceals the element that is in common between the two types of case: that in both, the conflict arises from a contingent impossibility. To take Agamemnon's case as example, the basic *oughts* that apply to the situation are presumably that he ought to discharge his responsibilities as a commander, further the expedition, and so forth; and that he ought not to kill his daughter. Between these two there is no inherent inconsistency. The conflict comes, once more, in the step to action: that as things are, there is no way of doing the first without doing the second. This should encourage us, I think, to recast it all in a more artificial, but perhaps more illuminating, way, and say that here again there is a double *ought*: the first, to further the expedition, the second, to refrain from the killing; and that as things are he cannot discharge both.

Seen in this way, it seems that the main weight of the problem descends on to '*ought* implies *can*' and its application to these cases; and from now on I shall consider both types together in this light. Now much could be said about '*ought* implies *can*', which is not a totally luminous principle, but I shall forgo any general discussion of it. I shall accept, in fact, one of its main applications to this problem, namely that from the fact that I cannot do both *a* and *b* it follows contrapositively that it is not the case that I ought to do both *a* and *b*. This is surely sound, but it does not dispose of the logical problems: for no agent, conscious of the situation of conflict, in fact thinks that he ought to do *both* of the things. What he thinks is that he ought to do *each* of them; and this is properly paralleled at the level of 'can' by the fact that while he cannot do both of the things, it is true of each of the things, taken separately, that he can do it.

If we want to emphasize the distinction between 'each' and 'both' here, we shall have to look again at the principle of agglomeration, since it is this that leads us from 'each' to 'both'. Now there are certainly many characterizations of actions in the general field of evaluation for which agglomeration does not hold, and for which what holds of each action taken separately does not hold for both taken together: thus it may be *desirable*, or *advisable*, or *sensible*, or *prudent*, to do *a*, and again desirable or advisable, etc., to do *b*, but not desirable, etc., to do both *a* and *b*. The same holds, obviously enough, for what a man wants; thus marrying Susan and marrying Joan may be things each of which Tom wants to do, but he certainly does not want to do both. Now the mere existence of such cases is obviously not enough to persuade anyone to give up agglomeration for *ought*, since he might reasonably argue that *ought* is different in this respect; though it is worth noting that anyone who is disposed to say that the sorts of characterizations of actions that I just mentioned are evaluative *because they entail 'ought'-statements* will be under some pressure to reconsider the agglomerative properties of *ought*. I do not want to claim, however, that I have some knock-down disproof of the agglomeration principle; I want to claim only that it is not a self-evident datum of the logic of *ought*, and that if a more realistic picture of moral thought emerges from abandoning it, we should have no qualms in abandoning it. We can in fact see the problem the other way round: the very fact that there can be two things, each of which I ought to do and each of which I can do, but of which I cannot do both, shows the weakness of the agglomeration principle.

Let us then try suspending the agglomeration principle, and see what results follow for the logical reconstruction of moral conflict. It is not immediately clear how '*ought* implies *can*' will now bear on the issue. On the one hand, we have the statement that I cannot do both *a* and *b*, which indeed disproves that I ought to do both *a* and *b*, but this is uninteresting: the statement it disproves is one that I am not disposed to make in its own right, and which does not follow (on the present assumptions) from those that I am disposed to make. On the other hand, we have the two *ought* statements and their associated 'can' statements, each of which, taken separately, I can assert. But this is not enough for the conflict, which precisely depends on the fact that I cannot go on taking the two sets separately. What we need here, to test the effect of '*ought* implies *can*', is a way of applying to each side the fact that I cannot satisfy both sides. Language provides such a way very readily, in a form which is in fact the most natural to use in such deliberations:

   (i) If I do *b*, I will not be able to do *a*;
   (ii) If I do *a*, I will not be able to do *b*.

Now (i) and (ii) appear to be genuine conditional statements; with suitable adjustment of tenses, they admit both of contraposition and of use in *modus ponens*. They are thus not like the curious non-conditional cases discussed by Austin.[6]

Consider now two apparently valid applications of '*ought* implies *can*':

   (iii) If I will not be able to do *a*, it will not be the case that I ought to do *a*;
   (iv) If I will not be able to do *b*, it will not be the case that I ought to do *b*.

Join (iii) and (iv) to (i) and (ii) respectively, and one reaches by transitivity:

   (v) If I do *b*, it will not be the case that I ought to do *a*;
   (vi) If I do *a*, it will not be the case that I ought to do *b*.

At first glance (v) and (vi) appear to offer a very surprising and reassuring result: that whichever of *a* and *b* I do, I shall get off the moral hook with respect to the other. This must surely be too good to be true; and suspicion that this is so must turn to certainty when one considers that the previous argument would apply just as well if the conflict between *a* and *b* were not a conflict between two *oughts* at all, but, say, a conflict between an *ought* and some gross inclination; the argument depends solely on the fact that *a* and *b* are empirically incompatible. This shows that the reassuring interpretation of (v) and (vi) must be wrong. There is a correct interpretation, which reveals (v) and (vi) as saying something true but less interesting: (taking (v) as example), that if I do *b*, it will then not be correct to say that I ought (then) to do *a*. And this is correct, since *a* will *then* not be a course of action open to me. It does not follow from this that I cannot correctly say then that *I ought to have done a*; nor yet that I was wrong in thinking earlier that *a* was something I ought to do. It seems, then, that if we waive the agglomeration principle, and just consider a natural way of applying to each course of action the consideration that I cannot do both it and the other one, we do not get an application of *ought* implies *can* that necessarily cancels out one or other of the original *oughts* regarded retrospectively. And this seems to me what we should want.

As I have tried to argue throughout, it is surely falsifying of moral thought to represent its logic as demanding that in a conflict situation one of the conflicting *oughts* must be totally rejected. One must, certainly, be rejected in the sense that not both can be acted upon; and this gives a (fairly weak) sense to saying that they are incompatible. But this does not mean they do not both (actually) *apply* to the situation; or that I was in some way mistaken in thinking that these were both things that I ought to do. I may continue to think this retrospectively, and hence have regrets; and I may even do this when I have found some moral reason for acting on one in preference to the other. For while there are some cases in which finding a moral reason for preference *does* cancel one of the *oughts*, this is not always so. I may use some emergency provision, of a utilitarian kind for example, which deals with the conflict of choice, and gives me a way of 'acting for the best'; but this is not the same as to revise or reconsider the reasons for the original *oughts*, nor does it provide me with the reflexion 'If I had thought of that in the first place, there need have been no conflict.' It seems to me impossible, then, to rest content with a logical picture which makes it a necessary consequence of conflict that one *ought* must be totally rejected in the sense that one becomes convinced that it did not actually apply. The condition of moving away from such a picture appears to be, at least within the limits of argument imposed by my rather crude use of *ought* implies *can*, the rejection of the agglomeration principle.

I have left until last what may seem to some the most obvious objection to my general line of argument. I have to act in the conflict; I can choose one course rather than the other; I can think about which to choose. In thinking about this, or asking another's advice on it, the question I may characteristically ask is 'what ought I to do?' The answer to this question, from myself or another, cannot be 'both', but must rather be (for instance) 'I (or you) ought to do *a*.' This (it will be said) just shows that to choose in a moral conflict, or at least to choose as a result of such deliberation, is to give up one of the *oughts* completely, to arrive at the conclusion that it does not apply; and that it cannot be, as I have been arguing that it may be, to decide not to act on it, while agreeing that it applies.

This objection rests squarely on identifying the *ought* that occurs in statements of moral principle, and in the sorts of moral judgements about particular situations that we have been considering, with the *ought* that occurs in the deliberative question 'what ought I to do?' and in answers to this question, given by myself or another. I think it can be shown that this identification is a mistake, and on grounds independent of the immediate issue. For suppose I am in a situation in which I think that I ought (morally) to do *a*, and would merely very much like to do *b*, and cannot do both. Here, too, I can presumably ask the deliberative question 'what ought I to do?' and get an answer to it. If this question meant 'Of which course of action is it the case that I ought (morally) to do it?', the answer is so patent that the question could not be worth asking: indeed, it would not be a deliberate question at all. But the deliberative question can be worth asking, and I can, moreover, intelligibly arrive at a decision, or receive advice, in answer to it which is offensive to morality. To identify the two *oughts* in this sort of case commits one to the necessary supremacy of the moral; it is not surprising if theories that tend to assimilate the two end up with the Socratic paradox. Indeed, one is led on this thesis not only to the supremacy, but to the ubiquity, of the moral; since the deliberate question can be asked and answered, presumably, in a situation where neither course of action involves originally a moral *ought*.

An answer to the deliberate question, by myself or another, can of course be supported by moral reasons, as by other sorts; but its role as a deliberate *ought* remains the same, and this role is not tied to morality. This remains so even in the case in which both the candidates for action that I am considering involve moral *oughts*. This, if not already clear, is revealed by the following possibility. I think that I ought to do *a* and that I ought to do *b*, and I ask of two friends 'what ought I to do?' One says 'You ought to do *a*,' and gives such-and-such moral reasons. The other says 'You ought to do neither: you ought to go to the pictures and give morality a rest.' The sense of *ought* in these two answers is the same: they are both answers to the unambiguous question that I asked.

All this makes clear, I think, that if I am confronted with two conflicting *oughts*, and the answer to the deliberative question by myself or another *coincides* with one of the original *oughts*, it does not represent a mere *iteration* of it. The decision or advice is decision or advice to act on that one; not a re-assertion of that one with an implicit denial of the other. This distinction may also clear up what may seem troubling in my approach, that a man who has had a moral conflict, has acted (as he supposes) for the best, yet has the sorts of regrets that I have discussed about the rejected course of action, would not most naturally express himself with respect to that course of action by saying 'I ought to have done the other.' This is because the standard function of such an expression in this sort of situation would be to suggest a deliberative mistake, and to imply that if he had the decision over again he would make it differently. That he cannot most naturally say this in the imagined case does not mean that he cannot think of the rejected action as something which, in a different sense, he ought to have done; this is to say, as something of which he was not wrong at the time in thinking that he ought to do it.

In fact, of course, it is not even true that *the* deliberative question is 'what ought I to do?' It may well be, for instance, 'what am I to do?'; and that question, and the answers to it—such as 'do *a*', or 'if I were you, I should . . .'—do not even make it look as though decision or advice to act on one of the *oughts* in a moral conflict necessarily involves deciding that the other one had no application.

---

[1] I shall in the rest of this paper generally use the phrase 'conflict of beliefs' for the situation in which a man has become conscious that his beliefs conflict.

[2] For a discussion of a similar notion, see A. Kenny, *Action, Emotion and Will* (London: Routledge & Kegan Paul, 1963), Ch. 5.

[3] Plato, incidentally, seems to have thought that all conflicts that did not involve a moral or similar motivation had a contingent basis. The argument of *Republic* IV which issues in the doctrine of the divisions of the soul bases the distinction between the rational and epithymetic parts on conflicts of desire and aversion directed towards the same object in the same respects. But not all conflicts establish different parts of the soul: the epithymetic part can be in conflict with itself. These latter conflicts, therefore, cannot be of desires directed towards the same object in the same respects; that is to say, purely epithymetic conflicts have a contingent basis.

[4] Aeschylus, *Agamemnon* 217.

[5] Cf. *The Foundations of Ethics* (Oxford: The Clarendon Press, 1938), pp. 84 *seq*. The passage is full of signs of unease; he uses, for instance, the unhappy expression 'the most right of the acts open to us', a strong indication that he is trying to have it both ways at once. Most of the difficulties, too, are wrapped up in the multiply ambiguous phrase 'laws stating the tendencies of actions to be obligatory in virtue of this characteristic or of that' (p. 86).

[6] *Ifs and Cans*, reprinted in his *Philosophical Papers* (Oxford: The Clarendon Press, 1961).

VII

REASONS

G. HARMAN

I

A NUMBER of ethical theories take the correctness of a moral 'ought' judgement to depend on how that judgement is related to certain practical principles, although the theories differ concerning what they take the relevant principles to be. Kant, for example, says that the relevant principles are the universal principles of pure practical reason. Hare says that they are whatever universalizable principles that the person making the 'ought' judgement subscribes to. Sartre says that they are the principles that are accepted by the person about whom the *ought* judgement is made. The convention theory says that the relevant principles are those conventionally accepted by the members of some contextually indicated group that includes both the person being judged and the person making the judgement.

Theories of this sort can also differ in what they say about the required relation between practical principles and moral judgement. For example, Hare's theory is that this is a logical relation that is to be explained within a logic of imperatives. An alternative and more plausible idea is that the relevant relation is a weaker nonlogical relation of the sort that holds between reasons and the thing for which the reasons are reasons.

According to Hare, the relevant principles can be formulated as general imperatives; and an 'ought' judgement is correct, in relation to a set of general imperatives, if a corresponding imperative follows logically from the set of general imperatives taken together with true factual assumptions. For example, suppose that the person making the judgement accepts the principle, 'Anyone, give someone what you owe him if you can and he asks for it back!' Suppose also that the facts include (1) that Jones owes Smith ten dollars and (2) that Smith has asked for the money back. Hare believes that from these suppositions we can derive the imperative 'Jones, pay Smith the ten dollars you owe him!' So, in Hare's view, the judgement that

From *Crítica*, Vol. VII, No. 21, December 1975, pp. 3–18. Reprinted by permission of the author and of The Instituto de Investigaciones Filosóficas of the Universidad Nacional Autónoma de México.

Jones ought to pay Smith the ten dollars he owes him is correct, in relation to that general principle, given those facts. This idea, about the required relation between particular 'ought' judgement and general principles, could also be accepted in a Kantian, Sartrean, or convention theory morality. Any of these theories could say that a moral 'ought' judgement is correct if, and only if, it is a logical consequence of the relevant practical principles and the facts of the case. The difference between the theories would then have to do with the nature of the relevant principles, and not with the required relation between principles and particular 'ought' judgements.

However, the idea that there must be this sort of logical relation between principles and particular judgements is not very plausible. For one thing, it implies that the relevant principles are so detailed that they determine logically exactly what we are to do in every possible circumstance. The idea that moral principles have this sort of precision has an air of unreality.

There is, furthermore, a looseness to 'ought' judgements that this idea fails to capture. 'P ought to do D' is not the only sort of judgement that we want to make in relation to the relevant practical principles. We also want to be able to say such things as, 'It would be good of P to do D', 'It would be wrong of P not to do D', 'P might do D', 'P must do D.' These judgements do not all mean the same thing. Some are appropriate where others are not. Hare's account seems on its face more appropriate for a judgement like 'P must do D' than for 'P ought to do D'. For, to say that P ought to do D is not necessarily to say that P's doing D is absolutely required.

It would be better, if that is what is meant, to say that P has to do D or that it would be wrong of P not to do D. We can suppose that P ought to do D without supposing that he absolutely must do D or even that it would be wrong of him not to do D. Saying that P ought to do D, on the other hand, is a stronger thing to say than saying simply that it would be good of P if he were to do D.

II

This suggests an alternative account according to which the relevant practical principles are vague and lack the sort of legalistic precision that would be required for Hare's account to work. In this alternative theory, the relevant principles commit us not so much to particular actions in particular circumstances as to certain general aims and goals. We are to respect others; we are to try not to harm them; if there is no great cost to ourselves involved, we are to try to help those who need help; and so forth. There are also principles regarding duties and divisions of responsibilities, e.g. within families—parents are to be responsible for the education and well-being of their children and so forth. In this view, the relevant moral principles are too vague to determine precisely what someone ought to do, if this has to be determined logically in the way that Hare suggests, since the relevant principles do not have the sort of precision necessary for us to be able to deduce what ought to be done, given the facts.

Still in this alternative view, as in Hare's view, to accept principles as practical principles is to be motivated to act in certain ways. It is to have certain goals and ends in addition to the goals and ends you would have if you had not accepted those principles. And, just as your other goals, ends, desires, and plans can give you reasons to do things, so too can the goals and ends that you have, e.g. as the result of accepting the conventions of society. But, to say that these principles give you reasons to do things is not just to say that these principles logically imply certain imperatives. The reason relation is weaker than, or at least different from, the relation of logical implication via a logic of imperatives. It is this vaguer relation of reasons that, in this view, correctly expresses the connection between the relevant practical principles and particular 'ought' judgements that are correct, in relation to those principles, given the facts.

In this view, then, to say that P ought to do D is to say that P has sufficient reasons to do D that are stronger than reasons he has to do something else. If what you mean is that P morally ought to do D, you mean that P has sufficient moral reasons to do D that are stronger than the reasons he has to do something else. In other words, given the relevant practical principles, for example the principles that P accepts as the conventions of society, P has sufficient reasons deriving from those principles for doing D, etc.

The relevant reasons can be of varying strengths, which accounts for the various sorts of judgement that might be made: 'P ought to do D', 'D is the best thing P can do', 'P must do D', 'P may do D', and so forth. For example, given that P intends to adhere to certain principles and given the facts, it may be that there are good reasons for P to do D, yet it would not all be a mistake for P not to do D. In that case, it may not be true that P positively ought to do D although it would be good of P to do D. On the other hand, if, given P's intention to adhere to those principles and given the facts, it would be a mistake for P not to do D, P ought to do D. And, if it would be irrational for P not to do D, given that he really does intend to adhere to those principles, he must do D. Not doing D in such a case would be incompatible with continuing to intend to adhere to those principles. To say, in relation to certain principles, that P must do D is to say that, if P does not do D, that will show that he does not in fact seriously intend to adhere to those principles. Finally, to say that P may do D or might do D

in relation to certain practical principles is to say that P's acceptance of those principles does not make it irrational for him to do D.

A theory of this sort is sometimes called a 'good-reasons' analysis of moral 'ought' judgements and related moral judgements. In this view, such judgements say something about the moral reasons a person has to do things. A similar analysis would be inappropriate for other sorts of moral judgement, such as the judgement that P is morally evil in doing D, since such judgements do not depend in the same way on assumptions about P's reasons to do things.

Good-reasons analyses can also be given for other senses of 'ought' and related words like 'may' and 'must'. Recall that the word 'ought' appears to have at least four different meanings. In addition to the moral 'ought' that we have been discussing, there is the simple 'ought' of rationality, as when we say that the bank robber ought to use the rear door; the evaluative 'ought', as in 'There ought to be more love in the world'; and the 'ought' of expectation, as in 'The train ought to be here in three minutes.' Corresponding to these different senses of 'ought' are different senses of 'must' and 'may'. There is, for example, a 'must' of expectation, as when we say, 'The train must have arrived by now', and there is a 'may' or 'might' of expectation, as when we say, 'The train may arrive in few minutes', or 'The train might have arrived at noon; I'm not sure.' Similarly, there are a 'must', a 'may', and a 'might' of evaluation and also of simple rationality. We say, for example, 'The hurricane mustn't hit Miami' or 'The bank robber must cut the alarm wires if he is to escape detection.'

Good-reasons analyses, suitably modified, are appropriate to these different cases. In the case of the 'ought', 'must' and 'may' of expectation, what is relevant are reasons to believe things. To say that the train ought to be here soon is to say that there are good reasons to think the train will be here soon. To say that the train must have arrived by noon is to say that the reasons for thinking this are conclusive. To say that the train may not have arrived at all is to say that it is not incompatible with the reasons we currently have to suppose that the train has not arrived at all. Similarly, to say that the hurricane mustn't hit Miami is to say that there are overwhelming reasons to hope that the hurricane will not hit Miami. To say that there ought to be more love in the world is to say that there are reasons for wishing that there were more love in the world. To say that the bank robber ought to use the back door is to say that he has good reasons to do that. To say that he must cut the alarm wires is to say that it would be irrational for him not to do so, given his ends and given the facts.

III

One advantage of such a good-reasons analysis is that it allows us to account in this way for various uses of 'ought', 'may', and 'must'. Another is that the good-reasons analysis helps to explicate an aspect of our use of 'ought' that was emphasized by W. D. Ross, who argued that there were two moral 'oughts', a *prima facie* 'ought' and an all-things-considered 'ought'. Ross argued that, if we try to state our moral principles using the word 'ought' we must use what he calls the *prima facie* 'ought'. For example, we say, 'You ought to keep your promises', 'You ought to tell the truth', 'You ought not to injure others', 'You ought to help those in need', and so forth. But we do not suppose that these principles are absolute. We do not suppose that you ought to keep every promise; we allow that there are circumstances in which you may break a promise—indeed there are circumstances in which you ought to break a promise. The same is true of other moral principles. 'All moral principles have exceptions.'

Hare's reaction to this point is to suppose that our moral principles are really much more complicated. For Hare, the 'exceptions' are built into the moral principles. But Ross took a different tack. According to him, a principle like 'You ought to keep your promises' is true as it stands; but this principle does not mean that there are no situations in which you may break your promise. According to Ross, the 'ought' used in stating this principle is the *prima facie* 'ought'. What the principle says is that you ought, *prima facie*, to keep your promises. More precisely, it means that, if you have promised to do something, that gives you a moral reason to do what you have promised to do. If you have no other reasons, then you should do what you have promised to do. If you have other reasons, then you must weigh your various reasons against each other in order to decide what you ought to do all things considered.

For example, you have promised to attend a meeting but your aunt has just died so you also have an obligation to attend the funeral. You therefore have conflicting obligations. Given that you have promised to go to the meeting, you ought (*prima facie*) to go to the meeting. Given that your aunt has died and your parents will be expecting you at the funeral, you ought (*prima facie*) to go to the funeral. These 'ought' statements do not contradict each other, since they are *prima facie* 'ought' statements. Neither statement says what you ought to do all-things-considered. This can be determined only by weighing your reasons against each other and deciding which is stronger.

Ross' theory of the *prima facie* 'ought' makes a great deal of sense from the point of view of the good-reasons analysis. In this view, moral principles indicate the sorts of things that you have moral reasons to do. What you should do all-things-considered is not determined by some further moral principle but is determined in whatever way conflicting reasons are weighed against each other, be they moral reasons or reasons of other sorts.

Putting this in another way, we might take Ross's theory to be a remark about the logical form of 'ought' statements. Strictly speaking, we can say, an 'ought' statement has the form, 'Given C (i.e. in relation to the fact that C), P ought to do D.' For example, 'Given that you have promised to do something, you ought to do it.' An all-things-considered 'ought' judgement would then have the form, 'All things considered, P ought to do D'—in other words, 'Given C, where C is all things considered, P ought to do D.' This amounts to the claim that the *prima facie* 'ought' is basic and that the all-things-considered 'ought' is to be defined in terms of the *prima facie* 'ought'. We might then define the basic, *prima facie* 'ought' like this: 'Given C, P ought to do D' means the same as 'C gives P a reason to do D'.

Exactly similar remarks can be made about the 'ought' of expectation. There is a *prima facie* 'ought' of expectation and an all-things-considered 'ought' of expectation. We say, 'Going by the timetable, the train ought to be here in five minutes; but, given that the engineer is new at the job, the train ought to be somewhat later than that.' We can define the basic form of the 'ought' of expectation as follows: 'Given C, it ought to be that S' means the same as 'C is a reason to believe that S.' Analogously, we might define the basic form of the evaluative 'ought' as follows: 'Given C, it ought to be that S' means the same as 'C is a reason to wish or hope that S'.

Finally, consider the 'ought' of simple rationality. Kant holds that moral requirements derive from reason alone; according to him it is irrational not to act morally. If that were true, there would be no reason to distinguish the moral 'ought' from the 'ought' of simple rationality. And, even if we suppose that Kant is wrong about the powers of reason, we might still suppose that the moral 'ought' is a special use of the 'ought' of rationality—not that it is irrational to fail to act in accordance with the moral law, but rather that moral 'ought' judgements are judgements using the 'ought' of rationality made about agents who are believed to intend to adhere to the relevant moral principles.

The basic logical form of an 'ought' statement, using the 'ought' of rationality, is 'Given C, P ought to do D.' The suggestion is that this is the moral 'ought' if the conditions C include P's intending to adhere to the relevant principles. In that case, in saying 'Given C, P ought morally to do D' we are saying 'Given both C and that P intends to adhere to the relevant principles, P ought to do D.' According to this suggestion, the difference between the judgement that the bank robber ought to give up his trade and the judgement that the bank robber ought to use the rear door is that in the former judgement but not in the latter we take the relevant conditions C to include the bank robber's acceptance of certain principles. What we mean is that, given his acceptance of those principles, he has reasons to go home rather than to continue robbing the bank.

This is to reduce the moral 'ought' of rationality. Analogous reductions of the other 'oughts' can also be given. The 'ought' of expectation in 'Given C, it ought to be that S,' becomes 'Given C, one ought to believe that S.' The evaluate 'ought' in 'Given C, it ought to be that S' becomes 'Given C, one ought to hope or wish that S.'

It still makes sense to say that the word 'ought' has four different meanings, since these reductions are not the same from one case to the next. A sentence of the form 'Given C, P ought to do D' might mean any of four different things, which can be expressed using the 'ought' of rationality as follows:

'Given C, P ought to do D', 'Given C and that P accepts the moral conventions we accept, P ought to do D', 'Given C, one ought to believe that P does D', 'Given C, one ought to hope or wish that P does D.' These are not equivalent. Nor is it quite correct to say that the moral 'ought' is just a special case of the 'ought' of rationality. The difference is that when we use the 'ought' of rationality to say that P ought to do D, we are not necessarily endorsing P's doing D, but, when we use the moral 'ought' to say that P ought to do D, we are normally endorsing P's doing D. When I judge that the bank robber ought to use the rear door, I do not endorse his doing so; I am not indicating that I am in favour of his doing so. But, when I say that the bank robber ought to give up his trade, I do endorse his doing that; I am indicating that I am in favour of his giving up his trade. The moral 'ought' is therefore the 'ought' of rationality plus something else. When I use the moral 'ought' I presuppose that the agent and my audience accept certain practical principles that I also accept, and I make my judgement in relation to those principles. Consider also the ways in which we react on learning that an agent does not have the goals we supposed that he had. I judge that a bank robber ought to use the rear door because I suppose that his goal is to rob the bank and get away unobserved. If I learn that he does not intend to rob this bank but is merely making a deposit, then I withdraw my judgement that he ought to use the rear door and I say that I was mistaken. On the other hand, suppose that I use the moral 'ought' to say that the bank robber ought to give up his trade. In saying this, I am presupposing that certain conventions that the bank robber accepts give him reasons to stop being a bank robber. If I learn that the bank robber is, however, totally amoral and that, given his goals and plans, he has absolutely no reason not to continue to be a bank robber, then although I will withdraw my judgement I will not do so by saying that I was *mistaken*. This difference indicates that the two sorts of judgement are not of the same kind. The moral sense of 'ought' is distinct from the sense of 'ought' of rationality, even though the two senses are closely related.

IV

It may seem, by the way, that I am oversimplifying when I speak of the *moral* 'ought', since the same sense of the word is used when it is said that someone has reasons to do something in relation to rules of law, club rules, conventions of etiquette, rules of a game, and so forth, which the speaker takes the agent to accept. If, for example, it turns out that the agent does not accept those rules or conventions, the speaker will not withdraw his original statement by saying that he was mistaken. I will, nevertheless, continue to speak of the moral 'ought'. The fact that 'ought' has the same sense in all of these cases is additional support for the social convention theory of morality. Given that theory, it seems appropriate to say that those who accept rules of law, club rules, or conventions of etiquette accept them in the way that they accept moral conventions; indeed, I would say that they accept them *as* moral conventions, as part of their moralities. Similarly, I would say that people playing a game have adopted a temporary morality of something quite like it.

Another complication is that the moral 'ought' can be used in relation to a morality that the speaker does not share and, in that case, in judging that *P* ought to do *D*, the speaker does not necessarily endorse *P*'s doing *D*. Consider such judgements as these; 'You, as a Christian, ought to turn the other cheek; I, however, propose to strike back.' A spy who has been found out by a friend might say, 'I hope that you will not turn me in, although I realize that, as a loyal citizen, you ought to do so.' In such a case, if it turns out that the agent is not a Christian, or is not a loyal citizen, the speaker can withdraw his original judgement by saying that he was mistaken. The difference between the moral 'ought' and the 'ought' of rationality does not emerge in such examples; it emerges only in the more usual case in which the speaker shares the relevant principles and endorses *P*'s doing *D*.

VIII

PRACTICAL REASON AND THE LOGIC OF REQUIREMENT

R. CHISHOLM

1. WE will consider the logic of the following types of argument:

(A)   (1) p occurs
     (2) p requires that S perform A
∴ (3) S has a duty to perform A

(B)   (1) q occurs
     (2) q requires that S perform an act incompatible
     with his performing A
∴ (3) S has a duty not to perform A

(C)   (1) r, as well as q, occurs
     (2) r and p does not require that S perform A
∴ (3) The requirement, imposed by p, that S perform A has been
     overridden

The second premiss in an argument of the form of (A) would formulate what Nelson calls a 'rule of morality'; the second premiss in an argument of the form of (B) could be said, in a certain sense, to formulate an extension of such a rule; and the second premiss in an argument of the form of (C) might be said to formulate a 'rule of moral permission'. The conclusions of arguments of the form of (A) and of (B) could be said to formulate '*prima facie* duties'. And the conclusion of an argument of the form of (C) could be said to describe a situation in which such a duty could be said, in Nelson's term, to be waived.

I would assert the following: (1) A significant part of our practical reasoning—our exhorting, justifying, and excusing, to ourselves and to others—can be cast in these three forms. (2) Each of the arguments is a valid logical argument. Moreover (3) the three arguments may be said to be

From S. Körner (ed.) *Practical Reason* (Basil Blackwell, 1974), pp. 2–13. Reprinted by permission of the publishers.

consistent with each other in the sense that one may consistently affirm the premisses and conclusions of all three arguments, where A, p, q, r, and S are replaced, completely and consistently, by actual terms. And, finally, (4) once we have made the explications that are necessary in order to see the second and third of these points, we will have grasped certain concepts which will help us in dealing with a number of fundamental puzzles about what we ought to do.

2. We must understand, then, the concept I have tried to single out with the term 'requirement'.

Examples of requirement, as here understood, are: making a promise requires keeping the promise; wronging a person requires compensating the person; virtue (if Kant is right) requires being rewarded; performing a sinful act requires punishment and repentance. Other examples of requirement have been studied by the Gestalt psychologists: 'It is a basic fact of perceptual experience that some things belong or fit together, and that others do not. A curve may demand a certain completion and seem to reject all others; this completion appears as appropriate to the nature of the curve.'[1] As the quotation suggests, the terms 'fitting' and 'unfitting' might also be used to express the phenomena of requirement. Thus 'p is fitting to q', in one of the senses in which philosophers have used this expression, could be taken to mean the same as 'p requires q'; in another one of the senses in which philosophers have used it, it might be taken to mean the same as 'p does not require not-q'.

We will take as our primitive locution the schema 'pRq'—'p when it obtains requires q'—where the letters p and q may be replaced by terms designating states of affairs. The schema 'pRq' may be read in English either as 'p would require q', or as 'p when it obtains requires q', or as 'p is such that if it were to obtain it would require q'. ('States of affairs' will be understood in what I take to be the usual way. For example: states of affairs stand in logical relations to other states of affairs; some of these logical relations constitute the subject-matter of the logic of propositions; for every state of affairs p, there is another state of affairs which is the negation of p and which obtains, takes place, or occurs when and only when p does not obtain, take place, or occur. I will use 'obtains', 'takes place' and 'occurs' interchangeably.)

To facilitate exposition let us begin with a definition:

D1 p requires q = Df p obtains and pRq

In other words, p does require q, or p in fact requires q, when p is such that (i) it obtains and (ii) if it were to obtain it would require q. Thus the defined '*p* requires *q*', unlike the undefined '*pRq*', implies that *p* obtains. (This contrast between the defined '*p* requires *q*' and the undefined '*pRq*' points to a certain ambiguity in the ordinary use of 'requires'. Sometimes philosophers who talk about the ethics of requirement use the locution '*p* requires *q*' in the sense here defined, and sometimes they use it in the sense of our undefined '*pRq*', i.e. '*p* when it obtains requires *q*'. The expression '*p* confirms *q*', which resembles '*pRq*' in a number of significant respects, has an analogous ambiguity. Sometimes '*p* confirms *q*' is used to refer to a relation that holds necessarily between propositions, or states of affairs, without implying anything as to the epistemic status of *p*; but sometimes '*p* confirms *q*' is used to imply, not only that a certain relation holds between *p* and *q*, but also that *p* is known to be true, or that it is evident that *p* is true.)

I will now attempt to set forth certain general principles that hold of requirement as here understood. I will presuppose a principle of substitutivity according to which logically equivalent expressions may replace each other in any *R*-formula. The list of principles is by no means exhaustive. Additional principles will suggest themselves when we consider some of the concepts that may be defined in terms of requirement. It will be simplest, I believe, to formulate the principles as axiom schemata:

The first principle reflects our commitment to states of affairs:

A1 $pRq \supset (\exists x)(\exists y)(xRy)$

Consider, for example, 'Jones promising to meet his friend, when it occurs, requires Jones meeting his friend.' This implies that there *is* something—namely, Jones promising to meet his friend, which is such that when it occurs it requires Jones meeting his friend; and it implies that there *is* something—namely, Jones meeting his friend, which is such that Jones promising to meet his friend, when it occurs, requires it. But when we say of the first of these two things that when it occurs it requires the second, our statement does not imply that either one occurs. More generally, '*pRq*' does not imply either that *p* obtains or that *q* obtains. And '*s* obtains and *pRq*' does not imply either '*(p&s)Rq*' or '*pR(q&s)*'.

Our second general principle tells us that the relation of requirement is like the relations of logic: if it holds between any two states of affairs, then it holds necessarily between those states of affairs.

A2 $pRq \supset N(pRq)$

Our third principle is reflected in the principle that 'ought' implies 'can'. If one state of affairs is such that when it occurs it requires a certain other, then the two states of affairs are logically compatible with each other

A3 $pRq \supset \sim N[(p\&q)$ does not obtain]

Our forth principle tells us, on the other hand, that two states of affairs that are logically compatible with each other may yet have requirements that are *not* logically compatible with each other:

A4 $(\exists x)(\exists y)(\exists z)\{\sim N[(x\&y)$ does not obtain]$\&xRz\&yR\sim z\}$

There is, therefore, the possibility of a *conflict* of actual requirements. That is to say, there may occur one state of affairs which requires a certain thing q and another state of affairs which requires not-q. If I promise one man to go and promise another man not to go, then there is something requiring me to go and something requiring me not to go. A man may be subject to conflicting requirements through no fault of his own. For example, he may find himself in the position of being the only one who is able to rescue either, but not both, of two equally worthy men in distress.

We may compare 'confirms' once again: one true proposition may confirm q, and another true proposition may confirm not-q. Indeed, one proposition that is known to be true may confirm q, and another proposition that is known to be true may confirm not-q.

We add two obvious principles pertaining to disjunctive and conjunctive states of affairs:

A5 $(pRs \& qRs) \supset (pvq)Rs$
A6 $(pRq \& pRs) \supset pR(q \& s)$

If two states of affairs are each such that they would require a given state of affairs, then their disjunction would also require that state of affairs (A5). Every state of affairs is such that it would require the conjunction of all those states of affairs it would require (A6).[2] It should be noted that we cannot affirm the converse of (A5), viz.,

$$(pvq)Rs \supset (pRs \& qRs)$$

For suppose, what (A4) allows, that (i) p would require s but (ii) the conjunction of p and r would not require s. Then the principle of substitutivity for logically equivalent expressions would allow us to infer, from (i), that $[(p \& r) v (p \& \sim r)]$ would require s. And then the converse, above, of (A5) would allow us to infer that $(p \& r)$ would require s, which contradicts (ii).

But the following, closely related formula would seem to be axiomatic:

A7 $(p v q)Rs \supset (pRs v qRs)$

One might put this principle, somewhat loosely, by saying that if a given state of affairs requires a certain other state of affairs, then, of the possible ways of extending or making 'more determinate' the first state of affairs, one at least will also require the second state of affairs.

3. Among the consequences that can readily be drawn from our axioms are the following:

T1 $pRq \supset \sim N(p$ does not obtain$)$
T2 $pRq \supset \sim N(q$ does not obtain$)$
T3 $pRq \supset \sim (pR \sim q)$
T4 $(pRq \& sR \sim q) \supset \{\sim [(p\&s)Rq] v \sim [(p\&s)R \sim q]\}$
T5 $pRq \supset [(p\&s)Rq v (p\& \sim s)Rq]$

A self-contradictory state of affairs would not require anything (T1) and would not be required by anything (T2). No state of affairs would impose incompatible requirements (T3). Thus if, in accordance with the possibility countenanced by (A3), two states of affairs that are compatible with each other happen to impose requirements that are incompatible with each other, then at least one of those requirements is not imposed by the conjunction of those two states of affairs (T4). Much of the sting of (A5), then, is removed by (T3) and (T4). Principle (T4), then, allows for the possibility that, although p is such that if it were to obtain it would require q, there occurs a wider state of affairs that entails p and that does not require q. But principle T5, which is a consequence of (A5), tells us that this is *only* a possibility. For, according to (T5), it is also possible that, if p requires q, then, for every wider state of affairs that obtains and entails p, that wider state of affairs also requires q.

We can say, then, that there may be requirements that conflict with each other (A4). But if there occurs something p which requires q, then this same thing p does not also require not-q (T3). Similarly, if there is a true proposition p which confirms another proposition q, then p does not also confirm not-q. If p and s have incompatible requirements, the larger situation, consisting of both p and s, will not have these incompatible requirements (T4). The analogy with confirmation is obvious, once again.

4. Our theorem T4, above, may be given this alternative formulation: if two states of affairs are such that they would impose incompatible requirements, then one or the other of those incompatible requirements would be *overridden* by the conjunction of the two states of affairs. The concept of a requirement being overridden is central to the logic of requirement and we will now consider it briefly.

Let us first define the case where one state of affairs is such that it *would* override the requirement that would be imposed by another:

> D2 The requirement for q, that would be imposed by p, would be overridden by $s = $ Df (i) pRq, (ii) $\sim[(p\&s)Rq]$, and (iii) $p\&s$ is logically compatible with q.

If s is such that it would override the requirement for q that would be imposed by p, then: p is such that it would require q, but the conjunction of p and s is *not* such that it would require q, and the conjunction of p and s does not entail the negation of q.[3]

We may now say that a state of affairs *does* in fact override a certain requirement if the state of affairs obtains and is such that it would override that requirement:

> D3 The requirement for q that is imposed by p is overridden by $s = $ Df (i) the requirement for q that would be imposed by p would be overridden by s and (ii) $p\&s$ obtains.

W. D. Ross has given us a clear example: 'If I have promised to meet a friend at a particular time for some trivial purpose, I should certainly think myself justified in breaking my engagement if by doing so I could prevent a serious accident or bring relief to the victims of one.'[4] His promise (p) to meet the friend requires his meeting the friend (q), but the accident or the dangerous situation (s) creates a new situation (p and s) which does not require that he meet the friend.

In Ross's example, of course, the new situation not only overrides a requirement but creates a new one—the requirement to prevent the accident or to relieve distress—and the new requirement is incompatible with the requirement that is overridden; the requirement for q is replaced by a requirement for not-q. But a requirement for something q may be overridden without being replaced by a requirement for not-q. If I am required to go to Boston in order to meet a friend, and then learn that he is dead, the requirement may be overridden without my being required not to go to Boston.

5. An overriding may itself be overridden. If, as I go to assist the man in distress, I learn than an even greater disaster will result should I fail to keep my appointment with the friend, then this new and more inclusive situation may require me once again to keep the appointment with the friend. Thus there may occur a set of events (there may be a set of true propositions) p, q, r, s, and t, such that:

> p requires q
> p and r requires not-q '
>
> p and r and s requires q
> p and r and s and t requires not-q

Once again, therefore, we find that requirement is like the logical concept of confirmation. For there may be true propositions, p, r, s, and t, such that:

> p confirms q
> p and r confirms not-q
> p and r and s confirms q
> p and r and s and t confirms not-q

The following propositions provide an example: 'Most of the people in this room are Democrats, and John is in this room' (p); 'John is a Democrat' (q); 'Most of the people on the left side of the room are not Democrats, and John is on the left side of the room' (r); '45 of the 50 people who arrived on time are Democrats, and John arrived on time' (s); '99 of the 100 people who voted for the measure are not Democrats, and John voted for the measure' (t). We do not say, in such cases, that one confirmation has been 'overridden' or 'defeated' in virtue of another, but we could.

Let us consider still another feature of this example of confirmation. Should we say that, in the situation described, the proposition q is probable, or should we say that it is improbable? One of the clearest answers to this question is suggested by Bernard Bolzano. We may say that a relational, or relative, probability of a proposition for a given person is the probability which the proposition has in relation to any part of what the person knows to be true. Thus, for a man who knows the propositions, p, r, s, and t, to be true, the proposition q has various relational probabilities— depending upon which of these propositions it is that q is being related to. But the absolute probability of a proposition, for any given person, is the probability which the proposition has in relation to the totality of those propositions which the person knows to be true.[5] Absolute probability is thus 'toti-resultant'. Normally, when we speak of 'the probability' of a proposition, we are referring to its absolute probability. And it is absolute probability that should constitute the guide of life.

6. From the fact that a state of affairs q is required by a certain state of affairs p such that p obtains, we may not infer that q is a state of affairs that *ought* to obtain. For the requirement imposed by p may be overridden by some other state of affairs s. But from the fact that a requirement for q has thus been overridden, we may not infer that q is a state of affairs that 'need not' obtain—i.e. a state of affairs such that it is not true that that state of affairs ought to obtain. For there may be some *other* state of affairs that requires q—indeed, some wider state of affairs that includes (entails) both p and s. We will say that a state of affairs ought to obtain provided there is a requirement for it that has not been overridden:

D4 It ought to be that q obtains = Df. There is an x such that x requires q and it is false that the requirement for q imposed by x is overridden.

The relation between what is merely required and what ought to be is thus analogous to the relation between what was called relative and absolute probability above. Thus one might also consider defining the 'ought to be' by reference to what is required by the totality of relevant considerations. But D4 is simpler and, I believe, accomplishes the same purpose.

7. Another pair of concepts that are useful in formulating certain ethical issues are singled out by the following definitions:

D5 p would indefeasibly require q = Df (i) pRq and (ii) there is no x such that the requirement for q that would be imposed by p would be overridden by x.

D6 p indefeasibly requires q = Df (i) p requires q and (ii) p would indefeasibly require q.

If we know that p indefeasibly requires q, then we can know that, no matter what wider states of affairs may happen to obtain, q is such that it ought to obtain.

There is a temptation to say that most ethical disputes are concerned, not merely with what requires what, but with what *indefeasibly* requires what. But any dispute about what indefeasibly requires what will turn upon some question about what requires what. (If you think, and I do not, that promise-making indefeasibly requires promise-keeping, then presumably there will be some state of affairs p which is such that I think, but you do not, that p would override the requirement imposed by promise-making. Our dispute would then turn on the question whether the conjunction of p and promise-making requires promise-keeping.)

The concept singled out in D6 is also relevant, of course, to the problems of theodicy.[6]

8. We are now in a position to introduce three definitions enabling us to see the validity of the three types of practical inference with which we began. The three types of inference were exhibited by:

(A)　(1) p occurs
　　　(2) p requires that S perform A
∴ (3) S has a duty to perform A

(B)　(1) q occurs
　　　(2) q requires that S perform an act logically
　　　incompatible with his performing A
∴ (3) S has a duty not to perform A

(C)　(1) r, as well as p, occurs
　　　(2) r and p does not require that S perform A
∴ (3) The requirement, imposed by p, that S perform A has been overridden.

To remove a certain ambiguity, to be noted below, let us re-express the conclusion of argument (A) by saying 'S has a *prima facie* duty to perform A' and that of argument (B) by saying 'S has a *prima facie* duty not to perform A'. We now add definitions of these two concepts:

D7 S has a *prima facie* duty to perform A = Df. There is an x such that x requires S's performing A.

D8 S has a *prima facie* duty not to perform A = Df. There is an x and a y such that (a) x requires S's performing y and (b) S's performing y is logically incompatible with S's performing A.

Definitions D7 and D8 enable us to see that arguments (A) and (B) are valid. Our earlier definition D3—the definition of the concept of *overriding* —enables us to see that argument (C) is valid. The three definitions together, taken with what we have said about the logic of requirement, are sufficient to justify the following remark that was made at the outset; namely, that the three arguments (A), (B), and (C), may be said to be consistent with each other in the sense that one may consistently affirm the premisses and conclusions of all three arguments, where A, p, q, r, and S are replaced, completely and consistently, by actual terms.

We may now define 'the ought to do' by reference to 'the ought to be':

D9 S ought to perform A = Df. It ought to be that S's performing A obtains.

Having defined 'the ought to be' in terms of requirement, and having characterized requirement in terms of relations holding necessarily among propositions or states of affairs, we may say, with Samuel Clarke, that our duties are a function of the eternal relations of fitness that hold among things.[7]

[1] Maurice Mandelbaum, *The Phenomenology of Moral Experience* (Glencoe, 1955), pp. 95–6. Compare Wolfgang Köhler, *The Place of Value in a World of Facts* (New York, 1938), especially ch. 3 ('An Analysis of Requiredness'). Köhler refers to M. Wertheimer, 'Some Problems in the Theory of Ethics', *Social Research*, vol. 2 (1935), pp. 353 ff.

[2] These two principles were suggested to me by Ernest Sosa.

[3] The third condition in the definiens of D2 is needed because of the consequences that would otherwise follow, given our general principles, from the assumption that a requirement for q had not been fulfilled. Without the third condition we would have to say that if p required q, and not-q obtained, then the conjunction of p and not-q would override the requirement q imposed by p.

[4] W. D. Ross, *The Right and the Good* (Oxford, 1930), p. 18.

[5] Bernard Bolzano, *Wissenschaftslehre*, vol. 3 (Leipzig, 1930), pp. 267–8. Bolzano also made a distinction between a real or objective probability and a supposed or subjective probability which we might put as follows: a real or objective probability of a proposition, for a given person, is the probability which that proposition bears to something that the person knows; the supposed or subjective probability is the probability the proposition bears to something the person thinks (possibly mistakenly) that he knows. (Unfortunately, Bolzano's own definitions are marred by the fact that he attempts to get along with an epistemic term which is weaker than 'knows'.) The more important parts of Bolzano's book have been translated by Rolf George as *Theory of Science*, The University of California Press: Berkeley and Los Angeles, 1972). Compare pp. 359–65 of the English edition.

[6] I have discussed this point in 'The Defeat of Good and Evil', in *Proceedings and Addresses of the American Philosophical Association*, vol. XLII (1968–9), pp. 21–38. This paper is reprinted in J. E. Smith, ed., *Contemporary American Philosophy: Second Series* (George Allen & Unwin: London, 1970), pp. 152–69.

7 Samuel Clarke, *Discourse upon Natural Religion* (London, 1706).

IX

REASONS FOR ACTION, DECISIONS AND NORMS

J. RAZ

THE purpose of this article is to draw attention to an important similarity between rules and decisions and to suggest a way in which both can be analysed in terms of reasons for action. Rules are not all of a kind. I shall confine myself to the kind of rules and principles with which moral, legal, and political philosophers have been most concerned. These may be called mandatory norms, and they can be affirmed in statements of the form 'x ought to (or should or must) do A and C'. In the terminology coined by von Wright, 'x' designates the norm-subject, 'A' the norm-act, and 'C' the condition of application.[1] 'Promises ought to be kept.' 'Parents should look after their children.' 'Nobody should commit adultery.' 'When insulted one should issue a challenge to a duel.' These are well-worn examples of mandatory rules.

1. EXCLUSIONARY REASONS

When conflicting reasons bear on a problem we determine what ought to be done by assessing the relative strength or weight of the conflicting reasons. In the presence of conflicting reasons we say, the agent should act on the balance of reasons. He should act on the reason or combination of reasons which override those conflicting reasons which apply to the problem facing him. These notions are interdefinable. If p is a reason to do A and q is a reason for not doing A (or, as we could for technical convenience say, for doing not-A) then if p is stronger than q it is also the more weighty reason and it overrides q and, therefore, on the balance of reasons it prevails and the agent ought, on the balance of reasons, to do A.

We thus have at our disposal a set of interlocking notions which we commonly employ to describe both the way in which conflicts of reasons are resolved ('He was aware of conflicting reasons but thought that the

From *Mind*, 1975, pp. 481, 482–8, 488–95, 496–9. Reprinted by permission of Basil Blackwell, Publisher.

need to look after his sick child overrides all other considerations') and the way in which such conflicts should be resolved. The pervasive use of this terminology suggests that all practical conflicts conform to one logical pattern: conflicts of reasons are resolved by the relative weight or strength of the conflicting reasons which determines which of them overrides the other. So long as we are content to handle such conflicts in an impressionistic way there is nothing wrong in this suggestion. But if we are concerned to construct a logical theory of practical conflicts we have to recognize that not all conflicts are of the same type. My claim, yet to be explained and defended, is that we should distinguish between first order and second order reasons for action and that conflicts between first order reasons are resolved by the relative strength of the conflicting reasons, but that this is not true of conflicts between first order and second order reasons.

The distinction between first order and second order reasons for action has not been recognized or discussed by philosophers. This is no doubt due at least in part to the fact that it is not reflected in any straightforward way in our use of the expressions of ordinary language. Reasons of both kinds are referred to as 'reasons', 'considerations', 'grounds', 'factors', etc. The resolution of conflicts of reasons belonging to different levels, just like the resolution of conflicts of reasons belonging to the same level, is described in terms of one reason prevailing over, or overriding, or being stronger than the other. So long as we are content to rely on our intuitive grasp of the sense and use of such expressions the distinction between first order and second order reasons need not concern us. My claim is that a useful explication of the notions of strength, weight and overriding is possible but only at the cost of restricting their scope of application and that if we embark on such an explication the theory of conflict must allow for the existence of other logical types of conflicts and of conflict resolution.

I shall proceed by first providing an explication of the notions of 'strength' and of 'overriding'. On the basis of these it will be possible to outline what I shall call the intuitive model of practical conflicts. I shall then provide two examples which do not conform to this model and finally I shall suggest briefly how the intuitive model should be modified to cope with them.

Let us say that p and q are conflicting reasons relative to x, A, and C, if and only if p is a reason for x to do A in C and q is a reason for x to do not-A in C.[2] Let us say that p overrides q relative to x, A, and C if and only if p and q are conflicting reasons relative to x, A, and C and if p & q is a reason for x to do A in C and it is not the case that p & q is a reason for x to do not-A in C.[3] In other words p overrides q if they conflict and if the complex fact which is the conjunction of both is a reason for the action for which p is a reason but not for the action for which q is a reason. The definition does not assume that of every pair of conflicting reasons one overrides the other. It may be that p & q is a reason both for doing A and for doing not-A or that it is a reason for neither. The definition does not and is not intended to help a man decide which reason overrides the other. All it does is explain what he is deciding when he decides that one reason overrides another.

If the reasons for x to do A in C override the reasons for x to do not-A in C then x has a conclusive reason to do A in C.[4] When a person has a conclusive reason to perform an action then on the balance of reasons he ought to do it. The intuitive model of the resolution of practical conflicts assumes that all practical conflicts are of the type described above and that one ought always to act on the conclusive reason. The intuitive model is represented by the following principle:

P1: It is always the case that one ought, all things considered,[5] to do whatever one ought to do on the balance of reasons.

I do not wish to challenge the validity of (P1) directly. Instead I shall show that it is not normally applied to many quite common conflict situations.

Imagine the case of Ann who is looking for a good way to invest her money. Late one evening a friend tells her of a possible investment. The snag is that she has to decide that same evening, for the offer to make the deal will be withdrawn at midnight. The proposed investment is a very complicated one, that much is clear to Ann. She is aware that it may be a very good investment, but there may be facts which may mean that it will not be a good bargain for her after all, and she is not certain whether it is better or worse than another proposition which was put to her a few days before and which she is still considering. All she requires is a couple of hours of thorough examination of the two propositions. All the relevant information is available in the mass of documents on her table. But Ann has had a long and strenuous day with more than the average amount of emotional upsets. She tells her friend that she can't take a rational decision on the merits of the case since even were she to try and work out the consequences of accepting the offer she would not succeed—she is too tired and upset to trust her own judgement. He replies that she can't avoid taking a decision. Refusing to consider the offer is tantamount to rejecting it. She admits that she rejects the offer but says that she is doing it not because she thinks the reasons against it override those in its favour but because she cannot trust her own judgement right now. He retorts that this violates (P1) and is unreasonable. Her weariness and her emotional state are not reasons for rejecting the offer. They do not establish that it would be wrong or undesirable to accept it, or that to do so would be contrary to her interests, etc. According to (P1) she should examine the offer on its merits. (P1) does not entail that she should disregard her present mental condition. She must, in following (P1), recognize that her judgement may be affected by her mental state and correct it to prevent this from happening. Ann, however, finds that this will only make things worse. She certainly cannot trust herself in her present state to work out how her mental state might taint her judgement. She insists that though she is taking a decision against the offer, she can rationally do so not on the ground that on the merits the offer ought to be rejected but because she has a reason not to act on the merits of the case. This, she concedes, is a kind of reason not recognized in (P1), but that only shows that (P1) is not valid.

Ann's case is interesting because she claims to be acting for a reason which is not taken into account in (P1). It may be that she is wrong in thinking that she has a valid reason for her action, but since the reason she relies on is not uncommon it deserves a closer study. The special feature of her case is not that she regards her mental state as a reason for action, but that she regards it as a reason for disregarding other reasons for action. (P1) allows her to take her fatigue as a reason for going to bed. But she regards it as a reason (or proof of a reason) for rejecting a business proposition despite the fact that her weariness does not bear at all on the merits of the proposition. She claims to have a reason for not acting on the balance of reasons.[6] Her reasoning is typical of situations in which the agent cannot trust his judgement because he is under pressure of time or because he is drunk or subject to a strong temptation or to threats or because he realizes that he is influenced by his emotions, etc. But such reasoning is not confined to situations of such a nature.

Consider the case of Colin who promised his wife that in all decisions affecting the education of his son he will act only for his son's interests and disregard all other reasons. Suppose Colin has now to decide whether or not to send his son to a public school. Among the relevant reasons are the fact that if he does he will be unable to resign his job in order to write the book he so much wants to write, and the fact that given his prominent position in his community his decision will affect the decisions of quite a few other parents, including some who could ill afford the expense. However, he believes that because of his promise he should disregard such considerations altogether (unless, that is, they have indirect consequences affecting his son's welfare). Again, some will think that his promise isn't binding, but that is besides the point. Our aim is simply to understand the reasoning of those who believe in such reasons, and it must be admitted that they are numerous. Colin's promise, like Ann's fatigue, does not affect the balance of reasons. It is not itself either a reason for sending his son to a public school or against doing so. Nor does it change whatever reasons there are. It does not mean that the consequences of Colin's decision on his chances to write his book or on the decisions of other parents are no longer relevant reasons. They are but Colin has, or believes he has, a reason to disregard them and not to act on them. Colin, like Ann, believes that he has a reason for not acting on certain reasons and that means that he believes that he may be justified in not acting on the balance of reasons.

To explain Colin's and Ann's reasoning several new concepts have to be introduced. Let us say that a person does A for the reason that p if and only if he does A because he believes that p is a reason for him to do A. A person refrains from doing A for the reason that p if and only if it is not the case that he does A for the reason that p. In other words a person refrains from acting for a reason if he does not do the act or does it but not for this reason. 'Refrains' is used here on an extended sense which does not imply that the agent intentionally avoids acting for the reason. A second order reason is any reason to act for a reason or to refrain from acting for a reason. An exclusionary reason is a second order reason to refrain from acting for some reason. Both Colin and Ann believe that their reasoning is sound because they believe that they have valid exlusionary reasons on which their decisions are partly based. Both reject (P1) because it does not take account of exclusionary reasons. Exclusionary reasons are the only type of second order reasons with which we will be here concerned.

If p is a reason for x to do A in C and q is an exclusionary reason for him not to act on p then p and q are not strictly conflicting reasons. q is not a reason for doing not-A in C. It is a reason for not doing A in C for the reason that p. The conflict between p and q is a conflict between a first order and a second order reason. Such conflicts are resolved not by the strength of the competing reasons but by a general principle of practical reasoning which determines that exclusionary reasons always prevail, when in conflict with first order reasons. It should be remembered that exclusionary reasons may vary in scope: They may exclude all or only some of the reasons which apply to certain practical problems. There may, for example, be some scope-affecting considerations to the effect that though Colin's promise apparently purports to exclude all the reasons not affecting his son's interests it does not in fact validly exclude considerations of justice to other people. An exclusionary reason may also conflict with and be over-ridden by another second order reason. Only an undefeated exclusionary reason succeeds in excluding. If exclusionary reasons are ever valid then the following principle is valid:

P2: One ought not to act on the balance of reasons if the reasons tipping the balance are excluded by an undefeated exlusionary reason.

(P2) contradicts (P1) and if valid should lead to the modification of (P1). The introduction of exclusionary reasons entails that there are two ways in which reasons can be defeated. They can be overridden by strictly conflicting reasons or excluded by an undefeated exclusionary reason.[7] It follows that if (P2) is valid then (P1) should be replaced with (P3).

P3: It is always the case that one ought, all things considered, to act for an undefeated reason for action.

2. DECISIONS

In what ways does a decision to perform an action differ from an intention to perform it? It is quite clear that often there is little difference. On many occasions 'He intends to' and 'He has decided to' are used interchangeably. Yet the central cases of decision differ from mere intentions in important respects and it is to these that we must turn.

Four features characterize fully fledged decisions:

(1) To decide is to form an intention. A decision may or may not involve a mental act of deciding. But even in those cases in which the decision is not crystallized in a mental act it is true that if a person decides at time t_1 to do A then for some time immediately before t_1 he did not intend to do A and for some time after t_1 he does intend to do A.

(2) Decisions are reached as a result of deliberations. x decides to do A only if he forms the intention to do A as a result of a process of deliberation whether to do A or how to solve a practical problem, where the doing of A is regarded by the agent as a solution to the problem. In most cases a decision results from deliberating on the reasons for or against the action. But a person may decide to perform an action without having first considered the reasons for it, if he has considered some alternative solutions to a practical problem and if the moment the thought of the action occurs to him it appears to him as the appropriate solution to that problem.[8]

'Decision' is sometimes used to apply to an intention formed without deliberation, usually when the agent is aware of conflicting pulls. One may even talk of an unconscious decision. But the central cases are those of intentions formed on the basis of deliberation. Not every intention to perform an action is a result of a decision. It is the process of deliberation as well as the fourth condition discussed below which distinguishes decision-based intentions from other intentions.

(3) Decisions are taken some time before the action. Occasionally we speak of a decision which is immediately carried out. But normally one decides to perform an action some time in the future. It is characteristic of decisions that one can change one's mind about them. In this decisions are similar to intentions and differ from straightforward cases of choosing. If Jones is offered a tray of different kinds of drinks and takes a martini it would be correct to say that he chose the martini but not that he decided to take the martini. 'If Jones decided to take a martini, then we expect that prior to the action there was deliberation, or at least preference and resolution, and *that between the time he decided and the time he acted we could correctly say that he intended to take the martini.*'[9]

(4) Decisions are reasons. The three features of decisions discussed above fail to account for some aspects of decisions. They do not explain why a decision is normally regarded as a stronger indication that the act will be done than an intention to do it which is not based on a decision. Nor do they explain why people often refuse to consider reasons for or against the action they have decided to take on the ground that the matter has already been settled by their decision. The explanation lies in the fourth feature of decisions: A decision is always for the agent a reason for performing the act he decided to perform and for disregarding further reasons and arguments. It is always both a first order and an exclusionary reason. Let me first argue that decisions are exclusionary reasons and then that they are first order reasons.

It should be remembered that a decision is reached only when the agent (1) reaches a conclusion as to what he ought to do and (2) forms the belief that it is time to terminate his deliberations. The first condition is not enough. Imagine a person who considers a problem for a while and then postpones the decision to the next day. At the time he concludes his deliberations for the day he may be as much in the dark as to which decision to take as when he began his deliberations. But it is also possible that he has already formed the view that the proper decision is to do A. That he hasn't yet decided to do A is not due to any hesitation or uncertainty on his part. He simply wants to consider another argument which he has no time to examine today, or he may want to hear the view of a friend whom he will meet tomorrow. He may be quite certain that the further argument or any facts to which his friend may draw his attention will make no difference to his decision. The reason for which we say that he has not yet reached a decision (and therefore also that he has not yet formed an intention) is not any uncertainty about what to decide or what to do, but only that he genuinely believes that he should consider some further reasons or facts or re-examine his reasoning—just in case. Indeed the following day he may decide that it would be futile to re-examine his reasoning, or that there is no point to wait for the advice of his friend, etc., and decide without further deliberation to do *A*. His decision consists simply in bringing the readiness to continue deliberation to an end.

To make a decision is to put an end to deliberation. It is also to refuse to go on looking for more information and arguments and to decline to listen to them when they crop up in one's mind or are suggested by other people. No doubt in most cases the refusal to re-open the case is not absolute. Usually it is accompanied by some unspecified rider—provided no new information becomes available, or, more strongly, provided no major change occurs, etc. Not all decisions are of the same strength, not all of them are subject to the same escape clause. But all of them are exclusionary reasons and it is this which distinguishes between them and mere intentions to act. An intention may often be less liable to change than a decision. But it is always (unless based on a decision) open to the competing claims of other reasons. To decide what to do is to rule out such a competition or at least to limit it.

Similarly though a decision is completely abandoned only when the agent abandons his decision-based intention, it is partly abandoned the moment the agent, still intending to perform the action, is ready to reconsider the case for doing it (unless, that is, his decision was never intended to exclude *this* factor). That explains why a person may refuse to discuss a problem with another on the grounds that he has already made his decision. That one has taken a decision means that one regards oneself as having an exclusionary reason to disregard further reasons or arguments. To convince another that we hold ourselves open to argument we have to make it clear that we are ready to change our mind and to do so is already partly to abandon the decision.

So far I have tried to show that decisions are exclusionary reasons in the sense that it is logically true that if *x* has decided to do *A* then *x believes* that his decision is a reason for him to disregard further reasons for or against doing *A*. It is not part of my claim that all decisions are valid exclusionary reasons, but only that whoever makes a decision regards it as such. A decision is a valid exclusionary reason only if the agent is justified in treating it as such. Often he is not. However, few would deny that sometimes there must rationally be an end to deliberation and indecisiveness even before the time for action. Hence it is clear that some decisions are valid exclusionary reasons. Paradoxical as this may seem reason sometimes requires disregarding reasons for action.

It could be claimed that though it is a necessary truth that whenever a person makes a decision he believes that he has exclusionary reasons to disregard further reasons, it is not the case that he regards the decision itself as an exclusionary reason. This seems to me wrong. To believe that one has a reason not to consider the matter any further is to believe that one ought to decide. One may of course believe that one ought to decide without being able to do so either because one does not know what to decide or because one cannot stop one's deliberations and form a firm intention. The interesting point is that having taken a decision a person may come to the view that it was a premature decision. He may become convinced not that the decision was wrong but rather that it was wrong to decide at that time. Nevertheless, since he has taken a decision, he now has an exclusionary reason not to reconsider the matter. That the decision was premature is a consideration which may lead the agent to reopen the matter for further consideration but this is never an automatic result. A decision to disregard a decision is itself a new step which should be based on reasons.

Furthermore a decision, like any other action, can be taken for a reason or for no reason. A person may take a decision even while believing that there is no reason for him to take a decision now. He may not believe that he has a reason to exclude other reasons from consideration and to bring his deliberation to an end and yet do so and make his decision. Once the decision is made it is a reason for him to avoid further consideration. If this were not the case it would have been impossible to make a decision without believing that one should decide. These facts show that the decision itself is an exclusionary reason.

The status of decisions as exclusionary reasons may be clarified by comparing them to promises. That a person promised to do A is a reason for him to do so. One should make a promise only if there are sufficient reasons to do so. But once a promise is made it is a reason for action even though it is a promise which should not have been made. Moreover, a person can promise knowing that he should not. Once the promise is made he has a reason to perform the promised act despite the fact that he made the promise knowing that he should not make it. The same is true of decisions. That a person has made a decision is for him an exclusionary reason not to consider further reasons. One should make a decision only if there are sufficient reasons to do so. But once a decision is made it is an exclusionary reason even though it is a decision which should not have been made. Moreover, a person can decide knowing that he should not.

Once he has decided, he has an exclusionary reason despite the fact that he decided while knowing that he should not do so.

A promise is a reason which can be defeated by other reasons and the fact that it should not have been made may be relevant to whether or not it is defeated. And this too is true of decisions. Some will think that a promise is a reason only in virtue of a general principle that promises ought to be kept. We could similarly regard decisions as exclusionary reasons in virtue of a general principle that decisions ought to be respected. Both principles need to be spelt out. Both are based on the idea that people should have a way of binding themselves by intentionally creating reasons for action. The Promise Keeping Principle states that they create a reason to do A if they express an intention to another person to be bound to do A.[10] The Decision Principle states that people can create an exclusionary reason to exclude further consideration by deciding, i.e. by meeting the first three conditions of a decision and forming an intention to stop deliberation. Both principles are sound practical principles, though both can be abused by making a promise or a decision which should not be made.

It should be remembered that the analogy I am discussing is between the formal features of promises and decisions. Materially they differ. Promises are designed to increase trust and predictability in inter-personal relations; Decisions—to enable people to settle matters in their own mind and put an end to deliberation. The reasons justifying them and determining their strength are entirely different. The formal analogy is, however, considerable. Its most important feature is that a person cannot make a promise without regarding it as a reason for him to behave in a certain way, nor can he make a decision without regarding himself as having an exclusionary reason. (In some institutional contexts such as the law one can both decide and promise without intending to bind oneself.)

That the analogy between decisions and promises is really a close one can be seen by comparing both with oaths and vows. These are often regarded as promises one makes to oneself. They can also be regarded as a kind of decision: a solemn and formal decision with very few escape clauses. I believe that the analogy between decisions and promises can be further explored. For example, both are content-independent reasons: regardless what you promise or decide to do you have a reason to do it because you have promised or decided. To examine the full scope of the analogy will involve establishing two things: (*a*) that promises are not only reasons to perform the promised act but also exclusionary reasons not to act for other, conflicting reasons; (*b*) that decisions are also reasons for performing the act one has decided to perform. This investigation cannot be undertaken here. I would like, however, to make a few inconclusive remarks in support of the view that decisions are reasons for performing the act decided upon.

Normally one decides to perform an action because one thinks that all things considered it ought to be done. In such circumstances it makes little difference whether the reasons for the decision are also regarded as the reasons for the action or whether the decision itself is regarded as the reason for the action and the reasons for it are only the reasons for the reason, so to speak, that is they are the grounds for which the reason is considered to be a valid one. Even in these circumstances the agent when asked for his reasons for performing or for intending to perform the action may refer to his decision. But more often than not he will refer to the reasons for his decision. It is tempting to regard such references to the decision as refusals to reveal the reasons or as assurances that the action was taken after serious consideration of the reasons. But an alternative interpretation is also available. We can regard the decision as the reason for the action and maintain that when the agent refers not to it but rather to the reasons for the decision this is because he knows that the purpose of the enquiry will be better served by stating the grounds on which his reason is based. My reason for not stealing may be that I believe that stealing is wrong but when asked why I did not steal I may say that God's commands must be observed—which is, I am assuming, my reason for believing that stealing is wrong.

A man may decide to do A even though he does not believe that all things considered he ought to do A. He may, for example, believe that he ought to decide and that it does not matter what he decides or he may believe that he ought to decide and not know what to decide. In such cases it is clear that the decision is regarded by the agent as a reason for action. Before he decided he saw no reason why he should do A rather than not-A. Having decided, he has a reason to do A—namely his decision. This argument suggests that at least in some cases decisions are reasons for the act decided upon.

3. MANDATORY NORMS

In the numerous discussions of the nature of rules the one subject that is rarely discussed is the relation between rules and reasons. Yet the relations between these notions must be clarified if the nature of rules is to be illuminated. What ought to be done, all things considered, is to perform that action for which there is an undefeated reason for action. Since there is no doubt that rules are relevant to what ought to be done, there must be a logical relation between rules and reasons. The nature of the relation is rather elusive. Are rules general statements of reasons? Does the statement that it is a moral rule that promises ought to be kept mean the same as the statement that there are reasons to keep promises? This cannot be true. We can state that there are rules but rules are not themselves statements. Statements, unlike rules, can be true or false. Rules, unlike statements, can be valid or void, they can be practised or followed or violated. Both statements and rules can be made, but each is made in a different sense. To make a rule is to change the reasons that people have. By making a statement one may draw attention to reasons but does not normally change them.

If to make rules is to change the reasons that people have then rules must themselves be reasons for action.[11] But obviously not every reason is a rule. So the question is what sort of reasons are rules? They cannot be reasons of great importance since some rules are of a fairly trivial nature— e.g. some rules of etiquette. Nor can they be reasons which result from the fact that someone in authority expresses the wish or his intention that some people shall behave in a certain way. Moral rules are not laid down by authority. Some have suggested that rules are social (or personal or institutional) practices. There is no doubt that the existence of some practices is a reason for action. One ought to drive on the left because everyone does so. The validity of rules of etiquette is based on the fact that they are practised. But not all rules are of this nature. Many moral rules are usually claimed to be of universal validity regardless of whether they are practised or not.

It may be useful to begin by noticing that the role mandatory norms play in affecting the behaviour of a person who believes in them is analogous to that of decisions. Suppose that I discover some mechanical fault in my car. I decide to take it to the garage the next morning, but to drive in it to a very important meeting today. It occurs to me that at the meeting some acquaintances of mine are likely to ask for a lift home. I do not want to take the risk of giving them a lift, even if they were ready to take it when told of the condition of the car. I know that if asked I will find it difficult to refuse. I therefore decide now not to take anybody in the car that day. I am taking a decision in advance, hoping that this will help me not to yield to requests when I am faced with them. When requested I will have to decide again. I cannot avoid this even if I want to. But this is a different decision—now I have only to decide whether to stick by my original decision. I am merely asking myself whether anything has happened which should make me reconsider the problem.

I may go further. I may, reflecting on the matter, decide on this occasion to make it a rule never to take anyone in my car when I suspect it has some mechanical fault. If so I am simply making a general decision. Of course even if I adopt the rule now I may have to decide again in the future what to do in particular cases, but my problem then will be different from what it would have been had I not adopted the rule. Having adopted the rule what I have to decide is whether to act on it in this particular case. What I am not doing is assessing the merits of the case taking all the relevant facts into consideration. I am not doing this for I have decided on a rule, that is, I have accepted an exclusionary reason, to guide my behaviour in such cases. I may occasionally, of course, examine the justification of the rule itself. If I re-examine the rule on every occasion to which it applies, however, then it is not a rule which I have adopted. I may on the other hand examine the rule occasionally even when not confronted with a case to which it applies. This is the test by which to determine whether a person follows a rule. It makes clear one advantage of having rules—it makes possible greater flexibility in making decisions, it allows for decisions to be made and revised in conditions other than the occasion for action.

Given our analysis of decisions there is little surprise that if a person decides to follow a rule he has an exclusionary reason to behave in accordance with the rule—the decision is his exclusionary reason. A person may, however, come to follow a rule without having decided to do so. He may have been brought up from early childhood to believe in the validity of the rule and to respect it. He may have drifted into following the rule as an adult gradually over a period of time without ever really making up his mind to do so. It is quite clear that the role a rule plays in the deliberations and behaviour of a person who follows it does not depend on whether he came to follow it one way or the other. A person who follows a rule without having decided to do so may one day critically examine his practice and decide to continue to follow the rule. But the role of the rule in his practical reasoning will not change, now that he has decided to follow it, from what it was before. Indeed this is precisely the purport of the decision—that he should continue to follow the rule as before.

The conclusion we are driven to is that mandatory norms in general play the same role as decisions in the practical reasoning of those who follow them. A person follows a mandatory norm if and only if he believes that the norm is a valid reason for him to do the norm-act when the conditions for application obtain and that it is a valid reason for disregarding conflicting reasons and if he acts on those beliefs. Compare two cases. Jack has friends in France whom he hasn't seen for many years. Jill has made a rule to spend her holidays in France. Both have a reason to spend the holidays in France this year, but there is a considerable difference between their reasons. Jack's desire to see his friends will have to compete with all the other reasons relevant to the problem. The trip will be expensive. His wife doesn't like his French friends and would rather buy a new washing machine. Going to France will mean that he won't be able to attend an important conference in the U.S., etc. Jack will go to France only if he finds that on the balance of reasons that is what he ought to do. Jill also faces many conflicting considerations, but she has no intention to act on the balance of reasons. She has adopted a rule to spend her holidays in France and she did so precisely in order to spare herself the necessity of deciding every year what to do during the holidays. She adopted the rule in order not to have to act on the balance of reasons on each occasion. Having the rule is like having decided in advance what to do. When the holidays come she is not going to reconsider the matter. Her mind is already made up. Her rule is for her an exclusionary reason for not acting on conflicting reasons as well as a reason to go to France for the holidays.[12]

This is the benefit of having rules and that is the difference between mandatory rules and other reasons for action. Mandatory rules are regarded by those who follow them as both a first order reason for performing the norm-act and a second order reason for not acting on conflicting reasons. That is why they are adopted and followed whenever the agent believes that he has a reason for disregarding certain reasons: This could be to save time, to avoid the danger of succumbing to temptation or the agony of indecision. Nor are these the only kinds of grounds which can justify mandatory norms. People often believe they have a reason in a particular situation to follow standards laid down by authority regardless of the balance of reasons which apply to that situation. They think that being subject to authority means precisely that. It means that they ought to follow the authority even if it is wrong. One is not submitting to authority if one does what one has reason to do anyway. Similarly one may regard oneself bound to disregard conflicting reasons because one has committed oneself to do so. To be sure rules, though exclusionary reasons, do not exclude all contrary considerations. Depending on the grounds for the rules, they may exclude a wider or a narrower range of conflicting reasons. But all mandatory rules exclude some conflicting reasons and that is the difference between them and ordinary first order reasons.

Not every rule is a valid reason. The point I am concerned to argue is that a person follows a rule only if he believes it to be a combination of valid first order and exclusionary reasons. He may be wrong but for him the rule is a rule only in being such a combination of reasons in the validity of which he believes. To explain what rules are one must do more than explain what it is to follow a rule. We are normally interested in rules either because they are valid or because they are practised by a certain community (or individual or institution) or because they were prescribed by a presumed authority. When the existence of rules is asserted the intention is normally to assert either the validity of the rule ('It is a moral rule that people should not kill other sentient beings'); or that it is practised ('The rule of vendetta still survives in many parts of the globe'); or that it was prescribed ('It is a statutory rule of English Law . . .'). It is not possible here to provide an analysis of the 3 dimensions of rules. Let me just say that all three dimensions can be easily explained once the notion of following rules has been explained. A rule is practised by a person if and only if he follows it. It is practised by a society if the bulk of its members follow it. Institutionalized rules, such as legal rules, are also to be explained by reference to the practices of individuals—in particular the practices of the officials of those institutions. Similarly the notion of a prescribed rule can be explained by reference to following rules. A person makes a new rule only if he expresses an intention that certain people should follow a certain pattern of behaviour as a rule. Finally a valid rule is a justified rule, i.e. a rule the norm-subjects of which should follow. So we see that the notion of following a rule provides the key to the explanation of rules. And this justifies the conclusion, based on the foregoing analysis of following rules, that rules are combinations of first order reasons for the norm-subjects to perform the norm-act when the conditions of application obtain, and exclusionary reasons for not acting on some conflicting reasons in those circumstances. If this is so then the analogy with decisions can contribute considerably to our understanding of the function of rules and their role in practical reasoning.

[1] G. von Wright, *Norm and Action*, 1963, chapter 5.

[2] Many first order reasons which are normally regarded as conflicting are not conflicting reasons according to this definition. We could regard the definition as defining 'strictly conflicting reasons'. Two first order reasons conflict if statements of these reasons themselves or in combination with other true statements conforming to some conditions entail the existence of strictly conflicting reasons. I shall continue to discuss only conflicting reasons as defined above. My conclusion can be easily adapted to conflicting reasons in the wider sense of the term.

[3] This definition is based on Prof. Chisholm's definition of one requirement overriding another, though it is not identical with it, cf. 'Practical Reason and the Logic of Requirement', p. 123 above.

[4] Unless the reasons for doing *A* are cancelled. Suppose I make a promise and that later keeping the promise becomes impossible or that the man to whom I made the promise releases me from it. The reason I had to do the promised act was cancelled. It was not overridden. Neither the impossibility of keeping the promise nor the fact that I was released from it is a reason for not doing the promised act. I do not have to assess which of several conflicting reasons overrides the other. The reason I had was simply cancelled.

[5] I am using 'ought, all things considered' to indicate what ought to be done on the basis of all the reasons for action which apply to the case, and not only on the basis of the reasons the agent in fact considered or could have considered.

[6] In my example Ann has not formed any view on the balance of reasons. But this is immaterial. She might have formed the opinion that the offer is a good one and refuse it all the same. She may distrust her judgement and refuse to act on it.

[7] Strictly speaking there is also a third way in which a reason can be defeated—it can be cancelled as explained in note 4.

[8] For a subtle and imaginative analysis of the first two conditions see: Meiland, *The Nature of Intention*, London, 1970, pp. 55–65. Meiland does not, however, recognize the importance of the other conditions.

[9] A. Oldenquist, 'Choosing, Deciding, and Doing' *Encyclopedia of Philosophy*, P. Edwards (editor in chief), New York, 1967, vol. 2. p. 98 (italics added).

[10] Cf. my 'Voluntary Obligations and Normative Powers', *Aristotelian Society* Supplementary Volume 46 (1972), pp. 96–100.

[11] Strictly speaking it is not the rule but the fact that there is a rule that . . . which is a reason. It is not, however, possible to explore this point here.

[12] Cf. D. P. Gauthier, *Practical Reasoning*, Oxford, 1963, pp. 160–3 for a similar account of rules.

X

DELIBERATION AND PRACTICAL REASON[1]

D. WIGGINS

1. THERE are theories of practical reason according to which the ordinary situation of an agent who deliberates resembles nothing so much as that of a snooker player who has to choose from a large number of possible shots that shot which rates highest when two products are added. The first product is the utility of the shot's success (a utility which in snooker depends upon the colour of the ball to be potted and the expected utility for purposes of the next shot of the resulting position), multiplied by the probability P of this player's potting the ball. The second product is the utility (negative) of his failure multiplied by $(1 - P)$. It is neither here nor there that it is not easy to determine the values of some of these elements for purposes of comparing prospects. There is no problem about the end itself, which is maximizing points.

2. There do exist a few deliberative situations outside snooker which are a bit like this. But in normal deliberation it is quite different. There is nothing which a man is under antecedent sentence to maximize; and probabilities, though difficult and relevant, need not be the one great crux of the matter. A man usually asks himself 'what shall I do?' not with a view to maximizing anything, but only in response to some historically determinate circumstance. This will make particular and contingent demands on his moral or practical perception, but the relevant features of the situation may not all jump to the eye. To see what they are, to prompt the imagination to play upon the question and let it activate in reflection and thought-experiment whatever concerns and passions it should activate, may require a high order of situational appreciation, or as Aristotle would say perception (*aisthesis*). We shall see that in this, and in the unfortunate fact that few situations come already inscribed with the names of all the human

From *Proceedings of the Aristotelian Society*, 1975–6, pp. 43–9 (© 1975 The Aristotelian Society). Reprinted by courtesy of the Editor of the Aristotelian Society.

concerns which they touch or impinge upon, resides the crucial importance of the minor premiss of the practical syllogism.[2]

3. When the relevant concerns are provisionally identified they may still be too unspecific for means-end reasoning to begin. *Pace* the utility and decision theorists, who concern themselves exclusively with what happens *after* this point, most of what is interesting and difficult in practical reason happens here. See paragraph 2 above. The difficult problem is not 'What will be casually efficacious in the promotion of these concerns?' but to see what really qualifies as an adequate and practically determinate specification of that which is here to be heeded or realized or safeguarded. Deliberation is still *zetesis*, a search, but it is not primarily, or at the point of difficulty, a search for means. It is a search for the *best specification* of what would honour or answer to the relevant concerns. Till the specification is available there is no room for the question of means. When this specification is reached, means-end deliberation can start, but difficulties which turn up in this means-end deliberation may send me back a finite number of times to the problem of a better or more practicable specification of the end. And the whole theoretical interest and difficulty of the matter is in the search for adequate specifications, not in the technical means-end sequel or sequels. It is here, as Aristotle finally recognized, that the analogy with the geometer's search, or the search of the inadequately clothed man, goes lame.[3] Their problem is practically determinate and, to that extent, is not such as to challenge philosophical reflection.

4. No theory, if it is to recapitulate or reconstruct practical reasoning even as well as mathematical logic recapitulates or reconstructs the actual experience of conducting or exploring deductive argument, can treat the concerns which an agent brings to any situation as forming a closed, complete, consistent system. For it is of the essence of these concerns to make competing and inconsistent claims. This is a mark not of human irrationality but of human rationality in the face of the plurality of human goods.[4]

5. The weight of the claims represented by these concerns is not necessarily fixed in advance. Nor need the concerns be hierarchically ordered. A man's reflection on a new situation which confronts him may disrupt such ordering and fixity as had previously existed, and bring a change in his evolving conception of the point (*to hou heneka*), or the several or many points, of living or acting. Any revealed preference theorist or other psychophysicist who seeks by extrapolation to 'take in the slack' which has been left by such indeterminacy or indecisiveness as this, or to tidy up as an 'inconsistency' the plurality of the concerns mentioned in paragraph 4, is preparing to deprive the subject of his autonomy, and to give him what he most likely wants not to have. If prediction were required, then a phenome-

nologist with a real interest in the value consciousness of his subject would do no worse. He could scarcely help but do better. But what is needed here is not prediction, but the subject's own decision processes, constantly re-deployed on new situations or on new understanding of old ones.

6. A man may think it is clear to him in a certain situation what is the relevant concern, yet find himself discontent with every practical syllogism promoting that concern (with major premiss representing the concern, that is). He may resile from the concern when he sees what it leads to, or what it costs, and start all over again. It is not necessarily true that he who wills the end must will the means.

7. The same would have to apply to public rationality, if we had that. In a bureaucracy, where action is not constantly referred back to what originally motivated it, the acute theoretical and practical problem is to make room for some such stepping back, and for the constant remaking and re-evaluation of concerns. (Also for the distinction which individual citizens make effortlessly for themselves between projects on the one hand and other concerns which define and set bounds upon the space within which deliberation operates unconstrained.)

In the difficulty of this referring back, and in the chronic inability of public agencies to render transitive between situations reviewed and/or brought about by planning the relation *is found better overall than*, lies one of the conceptual foundations for a reasoned hatred of bureaucracy, and for the demand for 'public participation' in planning. If one dislikes the last, or has no stomach for the expenditure of time and effort which it entails, then one should go back to the beginning, defy certain demands (even when they are represented as imperatives), and re-examine the ends for which a bureaucracy of such a size was taken to be needed, or at the very least the means chosen to realize the said ends. Nothing else can rescue and preserve civilization from the mounting irrationality of the public province (and its simultaneous enlargement, justified at each stage by the unsatisfactoriness of results at the previous stage) from Oppression exercised in the name of Management (to borrow Simone Weil's prescient phrase).

8. The unfinished or indeterminate character of our ideals and value structure is constitutive both of human freedom and, for finite creatures who face an indefinite or infinite range of contingencies with only finite powers of prediction and imagination (*NE* 1137°), of practical rationality itself.

9. The man of highest practical wisdom is the man who brings to bear upon a situation the greatest number of genuinely pertinent concerns and genuinely relevant considerations commensurate with the importance of

the deliberative context. The best practical syllogism is that whose minor premiss arises out of such a man's perceptions, concerns, and appreciations. It records what strikes such a man as the, in the situation, most salient feature of the context in which he has to act. This activates a corresponding major premiss which spells out the general import of the concern which makes this feature the salient feature in the situation. An analogy explored by Donald Davidson,[5] between a *judgement of probability*, taken in its relation to judgements of probability relative to evidence, and a *decision*, taken in its relation to judgements of the desirability of an action relative to such and such contextual facts, will suggest this idea; the larger the set of considerations which issue in the singling out of the said feature, the more compelling the syllogism. But there are no formal criteria by which to compare the claims of competing syllogisms. Inasmuch as the syllogism arises in a determinate context, the major premiss is evaluated not for its unconditional acceptability, or for embracing more considerations than its rivals, but for its adequacy to the situation. It will be adequate for the situation if and only if circumstances which could restrict or qualify it and defeat its applicability at a given juncture do not in the practical context of this syllogism obtain. Its evaluation is of its essence dialectical, and all of a piece with the perceptions and reasonings which gave rise to the syllogism in the first place. The analogy with probability is imperfect also because, as John McDowell has recently made clear, certain virtues may demand that we *count for nothing* certain pertinent facts—e.g. the likelihood of sustaining wounds in combating an adversary of implacably evil intent.[6] (In most cases of the proper exercise of a virtue we definitely do not want to say that the demands of the virtue are irrational. It is to be noted, though, that this is *not* to say that we shall expect there to be an *independent* account of prudence or rationality which itself shows these demands to be rational without reference to the virtue.)

10. Since the goals and concerns which an agent brings to a situation may be diverse and incommensurable, and may not in themselves dictate any decision, they need not constitute the materials for some psychological theory (or any empirical theory above the conceptual level of a theory of matter) to make a prediction of the action.[7] Nor need anything else constitute these materials. There is simply no reason to expect that it will be possible to construct an (however idealized) empirical theory of the rational agent to parallel the predictive power, explanatory non-vacuity and satisfactoriness for its purpose of (say) the economic hypothesis that, under a wide variety of specifiable circumstances, individual firms will push every line of action open to them to the point where marginal cost and marginal revenue are equal.

11. At this point I offer the reader an obscure but important passage of Aristotle. My translation *cum* paraphrase is of 11142^a 23 ff. of the *Nicomachean Ethics*:

> That practical wisdom is not deductive theoretical knowledge is plain. For practical wisdom is, as I have said, of the ultimate and particular—as is the whole subject matter of action. In this respect practical wisdom is the counterpart or dual of theoretical intuition. *Theoretical* intellect or intuition is of the ultimate in the sense that it is of ultimate universal concepts and axioms which are too primitive or fundamental to admit of further analysis or of justification from without. [At the opposite extreme] practical wisdom [as a counterpart of theoretical reason] also treats of matters which defy justification from without. Practical wisdom is of what is ultimate and particular in the different but analogously basic sense of needing to be simply perceived. By perception here I do not mean sense perception but the kind of perception or insight one needs to see that a triangle, say, is one of the basic or ultimate components [of a figure which is to be constructed with ruler and compass]. [For there is no routine *procedure* for analysing a problem figure into the components by which one may construct it with rule and compasses.] The analysis calls for insight and there is a limit to what one can say about it. But even this sort of insight is more akin to sense perception than practical wisdom is really akin to 'sense perception'.

Comment. On this reading the geometer example turns up again. Two things are worth noting, First, the analogy between the insight he requires and the analyzing-synthesizing grasp of the man of practical wisdom is eventually admitted by Aristotle to be rather lame. Note second, that, whatever else the allusion may accomplish, the example is well suited to effect a transition from technical (means-ends) deliberation to non-technical deliberation. The end proposed—that of drawing a prescribed figure with ruler and compasses—is absolutely specific, whereas in cases of deliberative specification it is not; but the method which the geometer discovers to construct the prescribed figure has a property unusual in a technical deliberation—that of being in some sense constitutive of the end in view. It counts as the answer to a question he was asked (and would be proved to count so). *Caution.* Paraphrase and interpretation is not here confined to square-bracketed portions.

12. The other paraphrase *cum* translation I offer is of *Nicomachean Ethnics* 1143^a 25 ff.:

> ... when we speak of judgement and understanding and practical wisdom and intuitive reason we credit the same people with possessing judgement and having reached years of reason and with having practical wisdom and understanding. For all these faculties deal with ultimates, i.e. with what is particular; and being a man of understanding and of good or sympathetic judgement consists in being able to judge about the things with which practical wisdom is concerned . . . . Now all action relates to the particular or ultimate; for not only must the man of practical wisdom know particular facts, but understanding and judgement are also concerned with

things to be done, and these are ultimates. And intuitive reason is concerned with ultimates in both directions [i.e. with ultimates in two senses and respects, in respect of extreme generality and in respect of extreme specificity]. For intuitive reason [the general faculty] is of both the most primitive and the most ultimate terms. Its proper province is where derivation or independent justification is impossible. In the case of that variety of intuitive reason which is the theoretical intuition pertaining to demonstrative proof, its object is the most fundamental concepts and axioms. In its practical variety, on the other hand, intuitive reason concerns the most particular and contingent and specific. This is the typical subject matter of the minor premiss of a practical syllogism [the one which is 'of the possible']. For here, in the capacity to pick out morally or practically salient features and form the corresponding practical syllogism, resides the understanding of the reason for performing an action, or its end. For the major premiss, and the generalizable concern which comes with it, arises from this perception of something particular. So one must have an appreciation or perception of the particular, and my name for this is intuitive reason. [It is the source both of particular syllogisms and of all the concerns however particular or general which give a man reason to act.]

Comment. It is the mark of the man of practical wisdom on this account to be able to select from the infinite number of features of a situation those features which bear upon the notion or ideal of human existence which it is his standing aim to make real. This conception of human life results in various evaluations of all kinds of things, in various sorts of cares and concerns, and in various projects. It does not reside in a set of maxims or precepts, useful though Aristotle would allow these to be at a certain stage in the education of the emotions. In no case will there be a rule to which a man can simply appeal to tell him what to do (except in the special case where an absolute prohibition operates). The man may have no other recourse but to invent the answer to the problem. As often as not, the inventing, like the frequent accommodation he has to effect between the claims of competing values, may count as a modification or innovation or further determination in the evolution of his view of what a good life is. *Caution.* As before, paraphrase has not been confined to square bracketed sentences.

13. *Conclusion.* Against this account, as I have explained it, it may be complained that in the end very little is said, because everything which is hard has been permitted to take refuge in the notion of *aisthēsis* or *situational appreciation* as I have paraphrased this. And in *aisthēsis*, as Aristotle says, explanations give out. I reply that, if there is no real prospect of an ordinary scientific or simply empirical theory of all of action and deliberation as such (see paragraphs 5, 6, 8, and 10 above), then the thing we should look for may be precisely what Aristotle provides—namely, a conceptual framework which we can apply to particular cases, which articulates the reciprocal relations of an agent's concerns and his

perception of how things objectively are in the world; and a schema of description *which relates the complex ideal the agent tries in the process of living to make real to the form which the world impresses, both by way of opportunity and by way of limitation, upon that ideal.* Here too, within the same schema, are knitted together, as von Wright says, 'the concepts of wanting an end, understanding a necessity, and setting oneself to act. It is a contribution to the moulding or shaping of these concepts.'[8] I entertain the unfriendly suspicion that those who feel they *must* seek more than all this provides want a scientific theory of rationality not so much from a passion for science, even where there can be no science, but because they hope and desire, by some conceptual alchemy, to turn such a theory into a regulative or normative discipline, or into a system of rules by which to spare themselves some of the agony of thinking and all the torment of feeling and understanding that is actually involved in reasoned deliberation.

---

[1] *Proceedings of the Aristotelian Society*, LXXVI, 1975–6, 29–51. The extract given here, with alterations required to make it self-sufficient, runs from pp. 43 to 51.

The author has supplied the following explanatory note: Kantians who have read the article to which this extract belongs are said to have been affronted by something pagan or unprincipled which they find in it. The explanation—not excuse—is easy to find. The subject of the article was the interpretation of Aristotle; and what most modern philosophers seek to bring under the general heading of principles Aristotle tended to account for (except in the special case of negative prescription for the most extreme cases, cf. *Nicomachean Ethics* 1110[ia] 26), not by judgements of the form 'nobody must ever, under circumstances ø, do an action of kind K', but by bringing action kinds under descriptions (pure evaluations) in the several modalities of good and evil: noble or honourable/base or ugly, courageous/cowardly, just/unjust, generous spirited/ mean spirited, truthful/deceitful, etc.

Aristotle still demands our attention in this subject because he perceived more clearly than have subsequent theorists of rationality, morality and the practical the openness, indefiniteness and unforeseeability of the subject-matter of *praxis* (cf. 1137[lbb]). Recognizing the systematic resistance of this subject-matter (in theory as well as in fact) to all attempts at generalized codification, the role of a philosopher of *praxis* is not to attempt the impossible task of codification or generalized prescription. Nor is it to codify some 'logic' of overall appreciation of practical situations. It is rather to describe, elucidate and amplify the concerns of human life, and to make transparent to theory the way in which these concerns necessitate, when they do necessitate, the actions or decisions in which they issue.

The original article was intended to suggest that Aristotle's description of practical reasoning, and of the process of deliberative specification (for this or that context of acting) of a man's standing ends or concerns, excels anything to be found in present day studies of the canons of public and private rationality. It was also claimed in sections I and II, not included here, that Aristotle has been incorrectly interpreted or translated (even in Book III of the *Ethics*) as saying that deliberation is not of ends. He is always prepared to describe practical reason not only in its connection with the realization of particular objectives already formed, but also in its concern with the question what objectives a man *is* to form (in general, or here and now), and what particular concerns he is to put first, in the light of how the Good appears to him. (Only the bare commitment to pursue the Good itself lies outside deliberation.) Aristotle simply stipulates: 'The theory of practice can only be schematic . . . Matters concerned with conduct and questions of what is good for us have no more rigidity than matters of health. The general account [of practical knowledge] being of this nature, the account of particular cases is yet more lacking in exactness; for they do not fall under any technical rule or prescription, but agents themselves in each case consider what is appropriate to the occasion, as happens also in the art of medicine and navigation' (1104^a, cf. 1107^a 28); 'It is difficult sometimes to decide what to choose at what sacrifice, or what to suffer for the sake of what good' (1110^a 29–30).

Those who have fallen under the spell of logical empiricism have arrived at a very different set of emphases. They have seen pure evaluation *per se* as non-descriptive in a manner alien to the context-conditioned evaluative objectivism of Aristotle, but looked for other ways, lying well outside the province supposedly put out of bounds by logical empiricism, of stiffening and objectifying certain principles of action and rationality. I have tried at *Proceedings of the British Academy* 1976 to defend against prescriptivist and neo-Kantian positions Aristotle's own emphasis, and to ground in the theory of truth Aristotle's theoretical preference for treating evaluation as descriptive, and practical judgement as problematic.

² See below, paragraphs 9 and 12. In Aristotelian action-syllogisms, the first or major premiss mentions something of which there could be a desire, *orexis*, transmissible to some practical conclusion (i.e. a desire convertible via some available minor premiss into action). The minor premiss details a circumstance pertaining to the feasibility in the particular situation of what must be done if the claim of the major premiss is to be heeded. In the light of the examples Aristotle gives in *De Motu Animalium*, nothing seems more natural than to describe the first premiss of a practical syllogism as *pertaining to the good* (the fact that it pertains to some good—either a general good or something which the agent has just resolved is good for this situation—is what can beckon to desire); and to describe the second or minor premiss as *pertaining to the possible* (where 'possible' connotes the feasibility *given* the circumstances registered by the minor premiss of the object of concern of the major premiss).

Aristotle calls such patterns of reasoning 'syllogisms' because of an analogy which interests him between *deductively concluding or asserting* and *coming to a practical conclusion or acting*. He says that the conclusion of a practical syllogizing is an action. It is highly questionable, especially given his view of the subject-matter of the practical (1137^b 17 ff.) and given his idea of what practical truth would have to be ($1139a$ 29–31), that Aristotle supposed such syllogisms could fall under some science of truth-preserving (or practical truth-preserving) inference. What matters is only that agents can see in the truth of the minor premiss a way of ministering to some concern to which the major affords expression.

³ See below paragraph 11. For the cloak syllogism, see *De Motu Animalium* 701^a. For the geometer see *Nicomachean Ethics* 1112^b: 'One assumes the end and considers by what means it is to be attained, and if it seems to be produced by several means he considers by which it is best and most easily produced, while if it is achieved by one only he considers how it will be achieved by this, and by what means that will be achieved till he comes to the first cause, which in the order of discovery is last. For the person who deliberates seems to investigate and analyse in the way described as though he were analysing a geometrical construction (not all seeking is deliberation but all deliberation is seeking), and what is last in the order of analysis seems to be first in the order of being brought about. And if one comes on an impossibility, he gives up the search, e.g. if he needs money and this cannot be got; but if a thing appears possible then he tries to do it.'

⁴ Jonathan Glover speaks at p. 183 of *Proceedings of the Aristotelian Society*, Suppl. Vol. 1975 of 'the aesthetic preference most of us have for economy of principles, the preference for ethical systems in the style of the Bauhaus rather than Baroque'. Against this, I say that only a confusion between the practical and the theoretical could even purport to provide reasoned grounds for such a preference. (For the beginnings of the distinction, see Bernard Williams, 'Consistency and Realism', *Proceedings of the Aristotelian Society*, Suppl. Vol. XL, 1966.) Why is an axiom system any better foundation for practice than e.g. a long and incomplete or open-ended list of (always at the limit conflicting) *desiderata*? The claims of all true *beliefs* (about how the world is) are reconcilable. Everything true must be consistent with everything else that is true. But not all the claims of all rational concerns or even all moral concerns (that the world *be* thus or so) need be reconcilable. There is no reason to expect they would be; and Aristotle gives at 1137^b the reason why we cannot expect to lay down a decision procedure for adjudication in advance between claims, or for prior mediation. By the dragooning of the plurality of goods into the order of an axiom system I think practice will be almost as rapidly and readily degraded (and almost as unexpectedly perhaps) as modern building, by exploitation of the well-intentioned

efforts of the Bauhaus, has been degraded into the single-minded pursuit of profit. The last phase of Walter Gropius's career, and the shady and incongruous company into which his ambitions for modern architecture drew him so irresistibly, will repay study by those drawn to Glover's analogy.

⁵ 'How is Weakness of Will Possible?', in Feinberg (ed.), *Moral Concepts*, Oxford, 1969.

⁶ 'Are Moral Requirements Hypothetical Imperatives?', *Proceedings of the Aristotelian Society*, Supp. Vol. XLXII (1978). The possibility of being wounded is in one way relevant—for the demands of courage presuppose that the evil to be avoided is commensurate with the risk—but in another way not relevant. Once the demand is there the brave man *par excellence* cannot as such allow the possibility to weigh.

⁷ See Donald Davidson, 'Mental Events' in *Experience and Theory*, ed. Foster and Swanson, Duckworth, London, 1971; also my 'Towards a Reasonable Libertarian', in *Essays on Freedom and Action*, ed. T. Honderich, Routledge, 1973, pp. 36–41.

⁸ *Varieties of Goodness*, p. 171. Both for the quotation and in the previous sentence I am indebted to M. L. C. Nussbaum. She writes (in an unpublished edition of *De Motu*): 'the appeal of this form of explanation for Aristotle may lie in its ability to link an agent's desires and his perceptions of how things are in the world around him, his subjective motivation and the objective limitations of his situation . . . animals are seen as acting in accordance with desire, but within the limits imposed by nature'.

XI

DESIRES, PRUDENTIAL MOTIVES, AND THE PRESENT

T. NAGEL

1. DESIRES

1. I SHALL argue that the superficially plausible method of accounting for all motivations in terms of the agent's desires will not work, and that the truth is considerably less obvious and more significant. It is therefore necessary to begin with an investigation of the role of desires in rational motivation generally, in order to demonstrate that what they can explain is limited, and that even in simple cases they produce action by a mechanism which is not itself explicable in terms of desires.

The attempt to derive all reasons from desires stems from the acknowledgement that reasons must be capable of motivating, together with an assumption which I shall attack—that all motivation has desire at its source. The natural position to be opposed is this: since all motivated action must result from the operation of some motivating factor within the agent, and since belief cannot by itself produce action, it follows that a desire of the agent must always be operative if the action is to be genuinely his. Anything else, any external factor or belief adduced in explanation of the action, must on this view be connceted with it through some desire which the agent has at the time, a desire which can take the action or its goal as object. So any apparently prudential or altruistic act must be explained by the connection between its goal—the agent's future interest or the interest of another—and a desire which activates him now. Essentially this view denies the possibility of motivational action at a distance, whether over time or between persons. It bridges any apparent gaps with desires of the agent, which are thought to supply the necessary links to the future and to external situations.

Prudence cannot on this view be explained merely by the perception that something is in one's future interest; there must be a desire to further one's future interests if the perception is to have an effect. What follows about altruism is similar: I cannot be motivated simply by the knowledge that an

From *The Possibility of Altruism* (Oxford University Press, 1970), pp. 27–32, 33–6, 37–45, 46. Reprinted by permission of the author and the publishers.

act of mine will have certain consequences for the interests of others; I must care what happens to them if this knowledge is to be effective. There seems little doubt that most people have the desire that makes prudence possible, though it is sometimes overcome by other, more immediate impulses. Altruistic or benevolent desires on the other hand seem less common. In neither case are we in any sense required to possess the desires in question: consequently we are not required to act on the specified considerations. If one lacks the relevant desire, there is nothing more to be said.

The consequence of this view, for a system of normative reasons, is that the interests of others, or his own future interests, cannot themselves provide a person with reasons for action unless we are prepared to admit also that reasons by themselves, or conditions sufficient for their presence, may provide us with no motivation for action whatever. The separation of normative from motivational discourse has of course been attempted. But if one finds that move implausible, and wishes some guarantee that reasons will provide a motive, then one is left with no alternative, on the motivational premisses already laid out, but to include a present desire of the agent, one with appropriate scope, among the conditions for the presence of any reason for action whatever. Therefore another's interest, or my own future interest, can provide me with a reason—a reason capable of motivating—only if a desire for that object is present in me at the time.

The consequences for any other-regarding morality are extreme, for if one wishes to guarantee its universal application, one must make the presence of reasons for altruistic behaviour depend on a desire present in all men. (No wonder self-interest has so often been preferred to altruism as the foundation for justice and the other social virtues.) This view eliminates the possibility of construing ethical principles so based as requirements on action, unless one can somehow show that the appropriate underlying *desires* are required of us.

2. The assumption that a motivating desire underlies every intentional act depends, I believe, on a confusion between two sorts of desires, motivated and unmotivated. It has been pointed out before[1] that many desires, like many beliefs, are *arrived at* by decision and after deliberation. They need not simply assail us, though there are certain desires that do, like the appetites and in certain cases the emotions. The same is true of beliefs, for often, as when we simply perceive something, we acquire a belief without arriving at it by decision. The desires which simply come to us are unmotivated though they can be explained. Hunger is produced by lack of food, but is not motivated thereby. A desire to shop for groceries, after discovering nothing appetizing in the refrigerator, is on the other

hand motivated by hunger. Rational or motivational explanation is just as much in order for that desire as for the action itself.

The claim that a desire underlies every act is true only if desires are taken to include motivated as well as unmotivated desires, and it is true only in the sense that *whatever* may be the motivation for someone's intentional pursuit of a goal, it becomes in virtue of his pursuit *ipso facto* appropriate to ascribe to him a desire for that goal. But if the desire is a motivated one, the explanation of it will be the same as the explanation of his pursuit, and it is by no means obvious that a desire must enter into this further explanation. Although it will no doubt be generally admitted that some desires are motivated, the issue is whether another desire always lies behind the motivated one, or whether sometimes the motivation of the initial desire involves no reference to another, unmotivated desire.

Therefore it may be admitted as trivial that, for example, considerations about my future welfare or about the interests of others cannot motivate me to act without a desire being present at the time of action. That I have the appropriate desire simply *follows* from the fact that these considerations motivate me; if the likelihood that an act will promote my future happiness motivates me to perform it now, then it is appropriate to ascribe to me a desire for my own future happiness. But nothing follows about the role of the desire as a condition contributing to the motivational efficacy of those considerations. It is a necessary condition of their efficacy to be sure, but only a logically necessary condition. It is not necessary either as a contributing influence, or as a causal condition.

In fact, if the desire is itself motivated, it and the corresponding motivation will presumably be possible for the same reasons. Thus it remains an open question whether an additional, unmotivated desire must always be found among the conditions of motivation by any other factor whatever. If considerations of future happiness can motivate by themselves, then they can explain and render intelligible the desire for future happiness which is ascribable to anyone whom they do motivate. Alternatively, there may be another factor operating in such cases, one which explains both the motivational influence of considerations about the future and the motivated desire which embodies that influence. But if a further, unmotivated desire is always among those further conditions, it has yet to be proved.

If we bring these observations to bear on the question whether desires are always among the necessary conditions of *reasons* for action, it becomes obvious that there is no reason to believe that they are. Often the desires which an agent necessarily experiences in acting will be motivated exactly as the action is. If the act is motivated by reasons stemming from certain external factors, and the desire to perform it is motivated by those same reasons, the desire obviously cannot be among the conditions for the presence of those reasons. This will be true of any motivated desire which is ascribable to someone simply in virtue of his intentional pursuit of a goal. The fact that the presence of a desire is a logically necessary condition (because it is a logical consequence) of a reason's motivating, does not entail that it is a necessary condition of the *presence* of the reason; and if it is motivated by that reason it *cannot* be among the reason's conditions.

3. As I have said earlier, the temptation to postulate a desire at the root of every motivation is similar to the temptation to postulate a belief behind every inference. Now we can see that the reply in both cases is the same: that this is true in the trivial sense that a desire or belief is always present when reasons motivate or convince—but not that the desire or belief explains the motivation or conclusion, or provides a reason for it. If someone draws conclusions in accordance with a principle of logic such as *modus ponens*, it is appropriate to ascribe to him the belief that the principle is true; but that belief is explained by the *same* thing which explains his inferences in accordance with the principle. The belief that this principle is true is certainly not among the *conditions* for having reasons to draw conclusions in accordance with it. Rather it is the perception of those reasons which explains both the belief and the particular conclusions drawn.

Beliefs provide the material for theoretical reasoning, but finally there is something besides belief, namely reason, which underlies our inferences from one set of beliefs to another, and explains both the conclusions and those logical beliefs which embody our inferential principles in general propositional form. Correspondingly, desires are among the materials for practical reasoning, but ultimately something besides desire explains how reasons function. This element accounts for many of the connections between reasons (including the reasons which stem from desires) and action. It also explains those general desires which embody our acceptance of the principles of practical reason.

The omnipresence of desires in action is misleading, for it suggests that a desire must form the basis of every motivation. But in fact, when we examine the logical reason why desire must always be present, we see that it may often be motivated by precisely what motivates the action. An alternative basis for that motivation must therefore be discovered. The alternative which I shall defend does not require one to abandon the assumption that reasons must be capable of motivating. It merely points out that they may have this capacity precisely because they are reasons, and not because a motivationally influential factor is among their conditions of application.

An account in terms of the structure of reasons and their relations to their conditions and to each other has the advantage of rendering the motivation of action by those conditions significantly more intelligible than does the mere postulation of intervening desires. It explains the peculiar intelligibility of prudential motivation, and also, I hope to show, the possibility of altruistic motivation—both without the assistance of intervening desires for future happiness or the welfare of others.

2. PRUDENTIAL MOTIVES AND THE PRESENT

1. Structural influences are apparent even when an unmotivated present desire motivates action. It will be useful to consider such a case before dealing with the more complex example of prudence.

If I am thirsty and a soft-drink machine is available, I shall feed it a dime, open the resulting bottle, and drink. In such a case desire, belief, and rudimentary theoretical reasoning evidently combine somehow to produce action. We should ordinarily say, moreover, that the circumstances provide at least *prima facie* reason for the act. So two questions must be answered: how does the motivation operate; and what provides the conditions for the presence of a reason?

I shall propose a single answer to both questions: Reasons are transmitted across the relation between ends and means, and that is also the commonest and simplest way that motivational influence is transmitted. No further desires are needed to explain this phenomenon, and moreover, attempts to explain it in such terms are bound to fail.

It must be realized that the case does require an explanation. Upon reflection, it can seem mysterious that *thirst* should be capable of motivating someone not just to drink, but to put a coin in a slot. Thirst by itself does not motivate such technical undertakings; an understanding of currency and the protocol of vending machines is essential. But when these factors have been added to the explanation, we still lack an account of how they combine with the thirst to produce action.

I think it is very important to resist the temptation to close this gap by expanding the original desire for drink, or by adding another desire. It is of course true that when one sees that the only way to get a drink is to put a coin in the slot, one then wants to put a coin in the slot. But that is what requires explanation: it is a desire *motivated* by thirst plus certain information. If we simply add it on as a further motive, we shall not do justice to its peculiar appropriateness; for *any arbitrary* desire might be added on in *that* capacity.

For example, it is imaginable that thirst should cause me to want to put a coin in my pencil sharpener, but this would be an obscure compulsion or the product of malicious conditioning, rather than a rational motivation. We should not say that thirst provided me with a *reason* to do such a thing, or even that thirst had motivated me to do it.

A theory of motivation is defective if it renders intelligible behaviour which is not intelligible. If we explain the ordinary case of adopting means to a desired end in terms of an additional desire or an extension of the original one, then we must allow a similar explanation for counter-rational cases.

But the fact is that such devices do not produce adequate motivational explanations of deranged behaviour. And if they do not yield adequate explanations in the peculiar case, there is reason to believe that their analogues are not the basis of intelligibility in the normal case. The analogous hypotheses seem to fill the motivational gap in the normal case only because they are not actually *needed* to make the behaviour intelligible, whereas in the abnormal case, where something more obviously *is* needed, they do not succeed. This leaves us, if we do not wish to be arbitrary, with the task of dividing the intelligible connections from the unintelligible ones and explaining why the former work and the latter do not.

2. The solution is to confer a privileged status on the relation between ends and means. This is easily incorporated into the definition of a reason. We may say that if being thirsty provides a reason to drink, then it also provides a reason for what enables one to drink. That can be regarded as the consequence of a perfectly general property of reasons for action: that they transmit their influence over the relation between ends and means. An exact statement of the thesis would have to include an analysis of that relation (or another better suited to the present purpose) as well as an account of what reasons are. Both of these questions will be treated at greater length eventually, but the position is clear enough in outline: all reasons are in some respect general, and this is merely part of the specification of how far their generality extends.

If there is a reason to do something on a particular occasion, it must be specifiable in general terms which allow that same reason to be present on different occasions, perhaps as a reason for doing other things. All such general specifications, whatever else may be true of them, will share a certain formal feature. They will never limit the application of the reason to acts of one sort only, but will always include other acts which promote those of the original kind. And in some cases the general specification will simply assign the reason to all acts that promote some end which is not itself an act. Intuitively, this means that when a person accepts a reason for doing something he attaches value to its occurrence, a value which is either intrinsic or instrumental. In either case the relation of means to ends is involved in the evaluative conception: if the value is intrinsic it attaches derivatively to what will promote the likelihood of the act; if instrumental, the act is valuable as a means to something else, and the same value attaches to other means as well.

In the case with which we began, a desire was among the antecedent conditions of a rational motivation, and the problem was to explain how that desire could extend its motivational influence beyond the scope of its immediate, spontaneous manifestations, through connection with certain beliefs. The system which accounts for this case is operative not only for reasons stemming from desires but for all other reasons as well. Hence it cannot be embodied merely in a constraint on the scope of desires—e.g. an insistence that to desire the end is always to desire the means. Any acceptance of a reason for action must conform to the general principle concerning means and ends. The full influence of desires and of other types of motivation is explained by their interaction with the system. Consequently desires cannot account for its operation.

3. What I propose to do now is to examine this system carefully, and to show how it can be extended to accommodate more complex rational motivations: first prudence and eventually altruism. I shall argue that structural accounts like this accommodate the phenomena of human motivation better than the natural alternatives, and that they reveal more about human beings.

In discussing prudence, we shall be concerned with the element of practical foresight, rather than with any special association the notion may have with self-interest. This must be mentioned because in philosophical usage the term 'prudential' has come to mean approximately the same as 'self-interested', losing even its special connection with provision for the future. This has some foundation in ordinary usage, for we often identify the prudent course of action with that which is personally expedient, and oppose it to selfless as well as to risky alternatives. But I believe that in the most general sense we can perfectly well speak of prudence (or its absence) in cases where the interest of the agent is not in question. When parents concern themselves with the welfare of their children, for example, they may be imprudent not only as regards their own future interests, but also in relation to their children's interests. A person's conduct of an organization's affairs, or his management of another person's investments, may be assessed in the same way. Whatever the case, it is the weight accorded to future consequences which is essential; one is judged imprudent if one disregards them or allows them to be outweighed by insufficient present considerations.

To explain prudential motives, I shall argue that the means-end relation enters into the generation of reasons in such a way as to extend the influence not only of reasons which are present, but also of reasons which are expected in the future. It is therefore a *formal* feature of the system that there is reason to do not only what will promote that for which there is presently a reason, but also what will promote something future for which it is expected that there *will* be a reason. This is, moreover, a perfectly general condition, applying to all reasons, and not just those which stem from desires or interests.

4. The issue is not whether prudence exists, but over its analysis: the analysis both of prudential motivation and of the conditions for the presence of prudential reasons. It is obvious that people are prudentially motivated and do care what will happen to them; someone who remained totally unmoved by the possibility of avertable future harm or accessible future benefits would be regarded as wildly peculiar by anyone, no matter what his theory of motivation. The issue, by now a familiar one, is whether the effect on present action of beliefs about my future interests must be explained by an intervening desire, or whether the connection can be made through a requirement of practical reason by which actions are governed. If there is such a requirement, codifiable as a condition on reasons, then its operation would take the place of desire in explaining certain motivational connections, connections which indeed could not be explained by a desire.

Against the neutral view that a covering prudential desire is operative, I contend first that it does not take care of the actual cases (i.e. what we can explain in terms of prudence and the actual prudential reasons which we believe to obtain); second, that the cases it does accommodate are not handled in the right way, so that their motivational nature is obscured by the theory; third, that my suggestion sheds more light on the operation of prudence and on human nature in general.

I have already inveighed against the position that a desire must always be present as the source of action and correlatively as a condition for the presence of reasons for action. The same difficulties apply in the present case, where some such conviction is certainly operative. One basis for the view that knowledge of my future desires cannot motivate me to act now without the *help* of a current motivating desire for future satisfaction is that in a trivial sense such knowledge cannot motivate me without a desire being *present*. But that is not because the desire's motivational force is necessary to enable the information to work, but rather because such a desire is ascribable to me *in virtue of* the operation of the motive. Once we have undercut that argument for the omnipresence of desires, we have no reason to believe that a desire must be present as the condition of every reason, in order to guarantee that the reason will, when present, be capable of motivating.

The same applies to the specific case of prudence, and to the insistence that a prudential desire must be present as the condition of both prudential motivation and prudential reasons. That may be true (in the familiar, trivial sense) of prudential *motivation*, but nothing in any case follows for prudential reasons.

One does not of course refute a position by showing that bad arguments may be offered in its support. Fortunately more direct criticisms are available. The hypothesis that all links to the future are made by present desires suggests that the agent at any specific time is insular, that he reaches outside himself to take an interest in his future as one may take an interest in the affairs of a distant country. The relation of a person to temporally distant stages of his life must be closer than that. His concern about his own future does not require an antecedent desire or interest to explain it. There must already be a connection which renders the interest intelligible, and which depends not on his present condition but on the future's being a part of his *life*. A life is not a momentary episode, nor a series of such episodes. I shall now elaborate on these criticisms.

5. The position I am attacking explains prudential conduct by saying that my future interests give me reasons to act because I have a present desire to further those interests. On this view future desires cannot by themselves provide reasons, but present desires can. I wish to begin by criticizing the normative system which embodies this contrast. Granted, on the view under discussion, there is usally in fact present a desire for the satisfaction of future desires, which allows the latter to give rise to reasons at one remove. But it is not unreasonable to examine the general system without reference to the particular prudential desire which it is designed to accommodate, for that after all is not part of the system but a motivational factor which allegedly operates through it. The system is supposed to define how reasons proceed from *any* desire, whether its object be present or future. It is therefore presumably meant to apply to situations in which the prudential desire is absent and other desires with future objects are present—whether or not such cases actually exist. Consequently we may begin by considering the rational system itself, without assuming the prudential desire.

The two features of the system to which I object are (*a*) that it does not allow the expectation of a future reason to provide by itself any reason for present action, and (*b*) that it does allow the present desire for a future object to provide by itself a reason for present action in pursuit of that object. All of the following constitute possibilities under the proposed system:

First, given that any desire with a future object provides a basis for reasons to do what will promote that object, it may happen that I now desire for the future something which I shall not and do not expect to desire then, and which I believe there will then be no reason to bring about. Consequently I may have reason now to prepare to do what I know I will have no reason to do when the time comes.[2]

Second, suppose that I expect to be assailed by a desire in the future: then I must acknowledge that in the future I will have *prima facie* reason to do what the desire indicates. But this reason does not obtain now, and cannot by itself apply derivatively to any presently available means to the satisfaction of the future desire. Thus in the absence of any further relevant desire in the present, I may have no reason to prepare for what I know I shall have reason to do tomorrow.

Third, expected future desires whose objects conflict with those of my present desires for the future do not in themselves provide any present countervailing reasons at all—not even *prima facie* reasons which may be outweighed. Any desires or reasons which are merely expected are motivationally irrelevant. I may now, therefore, have an unopposed reason to promote something future which I will, when it happens, have an unopposed reason to prevent—and if I know what my future desires will be, I may have reason now to do precisely what will ensure the failure of my future *rational* attempts; I may have reason to do what I know I will later have reason to try to undo, and will therefore have to be especially careful to lay traps and insurmountable obstacles in the way of my future self.[3]

A system with consequences such as this not only fails to require the most elementary consistency in conduct over time, but in fact sharpens the possibilities of conflict by grounding an individual's plottings against his future self in the apparatus of rationality. These are formal and extremely general difficulties about the system, since they concern the relation of what is rational to what will be rational, no matter what source of reasons is operative.

6. At the next stage of criticism we reintroduce the prudential desire postulated by proponents of such a system, and see how the system thus supplemented purports to account for the phenomena. But whatever the outcome of this enquiry, the objection of the preceding section remains valid. Addition of the proposed desire cannot dissolve the rational paradox which has been objected to in the theory, because the addition does not set a limit to what the theory allows as rational.[4]

In fact, postulation of a prudential desire does not deal satisfactorily with the problems which I have argued arise in the system without it. First of all, its formulation presents serious problems. Presumably the prudential desire is supposed to yield a result based on the consideration of all other desires (or alternative sources of reasons), past, present, and future. It should obtain the conclusion by striking a balance between claims from different times. However, it is itself simply *one* of the *present* desires, and operates as such. So if one of its objects is the satisfaction of those desires other than itself, they will enter the calculation of reasons twice: once in their own right, and once as objects of the prudential desire. To avoid this result, the objects of the prudential desire would have to be restricted to *future* satisfaction. But this would not be satisfactory either, for a further balancing mechanism would then be necessary in order to settle conflicts between considerations derived from ordinary present desires and those derived from the future via the prudential desire. Either this mechanism would be a further desire, in which case the same problems would arise all over again—or else it would be a structural feature of the system of reasons, in which case the project of accounting for prudence in terms of desires would have to be abandoned (as I have maintained).

Secondly, even if this problem could be surmounted, and there *were* a prudential desire, its presence would not alter the fact that the system through which it operates permits the derivation of reasons for action from *any* desire with a future object—not only the prudential one. A desire with a future object does not on this view have to be justified in order to provide reasons for action. Therefore it remains the case, even if the prudential desire is present, that other desires with future objects can provide me with reasons to bring about what I know I shall have no reason to want when the time comes. This will occur if I have a desire for a future object to which I shall in the future be entirely indifferent (and about which the prudential desire is therefore neutral). The system cannot be prevented from generating these unwelcome reasons.

Thirdly, although introduction of a prudential desire may accomplish the primary aim of generating reasons to prepare now for future satisfaction, it at the same time creates new counter-intuitive results. For if it has among its objects the satisfaction of all future desires, this could include the satisfaction of a future desire for a still more future object. So if on Monday I expect that on Tuesday I shall want to eat a persimmon on Wednesday, although I also expect that on Wednesday I shall be indifferent to persimmons (as I am on Monday)—then on Monday I have a clear *prudential* reason to make sure I have a persimmon available on Wednesday, though I will not have any reason to want it then, and I do not on Monday want to have it then.

In other words, the proposed system continues to yield paradoxical results, even after the (unformulable) prudential desire has been added. But finally, even if these problems are set aside, there remains what I regard as the central objection: that even when the proposed view does accommodate the phenomena of rational motivation extensionally, so to speak, it accommodates them in the wrong way, and makes the wrong kind of sense out of them. A person's future should be of interest to him not because it is among his present interests, but because it is *his future*. He already stands in a far stronger and more important relation to his future and the desires he can expect to experience than could possibly be established by any desire which might assail him in the present. The latter sort of connection enables him to reach towards something outside himself; the former depends on an acknowledgement that certain things are not outside to begin with, and that events in his future hold an interest for him now because they belong to a single person of whom his present segment is merely one stage. (This will be elaborated subsequently, and, I hope, rendered less metaphorical.)

7. The above point is reinforced by our final criticism of the view under attack: we must raise the question whether desires with future objects ever give rise to important reasons at all. I have claimed that a prudential desire is *unnecessary* as a bridge to one's own future, because the connection is already guaranteed by formal conditions on practical reason. But even if it were present, it would not be sufficient to yield serious reasons, simply *because* it is a desire with a future object. I have already expressed doubt that desires are the most important sources of motivation. I now wish to extend this doubt, with particular emphasis, to the case of unmotivated desires with future objects. The reasons for action which they provide are insignificant at best. Since the system under attack demands that desires with future objects should be admitted in general as an important source of reasons, if this can be called in question, the system will be further discredited.

It must be emphasized that I am discussing *unmotivated* desires for the future which are supposed to operate as *sources* of motivation: I am not talking about the motivated pursuit of future goals selected for independent reasons. Nothing is commoner than desires for what is future, but they are nearly always motivated by reasons which will *obtain* in the future, in which case the desires do not originate the motivation.

Consider, however, the hypothetical example of a (non-prudential) desire for the future not dependent on any reasons for action which will obtain then. Suppose that, for no reason having to do with the future, I conceive now a desire to become a policeman on my 35th birthday. If I do not believe that the desire will persist, or that any circumstances then obtaining will provide me with reason for being or becoming a policeman, is it possible to maintain nevertheless that the desire itself gives me reason to do what will promote its realization? It would be extremely peculiar if anyone allowed himself to be moved to action by such a desire, or regarded it as anything but a nervous symptom to be looked on with suspicion and got rid of as soon as possible. In general, no one wants anything future in this way, without a reason derived from the expectation of a reason.

There are occasional exceptions—whims about minor matters. One does for example find provisions in wills about where the deceased wants his ashes scattered, and it would be stretching a point to argue that this must always be explained in terms of reasons which he thinks will obtain *after his death* for committing his remains to the Potomac. Such a fancy, reaching out from the present to the future, may justify limited measures to ensure its fulfilment, but even if it is very strongly felt, the reasons which it provides are certainly not strong enough to support the extensive array of rational conduct by which ordinary prudential foresight is manifested and which would have to be supported by reasons stemming from an imagined general prudential desire.

I do not claim that it is impossible or incoherent to ascribe to a person significant and powerful, but unmotivated desires with future objects. Any sufficiently directed behaviour permits us to ascribe a desire, and concerted behaviour might in principle be directed at almost any goal. I claim that such desires for the future are rare, and that the reasons they provide are weak at best. The desires may indeed be motivationally unintelligible. And we cannot make unintelligible directed behaviour intelligible by explaining it in terms of an equally unintelligible desire ascribed on the basis of exactly that behaviour.[5]

8. If it appears that the presence of an unmotivated desire for something future is in most cases not a good reason for pursuing that object, doubt is cast on the suggestion that a present desire for future satisfaction or well-being can be the source of reasons for prudential conduct. Even when such desires do provide reasons they are merely whims, to which it is irrational to attach excessive importance. One *might* for no reason at all conceive a desire that there should be parsley on the moon, and do what one could to smuggle some into the next available rocket; one might simply like the idea. But this is not the alleged status of the proposed prudential desire; it is supposed to be something far more serious than a whim, something which exerts decisive claims on our rational conduct. We do not merely *like* the idea of our own future happiness.

The hypothesis might be saved if we could discover something about this particular desire which explains why it provides serious reasons. But there is a much simpler alternative: namely, that something besides a prudential desire lies at the source of prudential reasons, something that accounts for the rationality both of prudential conduct and of prudential desires, which turn out to be motivated as well. All these conditions are met by the structural factor already mentioned. A desire for one's future well-being, unlike certain other desires for the future, is perfectly intelligible, and therefore an apparent candidate for the source of prudential reasons and prudential motivation, because it already *has* perfectly good reason, in the form of its future objects. Desire for the satisfaction of future desires is justified and motivated by reasons which the expectation of such future desires provides. But if we remove the support of such reasons (as we must if we make the desire their basis) then it becomes a detached whim, unworthy of any strong rational influence on conduct.[6]

The structural condition which accounts for prudence is a general one, and does not apply only to reasons stemming from desires. It entails that the influence of reasons can extend over time, because there is reason to *promote* that for which there is *or will be* a reason. The influence of reasons is transmitted over time because reasons represent values which are not time-dependent. One might even describe them as timeless values. So if a given condition creates a reason for something to happen, there is not only a reason to bring that thing about when the condition is present; there is also a reason to promote its future occurrence if the condition is expected to obtain later on. An expected reason is a reason none the less.[7]

1 For example by Aristotle: *Nicomachean Ethics*, Book III, Chapter 3.

2 There is one way in which an irrational desire like this might provide legitimate reasons for action: namely, as a source of anxiety troublesome enough to be worth appeasing. Thus if on Saturday I conceive for no reason a strong desire to eat a persimmon on Sunday, although I know I shall not want it on Sunday and shall have no other reason to eat it then (perhaps the same thing happens to me every weekend), I may have *some* reason to buy a persimmon on Saturday (assuming they cannot be purchased on Sunday) simply to preserve my peace of mind on *Saturday*. Note, however, that in this case the desire does not directly provide a reason for pursuit of its object; rather it creates an anxiety which there is reason to dissipate, and which it may be impossible to dissipate except by ensuring the availability of the future object of the desire.

3 This must not be confused with the perfectly unobjectionable and not uncommon case in which someone puts obstacles in his way knowing that he will *want* something in the future which he should not have. This may induce him to put a time lock on the liquor cabinet, for example. But that is because he expects to want to do what he will *at that time* have reason *not* to do. There is thus a straightforward link in such cases between present and future reasons. One does not have reason now to ensure the frustration of what it will be *rational* to do in the future.

4 It may be suggested that the dissociated behaviour could be denied to be rational even by this theory, on the ground that the *desires* from which that behaviour derives are so peculiar. But this is to concede my point. For it must mean that while a desire for future satisfaction is rational, certain other desires, namely those for future objects which one knows there will be no reason to pursue in the future, are themselves irrational and confer this irrationality on their behavioural consequences. And the principle which entails the irrationality of those desires will be the same as the one I am defending: namely, that desires for the future *per se* do not

ordinarily provide reasons for action, and that action deriving from such desires is rational only when it, and the desires themselves, are justified by reasons expected to hold in the future.

[5] This is connected with G. E. M. Anscombe's contention that one cannot 'just want' just anything. The reply 'I just wanted to', offered as a *reason* for doing something, has only a very limited application. See *Intention* (Oxford: Blackwell, 1957), pp. 69–71.

[6] It may be added parenthetically that the same can be said of other desires, including many with present objects. They are often motivated by reasons deriving from their objects, rather than being original sources of reasons and motivation. I have focused on the queerness of desires for the future unaccompanied by reasons stemming from the future, because a desire of that sort plays the crucial role in the theory I am attacking.

[7] The general principles which yield this consequence imply that the circumstances that create a reason may occur either earlier or later than the time of action. They therefore permit a new understanding of the reasons provided by those whims about the future which we discussed above. A man who buys himself a cemetery plot and the widow who later ensures that he gets into it may be acting for the same reason: namely, the one provided by his original wish to be buried there. Neither of them need believe that a further reason is provided by circumstances obtaining at the time of burial. Revenge and retribution are further examples of reasons which span time; they may not be good reasons, but their form becomes intelligible if we give up the assumption that a reason must always be the product of circumstances existing at the time of action. A substantive account of such backward-looking reasons would of course require more work.

XII

MOTIVE AND REASON

G. R GRICE

1. REASON FOR ACTING AND DESIRE

I T is wrong to hold that a proposition can be a reason for acting only for a man who wants something to be attained by the action. Reasons for acting are logically independent of desires. Suppose James is home from school for the summer holidays. It is a beautiful day and the river is at its best. One of James's delights is punting. His friends, home from other schools, are all going on the river, taking a picnic with them. There are girls in the party too, and James likes girls. But alas! he is in one of those dreadful moods of ennui. He is consumed with lethargy and as miserable as sin. He is in the kind of mood which we all know and which most of us sometimes suffer. He does not want to go on the river. All he wants to do is slouch around at home. Despite his lack of desire, we can suppose that he would enjoy it on the river if he would make the effort to conquer his present mood. We can suppose that he would enjoy it more than anything else he could do and certainly much more than a day spent moping. If this is so, there is good reason for his going on the river even though he does not want to. In staying at home, he is being stupid, foolish, and unreasonable. He is wasting his time. The case shows that there being good reason for a man's doing so-and-so is logically independent of his wanting to do it or wanting to achieve anything to be attained by doing it.

The conclusion of the previous paragraph may be reached by a more direct route. Suppose a man would enjoy a certain activity more than any other he could do at the time. If this is so, there is a reason for his doing it. It follows immediately that there can be a reason for a man's doing something even though he does not want to do it, for it may not have crossed his mind to do it. And if it has not crossed his mind, he cannot want to do it. Whether there is a reason or not is logically independent of his desires. It may seem that this argument applies only if 'want' is used episodically, and that the fact adduced is no reason for acting unless he has a disposition to

From *The Grounds of Moral Judgement* (Cambridge University Press, 1967), pp. 10–20, 21. Reprinted by permission of the author and the publishers.

want to do the kind of action in question. But the truth is that a disposition to want is no more necessary than his wanting episodically. It may be possible to establish that a man would most enjoy playing golf one afternoon even though he has never in his life thought of playing golf and never wanted to do so: it may be an afternoon on which the alternatives are not exciting; it may be possible to infer from his known skills that he would be good at golf, and known that he enjoys activities which he does well. This is enough to establish that there is good reason for his playing golf. Yet, *ex hypothesi*, he has no disposition to want to: the thought of playing golf has *never* crossed his mind.

As a final illustration, suppose a certain action would win a man promotion. If it has not occurred to him to do it, he cannot want (episodically) to do it. But it may seem that there is a reason for his doing it only if he (dispositionally) wants promotion. This again is false. Whether there is a reason for his doing the action or not depends not upon whether he *wants* promotion but upon whether it is in his *interest* to have it. He may be perfectly contented in his rut and have no desire to emerge. But it remains possible that he would be happier if promoted, and to establish that he would is to establish that there is a reason for his doing the action whatever his desires may be.

I have spoken throughout this section of *there being* a reason for a man's acting in a certain way and not of *his having* a reason. At a later stage, I shall draw a distinction between A's *having* a reason for doing x and *there being* a reason for A's doing x, where 'A' represents, as throughout, any agent and 'x' any action. But for the moment I want to consider the objection that the point about the independence of reasons and desires holds only for the latter and not for the former, i.e. that a man cannot *have* a reason for doing x unless he wants something to be attained by the action, although it is conceded that there can *be* a reason for his doing it even if he does not want any such thing. This objection arises only because reasons are confused with motives. It may be seen to be unfounded by considering again the case of the boy suffering from ennui. Suppose he knows all the facts of the case as set out. It is conceded that there is a reason for his going on the river. It follows that, if he knows all the facts, he knows that there is. It cannot now be said that he does not have a reason for going on the river: there is a reason, and he knows it. Any inclination to object to this is the result, as will be seen, of confusing the proposition that he does not have a *reason* with the proposition that he does not have a *motive*. He does not have a motive because he does not *want* to go on the river: all he wants to do is mope. When this confusion of reason with motive is avoided the temptation to say that he has no reason for going on the river if he does not want to is overcome. He does not have a motive, but he does have a reason. The formula *No reason without a desire* is false. But the formula *No motive without a desire* is true. This is the first important point of distinction between a reason for acting and a motive.

2. MOTIVE

Bentham held that avarice, indolence, benevolence, and such like are motives only in a figurative sense of the term.[1] A motive in the unfigurative sense is the expectation of an 'individual lot of pleasure or pain'. If we abandon Bentham's view about the omnipotence of pleasure and pain, and substitute 'belief' for 'expectation', his position takes the form that to have a motive for an action is to believe that some end will be furthered by doing it. This is a necessary condition of having a motive, but it is not sufficient. It is also necessary to *want* to further that end. *A* and *B* may both believe that the action would lead to their children's happiness, but *A* can have a motive for doing it while *B* has not: *A* may want his children to be happy while *B* does not. Again, *A* and *B* may both believe a certain action would lead to riches. But if *A* wants riches and *B* does not, *A* has a motive for the action while *B* does not. The formula *No motive without a desire* is true.

In both these cases, the question whether *A* and *B* have motives is independent of whether there is a reason for their acting in certain ways. In the latter case, it may be possible to show that *B* would be happier if he were possessed of riches, and if this is so, there is a reason for his doing the action whatever he may think and whatever he may want. This is a prudential case in which it is easy to see what the reason might be. The former case is moral, and the kind of reason appropriate cannot be given yet. But it is clear that it may be possible, as it is in the prudential case, to give a reason for *B*'s acting so as to make his children happy even though he does not wish to make them happy and has no motive for doing so. Whether, in showing him that there was such a reason, we should supply him with a motive is another question again. The answer to it depends upon how his desires are affected when he is shown that there are reasons for acting in certain ways. It is indeed true that the intellect alone cannot move the will to action; but it is also true that the intellect alone supplies us with reasons for action.

Suppose a man has acted so to ease his neighbour's burden and that his action is explained as done from considerateness. The suggestion that the motive is explicitly named has been rejected, and it remains to show how the explanation functions. It functions in a two-fold way. First, it explains why the belief that a certain action would ease his neighbour's burden was a motive for this man whereas there are many others for whom it would not be a motive. It does this by pointing out that the former man is considerate whereas some others are not; by pointing out that it is characteristic of him to be moved by such a belief. But secondly it explains by revealing the kind of belief which provided the motive for the action. In being told that it was done out of considerateness, we are being told that he was moved by the belief that the action would help his neighbour and not by the belief that he would be judged a benevolent man, nor that his neighbour would return the kindness to him. Had one of the latter pair been the case, the explanation would have been not 'Out of considerateness' but perhaps, 'Out of vanity' or 'Out of prudence' respectively. Similarly, when an action is explained in terms of lust, greed, curiosity, sympathy, or benevolence the explanation singles out the kind of belief involved in the motive. The second of these two elements has more explanatory force than the first, and together they do just about as much to explain a man's actions as we think is done by answers of this kind.

I have been arguing for the truth of the formula *No motive without a desire* and the falsity of the formula *No reason without a desire*. To establish that the second formula is false is to establish that the question whether a man can be given reasons for acting in certain ways is indepencent of any question about his desires. This is not to say that it is independent of his interests, considered either independently of the interests of other people or in conjunction with them. Reasons for acting and people's interests are intimately connected in ways to be seen. But reasons are independent of desires, and this is one of the ways in which the concepts of reason for acting and motive differ.

It may be objected to this thesis that 'I want to do *x*' is itself a reason for doing *x*. But the truth is that it is not. It appears to be only because it is usually a fair assumption that it is in a man's interest to do what he wants to do. If it is to be established that there is a (prudential) reason for a man's doing *x*, it has to be established that it is in his interest to do *x*. Given that he wants to do *x*, it has to be established that, in the case in question, it is in his interest to do what he wants to do. That he wants to do it is not a reason. To say, 'I want to do *x*' is not to contribute to a discussion of whether it is rational for me to do *x*. It is to exhibit truculence—unless it is brought forward because, in the particular case, it is understood that it is in my interest to have what I want.

3. DESIRE AND INTEREST

In the previous sections, I have drawn a distinction between a man's desires and his interests. And I have argued that although his having a reason for doing x, and there being a reason for his doing x, are independent of his desires, they are not independent of his interests and the interests of other people; while, on the other hand, his having a motive for doing x is not independent of his desires, but is independent of his interests. To have a motive for doing x, it is not, of course, necessary that he should want to do that action. For example, we often have motives for doing morally right actions without wanting to do those actions. But it is necessary that something is wanted: to see oneself as a moral person, for example, or to enjoy the good opinion of one's neighbours.

Now plainly it may be in a man's interest to do an action even though he does not want to do it: it may be in his interest to invest his inheritance even though he wants to exhaust it in purchasing an expensive car. Certainly there may be a reason for a man's acting in a certain way even though he does not want to do that *action*. But so tame a truth is a far cry from the claim that his having a reason, or there being a reason, for his doing the action is totally independent of his desires. And it may seem that the only way of establishing that it is in his interest to invest his inheritance, that there is a reason for his doing so, is by drawing attention to other things which he desires, e.g. the improvement in his standard of living which an additional income would make possible. Thus, it may appear that the distinction between interests and desires cannot be driven home, and that the distinction between reasons and motives, so far as it rests upon it, breaks down. A man may have a motive for doing x or he may have a reason for doing x: in neither case is it necessary that he should want to do x; but in both cases it is necessary that something should be wanted which will be attained by doing x.

The reply to this objection is that the premiss on which it rests is false. It is not true that when a man does not want to do something we can show that it is in his interest to do it only by appealing to other desires which he has. Suppose a man of no talent and no financial resources is embarked upon a wretched career as an actor. He lives in poverty. He has no chance of success. He is thoroughly discontented and unhappy. It may be that despite his discontent and unhappiness, despite his poverty and the certainty of failure, he wants, and wants more than anything else, to persist in the life he has chosen. But it may also be that, despite his desires, and in addition to the facts cited, there are all sorts of hints to be found in his life that it is in his interest to tear himself away from the stage and sink himself in some other career. It would need a novelist, not a philosopher, to do justice to the description of such hints, but they need not be any facts about what he wants in his present condition: if, of any consequence of the alternative career, we were to ask, 'And don't you want that?' he may reply correctly, 'No, not if it is incompatible with my being an actor.' I am not saying that we can establish that it is in his interest to abandon the stage without also establishing that, if he would make the break, he would *come to want* the alternative career rather than his acting career. But the fact remains that, whatever his desires may *be*, it may be possible to establish that it is in his interest to make the break; and thus there may be a reason for his acting in a certain way even though he wants nothing to be attained by acting in that way. On the other hand, he cannot have a motive for an action unless he does, there and then, desire something to be attained by the action. The distinction between the notions of reason and motive does not break down in the way alleged.

4. REASON FOR ACTING

So far the only examples given of reasons for acting have been that A would enjoy doing x, and that it is in A's interest to have the promotion to which x would lead. Consider now the very general reason that it is in A's interest to do x, and let this proposition be represented by 'P'. The truth of P is a reason for A's doing x, but it is not the only reason in terms of P. The truth of the proposition that A has good reason for judging that P is also a reason. To deny this leads to paradox. Suppose A decides to catch the 3.05 train to London. It may be true that the train is going to crash with the death of all passengers and therefore false that it is in his interest to catch it. But if he has no good reason for thinking it will crash, and good reason to think that by catching it he will reach London in time for an appointment, then he has good reason for judging that it is in his interest to catch it. And if this is so, it cannot be denied that he has a reason, and good reason, for catching that train. The use which is required of 'A has good reason for judging that P' allows for the individuality of A's situation—that it is different, for example, from the situation of those about to engineer the destruction of the train. At the same time, it is necessary that certain canons of judgement are satisfied. These canons are such that, if they are satisfied, we can say that the judgements A made on this occasion were beyond criticism. I shall say that if P is true, *there is* a reason for A's doing x; and that if A has good reason for judging that P is true, A *has* (given the individuality of his situation) a reason for doing x.

Thus the truth of P and the truth of the proposition that A has good reason for judging that P are both reasons for A's acting. It will save verbiage if I speak of the proposition as a reason for acting, and this device will be adopted frequently. Whenever I speak in this way, it is a shorthand for referring to either the truth of the proposition or the truth of the

proposition that A has good reason for judging it true. With this understanding, it is false to say that *any* proposition can be a reason for acting. It
is false, for example, of the propositions that it is a beautiful day, that the
specific heat of copper is $0 \cdot 1$, that the ice is thin and that Bentleys are
expensive. It may seem that circumstances can be imagined in which any of
these propositions is a reason for acting, but the fact is that circumstances
can be imagined in which any of them may provide inductive support for a
proposition which is a reason for acting. At this point the discussion under
the heading *Reason for Acting and Reason for Judging*[2] is taken a stage
further. I said in that earlier discussion that philosophers often apply the
term 'reason for acting' to propositions which are not reasons for acting
but which provide inductive support for propositions which are; and that
this was a confusion which must be avoided if the concept of reason for
acting is to be isolated. I must now try to make clear my view upon what
kinds of proposition can be reasons for acting.

In the section *Reason for Acting and Desire* we say that the question of
whether or not there is a reason for A's doing x is independent of his
desires. But there was no suggestion that it was independent of his interests. Quite the reverse: in each case discussed the question depended upon
whether A would enjoy doing x, or, more generally, whether it was in his
interest to do x. The only propositions which are properly understood as
reasons for acting—as reasons for A's doing x—are propositions which
state either that x is *in some way* in accordance with A's interests or that x
conduces to A's aims. One such proposition is that it is in A's interest to do
x, but the action is not always related to the agent's aims or interests in this
simple way. In the case of moral reasons a more complex relation holds
between the interests of A, the interests of other people, and the action; but
it still asserts that x is *in some way* in A's interests. The truth of a proposition of one of these kinds is a reason for acting; and so is A's having
good reason for judging it true. The truth of any other kind of proposition
is not; nor is A's having good reason for judging it true. Many other kinds
of proposition may indeed, in various circumstances, provide inductive
support for a proposition which is a reason for acting. But this is not to say
that they are themselves reasons for acting.

This may seem like dogmatic assertion, or it may seem obvious once
stated, or it may have seemed obvious before it was stated. But in any case
I had better defend the position adopted. It can only be done at this stage
by considering a prudential case in which no moral factors are involved.
The claim will be argued independently for moral cases at a later stage.
Suppose I establish to a man's satisfaction that it is going to be a beautiful
day. It does not follow that I have established that there is a reason for his

doing anything: he may be oblivious to the weather. Suppose I prove to him that the ice is thin. I have again not proved that there is a reason for his acting in any way; he may be in bed with a sprained ankle. Again, if I establish that there is a restaurant nearby, I have not established that there is a reason for his doing anything: he may be an ascetic who is not hungry. It is only when I have shown that it is in his interest to do something that I have shown that there is a reason for his doing it. I can establish any proposition I like which does not state that an action is in his interest and he can always intelligibly reply, 'You have not yet given me a reason for acting.' It is only when I have established that it is in his interest to act in a certain way that he cannot make this reply. 'It is in my interest to do x, but that is no reason for my doing x' is self-contradictory, while 'It is a beautiful day, but that is no reason for my doing x' is not.

The point is concealed in day to day discussions because so much is usually taken for granted. For example, when someone states that the ice is thin, other propositions are often taken for granted which, together with the one asserted, provide sufficient inductive support for the proposition that it is in the interest of all concerned to keep off. In such a case, it is established that there is a reason for doing so, though the argument is not explicitly set out. It thus seems that the proposition that the ice is thin is a reason for acting, because it is the only proposition asserted. But the fact is that it is part of the inductive support, the rest being implicit, for the proposition that it is in the interest of all concerned to keep off the ice. And this latter proposition is the reason for acting.

The most important point to be considered about reasons for acting is their assessment as good or bad. Two elements are involved in such an assessment. To avoid verbiage again, I shall let 'S' represent any proposition which asserts that x is *in some way* in accordance with A's interest or conduces to A's aims. Thus 'S' represents the kind of proposition which I have just been arguing can be a reason for acting. (Strictly speaking, as already explained, the truth of S and the truth of the proposition that A has good reason for judging that S are reasons for acting.) 'S' may represent any of a number of propositions, for there are many ways, as we are to see, in which x can be in accordance with A's interest.

The first element involved in the assessment of a reason for acting as good or bad is as follows. It is a necessary and sufficient condition of *there being* a reason for A's doing x that some S is true. And it is a necessary and sufficient condition of *A's having* a reason for doing x that he should have good reason for judging some S true. These are necessary and sufficient for there being *a* reason and for A's having *a* reason respectively. They are necessary but not sufficient for there being *good* reason for A's doing x and for A's having *good* reason for doing x. It is a further necessary condition, that the S involved is of a certain kind. But before dealing with this point, which deserves a separate section, I must draw attention to the second way in which a reason for acting differs from a motive.

It has already been argued that having a motive implies having a desire but that neither having a reason nor there being a reason implies having a desire. Leaving there being a reason on one side—precisely parallel remarks apply to it—we now see that it is a necessary condition of A's having a reason for doing x that he has good reason for judging some S true. It is plain that this is not a necessary condition of his having a motive for doing x. It is sufficient for his having a motive that he should *believe* that some aim is furthered by his doing x and that he should want to further that aim. It is irrelevant whether he has good reason for his belief; his reasons may be abysmal, but it has no bearing upon whether or not he has a motive. It follows that one of the elements involved in the assessment of a reason for acting as good or bad, viz., that some S is true, or that he has good reason for judging some S true, is not available for the assessment of motives. Motives cannot be good or bad in the way that reasons for acting can. Motives can be assessed as morally good or bad, but that is a different matter.

5. BETTER REASON THAN

The truth of some S is a necessary condition of there being good reason for A's doing x, but it is not sufficient. It is not sufficient because the truth of some S's is better reason for acting than the truth of some others. If an S is true of x it does not follow that there is good reason for A's doing x because another S may be true of not-x, *and the truth of the second S may be a better reason for acting than the truth of the first.*

A distinction can be drawn between a man's present and his future interests. An action may be in his present interest because he would enjoy it, because it would give him immediate satisfaction, relieve an uneasy conscience, cure a pain or rid him of some other unpleasant sensation. It may be in his future interest because it will lead to an annual income of £5,000 later, or to a happy retirement, or to his marrying the girl he wants, and so on. The distinction between present and future interests is not, of course, sharp. An action which is in his present interest may also be in his future interest and vice versa; but an action which is in his present interest may be against his future interest and an action which is in his future interest may be against his present interest. When such conflicts occur we need a way of referring to the action it is in his interest to do, and for this purpose I speak of his overall interest. The action which is in his overall interest is the action it is in his interest to do when his present and future interests conflict. It is not always in a man's overall interest to do the action which is in his future interest. 'One splendid indiscretion,' Ernest de Selincourt said, 'is worth a world of caution.' It can be in a man's overall interest to cater for either his present or future interests. There need be nothing momentous about deciding an action to be in one's overall interest. I may decide that it is in my overall interest to go for a walk one afternoon because I would enjoy it and doing so will have no effect upon my future life. Vast numbers of decisions which we take are like this. On the other hand, such decisions are sometimes immensely important.

¹ *Principles of Morals and Legislation*, 1879, p. 99.
² [It is not reprinted here—Ed.]

XIII

REASONS FOR ACTION
AND DESIRES

P. R. FOOT

MR. WOODS[1] wants to disprove a certain theory of what it is for an agent
to have a reason for acting. This theory is the one that makes reasons
dependent on desires, saying that every statement of a reason, when fully
spelled out, must contain a reference to something wanted or desired by the
person whose reason it is to be. As an account of sufficient conditions this
is quite implausible, as Mr. Woods shows. Nevertheless it might truly state
a necessary condition, and it is to this suggestion that Mr. Woods
addresses himself. He wants to show, by producing examples, that there
are reasons for acting not dependent on the agent's desires.

Two questions arise, first whether Mr. Woods is right in rejecting the
theory he rejects, and secondly whether his arguments are sound. It will be
argued here that the answer to the first question is 'yes' and the answer to
the second 'no'. I shall first give my own counter-example and then go on
to say why I reject those put forward by Mr. Woods.

Prudential reasons seem to me to provide the most obvious counter-
example to the thesis that all reasons for action depend on the agent's
desires. By 'prudential reasons' I mean those having to do with the agent's
interests. There are, of course, problems about the limits of this class, but
these need not concern us here. It will be enough to take some uncon-
troversial example of a prudential reason.

Let us, then, consider the case of a man who knows he will go hungry
tomorrow unless he goes shopping today. We will suppose that circumstances are normal; he has no reason for wanting to be hungry tomorrow,
and his house is not on fire. He has a prudential reason for visiting the
shops. Now according to the theory we are discussing, the statement of his
reason, if fully spelled out, must contain a reference to one of his desires.

From *Proceedings of the Aristotelian Society*, Supp. Vol. 1972 (© 1972 The
Aristotelian Society). Reprinted by courtesy of the Editor of the Aristotelian
Society.

What desire will this be? The desire *not to be hungry tomorrow* seems the most obvious candidate. For we may tell ourselves that this is the desire that will be present in every case. We should pause, however, and ask why we say that the man who has reason to go shopping today has a *desire* not to be hungry tomorrow. Do we find ourselves, in such circumstances, with thoughts and feelings that allow us to speak of 'desire'? Sometimes this is exactly how it is; the prospect for tomorrow fills us with anxiety and apprehension, together with a lovely hope that the evil may be averted. But in most ordinary cases we would have nothing of the kind to report; it is not on such grounds that we can speak of a desire, and if reasons depended on such things there would be few reasons indeed. Yet surely we cannot deny that when a man goes shopping today because otherwise he will be hungry tomorrow he wants, or has a desire to, avoid being hungry? This is true, but an analysis of the use of expressions such as 'want' and 'has a desire to' in such contexts shows that these 'desires' cannot be the basis of the reason for acting. Thomas Nagel, in an excellent discussion of prudence, has explained the matter in the following way:

> That I have the appropriate desire simply *follows* from the fact that these considerations motivate me; if the likelihood that an act will promote my future happiness motivates me to perform it now, then it is appropriate to ascribe to me a desire for my own future happiness.[2]

What we have here is a use of 'desire' which indicates a motivational direction and nothing more. One may compare it with the use of 'want' in 'I want to ϕ' where only intentionality is implied. Can *wanting* in this sense create the reason for acting? It seems that it cannot. For in the first place the desires of which we are now speaking are to be attributed to the agent only in case he is moved to action, or would be so moved in the absence of counteracting reasons or causes, and it is a mistake to set corresponding limits to the scope of reasons for acting. Moreover a false account is given even of the cases in which action occurs. For what happens there is that a man is moved to action by the recognition that he has reason to act. This would be impossible if there were no reason to be recognized until the agent has been moved.

It seems, then, that the agent's present desire to avert the future evil cannot be the basis of his prudential reason for acting. Would it be more plausible to suggest that it is on future desires that prudential reasons depend? It might be said, for instance, that suffering is something we necessarily want away *at the time we are suffering*, so the thought of future suffering contains the thought of future desire. Whether or not it is right to see a connection as close as this between every prudential consideration and future desire, the theory seems to put the emphasis in the wrong place. For it is not as implying a desire, but rather *as suffering*, that future pain is something we have reason to avoid. If we postulate the future desire alone it is not at all certain that a reason for action in the present remains, as we can see by considering the case of future *whims*. Suppose we believe today that tomorrow we shall want to do something, which will, however, be a mere whim. Suppose, moreover, that we do not expect to get pleasure from the satisfaction of our whim, and do not think we will feel frustrated or annoyed if the whim is not gratified. Have we any reason to make provision now for the satisfaction of this future desire? We are inclined to say that we have not; at the very least our intuitions become uncertain, and even this suggests that in stripping down to future desire we have not reached the essential factor in prudential reasoning.

Mr. Woods himself did not discuss prudential reasons except as refuting the suggestion that reasons must necessarily move to action. I hope he may agree with most of what I have said up to this point. But whether or not he thinks that prudential reasons could be used as a counter-example to the thesis that statements of reason, when fully spelled out, must contain a reference to the desires of the person for whom they are to be reasons, he himself relied on examples of another kind. He believes that the theory can be refuted by showing that moral beliefs, aesthetic opinions and 'evaluative beliefs in general' give reasons that are not dependent on the agent's desires. I want to show that Mr. Woods is mistaken in thinking that evaluative beliefs give reasons in this special way. They have a special connection with reasons for action, but this depends on their special connections with interests and desires.

How, then, do evaluative judgements give reasons for acting? Let us put aside moral and aesthetic examples for the moment, and look at familiar everyday instances of evaluation outside these fields. We may think, for instance, about good doctors and good philosophers, good arguments and good parties, good houses and good land. If a patient has a reason to choose a good doctor, and a tenant a good house, why is this so? Obviously it is because the qualities by which a doctor is judged a good doctor, and a house a good house, are those which make them useful to patients and tenants respectively. Good qualities are exactly those which are of some interest or use, and it is not surprising that *someone* has a reason to choose good Fs and good Gs where Fs and Gs are the kind of things one can choose. In general very many people will have reason to choose to have good ones, or, in some cases, to choose to be good ones, since the good will be judged from some standard point of view. But not everyone will have these reasons, since he may not have standard desires and interests, and may not be the one whose desires and interests are taken into account. There is no magical reason-giving force in evaluative judgements, and it would be ludicrous carefully to choose a good *F* or a good *G*, rather than a bad *F* or a bad *G*, if one's own desires and interests were not such as to provide a reason in one's own case.

The reason-giving force of aesthetic judgement has a similar dependence on interests and desires. A man has reason to read an interesting book just so far as he thinks it will interest him, or if he expects the reading to be pleasing or profitable in some other way. The idea that one should have good works of art around just because they are good works of art, and even if one can get nothing from them, must depend on hopes of improvement in one's taste. This is probably bad policy, and in any case does nothing to support the thesis that aesthetic beliefs provide reasons for action that are independent of what the agent wants.

Are moral evaluations linked with reasons for acting only when connected with the agent's interests and desires? There are many who will refuse to admit that it is so, agreeing with Mr. Woods at least so far as this class of evaluations is concerned. It seems to them essential that moral considerations give reason for acting to each and every man, and they rightly say that such universal reasons cannot be provided for moral action if the basis is interest and desire. Why, however, do they insist that each and every man, whatever his situation and whatever his nature, must have reason to do what morality requires? Is there perhaps some confusion between the moral judgement, which undoubtedly stands for any man, and the judgement about reasons which may not? Or is it that they want to be able to call a wicked amoral man irrational, as if by that they can hit him where it will hurt? Some would admit that the cool calculating amoral man is not to be called *irrational*, but nevertheless say that he has reason to act morally whatever his interests and desires. This seems to be an inconsistent position, as we may show in the following way.

Suppose a man to assert these propositions:

A. 1. I have a reason to do action *a*.
   2. I have no reason not to do *a*.
   3. I am not going to do *a*.

From these premises he must conclude

   4. I am going to act irrationally.

On the other hand the following are admitted consistent:

B. 1. I shall act immorally unless I do *a*.
   2. I have no reason not to do *a*.

3. I am not going to do *a*.
4. I am not going to act irrationally.

We can show by a simple argument that when B. 1–4 are true, A. 1 is false; from which it follows that B. 1 cannot entail A. 1.

What proof can be given of the special reason-giving force of moral considerations? What is its source supposed to be? Mr. Woods is impressed by the fact that moral judgement, and evaluation generally, is connected with 'intelligible human pursuits and practices'. But as we saw in discussing non-moral evaluations this will not guarantee that every man has a reason to choose what is properly called good. Perhaps good men are those who have qualities useful to society, not to themselves; perhaps it is others who have reason to want them to be good? Or perhaps it is sometimes one and sometimes another, with no guarantee that on each occasion each man will have reason to do what morality requires.

Why is it, one may ask, that these particular evaluations—moral evaluations—are supposed by so many people to be different from the rest? The reason why they should be *thought* to be different is not hard to find. For moral judgements are not only evaluative but also normative. Moral language is used not simply to pick out actions and qualities which are of interest or use, but also to teach that these actions should be performed, and these qualities acquired. Moral behaviour is the subject of social teaching and social demand. There is thus no doubt that people are taught to *take* moral considerations as reasons for acting, without any reference to what they want, or what their interests are. They are to say 'It's immoral, so I won't do it' or 'Justice requires that I act in this way, so that is what I shall do.' This kind of teaching explains why it should be thought that moral judgements give reasons for acting which are independent of interests and desires, but it does nothing to prove that it is so. For we certainly do not think that independent reasons could be created by social pressures, and elsewhere we are quite ready to throw over the rules of behaviour that we were taught when we were young. We were taught, for instance, that we should follow rules of etiquette. Later we ask whether there is any reason to do what we were taught.

It may be suggested that we are looking for the special connection between reason for acting and morality in the wrong place. Perhaps it is to be found not in the form of moral judgements but rather in their content. Morality, or a large part of morality, has to do with a man's actions so far as these affect other men for good or ill. If it can be shown that we have reason to aim at the good of others, as much as we have reason to aim at our own, then we shall have reason to follow a great many of morality's laws. Theories have, of course, been constructed along these lines. A version of the argument was put forward by G. E. Moore in the following well-known passage:

... The only reason I can have for aiming at 'my own good' is that it is *good absolutely* that what I so call should belong to me ... But if it is *good absolutely* that I should have it, then everyone else has as much reason for aiming at *my* having it, as I have myself.[3]

What Moore is saying is that if I have reason to promote state *S* then *it is good* that state *S* comes about, and if *it is good* that *S* comes about then anyone has reason to promote *S*. The argument is faulty because there is no such thing as an objectively good *state of affairs*. Such constructions as 'a good state of affairs', 'a good thing that *p*', are used subjectively, to mark what fits in with the aims and interests of a particular individual or group. Divorced from such a background these expressions lose their sense, and an argument of the type that Moore suggested will not, for this reason, go through.

Thomas Nagel, who has recently argued the case against rational egoism with much subtlety, employs what is basically the same argument as Moore's. When anyone has a reason for bringing anything about there has to be a reason for that thing 'to happen', and Nagel says that in acting for a reason one must be able to regard oneself as 'promoting an objectively valuable end'.[4] But if it means nothing to speak of an 'objectively valuable end' then there are no reasons such as Nagel describes and I may say that another has reason to aim at his own good without implying that I too have reason to promote this end.

It seems, then, that we lack a convincing argument for the special, automatic reason giving force of moral judgement, and should be prepared to think that moral considerations give reasons for action only in ordinary ways. Can we explain how men do have reasons for acting morally if we confine ourselves to reasons based on interests and desires? It seems that we can do so, and that without placing too much emphasis on self-interested reasons for doing what ought to be done. One does not want to deny a general connection between virtue and happiness, but no one who acts justly or charitably only where it pays him to do so will qualify as a just or benevolent man. A moral man must be ready to go against his interests in the particular case, and if he has reason to act morally the reason will lie rather in what he wants than in what is to his advantage. On this basis reasons will exist for many kind and upright men. We readily accept private affection as giving reasons for actions without the least hint of self-interest; why should a more extended fellow-feeling not do the same? If a man has that basic sense of identification with others that makes him care whether or not they live wretched lives, has he not the best possible reason for charitable action? And would it not be misrepresentation to speak of this as a charity dependent on the feelings and inclinations of the moment, since both public and private affections endure through periods of coldness, and lack of inclination never destroys the reason to act?

The case of justice may be thought to present greater difficulties for such an account of moral reasons for acting, since justice is notoriously not to be reduced to benevolence, and a man's affections, however extended, would not necessarily lead him to be just. Two different types of example have to be considered. There is first the case where the life or liberty of an individual is set against the good of the majority. This seems to pose no special problems. There are some who have a special concern for those who are vulnerable to oppression, and one who is a lover of justice will be a man such as this. The second case is more puzzling: it is that of Hume's profligate creditor to whom a debt should be paid though no good is foreseen. Why does anyone think that he has reason to be honest in such a case? It could be mere superstition. Perhaps we have been bewitched by the idea that we *just do* have reason to obey this part of our moral code. But such a suggestion may well be wrong. It seems that we cannot get on well without the kind of justice that is 'without reason' in the particular case. We need *just men* who are prepared to follow rules of justice even where these are not coincident with any benevolence, and men act justly because they believe that this is so. We should also take into account, here and elsewhere, the desires that people have to live a certain kind of life. Of course these desires vary greatly from person to person. One man likes to be useful; another demands a part in some great or noble cause. Perhaps it will be said that such people choose the life they choose because they think they *ought* to do so—because this is how a man ought to live. But perhaps no such thought, with its problematic reason-giving force, enters into the matter at all. Without any moral imperatives a man may have such desires.

[1] The reference is to M. Woods, 'Reasons for Action and Desires', ibid., to which Mrs Foote's article is a reply—Ed.

[2] *The Possibility of Altruism* (O.U.P., 1970), pp. 29–30.

[3] *Principia Ethica* (Cambridge, 1903), p. 99.

[4] *The Possibility of Altruism*, pp. 96–7.

XIV

MORALITY AND ADVANTAGE

D. P. GAUTHIER

I

HUME asks, rhetorically, 'what theory of morals can ever serve any useful purpose, unless it can show, by a particular detail, that all the duties which it recommends, are also the true interest of each individual?'[1] But there are many to whom this question does not seem rhetorical. Why, they ask, do we speak the language of morality, impressing upon our fellows their duties and obligations, urging them with appeals to what is right and good, if we could speak to the same effect in the language of prudence, appealing to considerations of interest and advantage? When the poet, Ogden Nash, is moved by the muse to cry out:

> O Duty,
> Why hast thou not the visage of a sweetie or a cutie?[2]

we do not anticipate the reply:

> O Poet,
> I really am a cutie and I think you ought to know it.

The belief that duty cannot be reduced to interest, or that morality may require the agent to subordinate all considerations of advantage, is one which has withstood the assaults of contrary-minded philosophers from Plato to the present. Indeed, were it not for the conviction that only interest and advantage can motivate human actions, it would be difficult to understand philosophers contending so vigorously for the identity, or at least compatibility, of morality with prudence.

Yet if morality is not true prudence it would be wrong to suppose that those philosophers who have sought some connection between morality and advantage have been merely misguided. For it is a truism that we should all expect to be worse off if men were to substitute prudence, even of the most enlightened kind, for morality in all of their deliberations. And

From *The Philosophical Review*, October 1967, pp. 460–75. Reprinted by permission of the author and the editor of the journal.

this truism demands not only some connection between morality and advantage, but a seemingly paradoxical connection. For if we should all expect to suffer, were men to be prudent instead of moral, then morality must contribute to advantage in a unique way, a way in which prudence— following reasons of advantage—cannot.

Thomas Hobbes is perhaps the first philosopher who tried to develop this seemingly paradoxical connection between ,morality and advantage. But since he could not admit that a man might ever reasonably subordinate considerations of advantage to the dictates of obligation, he was led to deny the possibility of real conflict between morality and prudence. So his argument fails to clarify the distinction between the view that claims of obligation reduce to considerations of interest and the view that claims of obligation promote advantage in a way in which considerations of interest cannot.

More recently, Kurt Baier has argued that 'being moral is following rules designed to overrule self-interest whenever it is in the interest of everyone alike that everyone should set aside his interest'.[3] Since prudence is follow-ing rules of (enlightened) self-interest, Baier is arguing that morality is designed to overrule prudence when it is to everyone's advantage that it do so—or, in other words, that morality contributes to advantage in a way in which prudence cannot.[4]

Baier does not actually demonstrate that morality contributes to advantage in this unique and seemingly paradoxical way. Indeed, he does not ask how it is possible that morality should do this. It is this possibility which I propose to demonstrate.

II

Let us examine the following proposition, which will be referred to as 'the thesis': *Morality is a system of principles such that it is advantageous for everyone if everyone accepts and acts on it, yet acting on the system of principles requires that some persons perform disadvantageous acts.*[5]

What I wish to show is that this thesis *could be true*, that morality could possess those characteristics attributed to it by the thesis. I shall not try to show that the thesis is true—indeed, I shall argue in Section V that it presents at best an inadequate conception of morality. But it is plausible to suppose that a modified form of the thesis states a necessary, although not a sufficient, condition for a moral system.

Two phrases in the thesis require elucidation. The first is 'advantageous for everyone'. I use this phrase to mean that *each* person will do better if the system is accepted and acted on than if *either* no system is accepted and acted on *or* a system is accepted and acted on which is similar, save that it never requires any person to perform disadvantageous acts.

Clearly, then, the claim that it is advantageous for everyone to accept and act on the system is a very strong one; it may be so strong that no system of principles which might be generally adopted could meet it. But I shall consider in Section V one among the possible ways of weakening the claim.

The second phrase requiring elucidation is 'disadvantageous acts'. I use this phrase to refer to acts which, in the context of their performance, would be less advantageous to the performer than some other act open to him in the same context. The phrase does not refer to acts which merely impose on the performer some short-term disadvantage that is recouped or outweighed in the long run. Rather it refers to acts which impose a disadvantage that is never recouped. It follows that the performer may say to himself, when confronted with the requirement to perform such an act, that it would be better *for him* not to perform it.

It is essential to note that the thesis, as elucidated, does not maintain that morality is advantageous for everyone in the sense that each person will do *best* if the system of principles is accepted and acted on. Each person will do better than if no system is adopted, or than if the one particular alternative mentioned above is adopted, but not than if any alternative is adopted.

Indeed, for each person required by the system to perform some disadvantageous act, it is easy to specify a better alternative—namely, the system modified so that it does not require *him* to perform any act disadvantageous to himself. Of course, there is no reason to expect such an alternative to be better than the moral system for everyone, or in fact for anyone other than the person granted the special exemption.

A second point to note is that each person must gain more from the disadvantageous acts performed by others than he loses from the disadvantageous acts performed by himself. If this were not the case, then some person would do better if a system were adopted exactly like the moral system save that it never requires *any* person to perform disadvantageous acts. This is ruled out by the force of 'advantageous for everyone'.

This point may be clarified by an example. Suppose that the system contains exactly one principle. Everyone is always to tell the truth. It follows from the thesis that each person gains more from those occasions on which others tell the truth, even though it is disadvantageous to them to do so, than he loses from those occasions on which he tells the truth even though it is disadvantageous to him to do so.

Now this is not to say that each person gains by telling others the truth in order to ensure that in return they tell him the truth. Such gains would merely be the result of accepting certain short-term disadvantages (those associated with truth-telling) in order to reap long-term benefits (those associated with being told the truth). Rather, what is required by the thesis is that those disadvantages which a person incurs in telling the truth, when he can expect neither short-term nor long-term benefits to accrue to him from truth-telling, are outweighed by those advantages he receives when others tell him the truth when they can expect no benefits to accrue to them from truth-telling.

The principle enjoins truth-telling in those cases in which whether one tells the truth or not will have no effect on whether others tell the truth. Such cases include those in which others have no way of knowing whether or not they are being told the truth. The thesis requires that the disadvantages one incurs in telling the truth in these cases are less than the advantages one receives in being told the truth by others in parallel cases; and the thesis requires that this holds for everyone.

Thus we see that although the disadvantages imposed by the system on any person are less than the advantages secured him through the imposition of disadvantages on others, yet the disadvantages are real in that incurring them is *unrelated* to receiving the advantages. The argument of long-term prudence, that I ought to incur some immediate disadvantage *so that* I shall receive compensating advantages later on, is entirely inapplicable here.

III

It will be useful to examine in some detail an example of a system which possesses those characteristics ascribed by the thesis to morality. This example, abstracted from the field of international relations, will enable us more clearly to distinguish, first, conduct based on immediate interest; second, conduct which is truly prudent; and third, conduct which promotes mutual advantage but is not prudent.

A and *B* are two nations with substantially opposed interests, who find themselves engaged in an arms race against each other. Both possess the latest in weaponry, so that each recognizes that the actual outbreak of full-scale war between them would be mutually disastrous. This recognition leads *A* and *B* to agree that each would be better off if they were mutually disarming instead of mutually arming. For mutual disarmament would preserve the balance of power between them while reducing the risk of war.

Hence *A* and *B* enter into a disarmament pact. The pact is advantageous for both if both accept and act on it, although clearly it is not advantageous for either to act on it if the other does not.

Let *A* be considering whether or not to adhere to the pact in some particular situation, whether or not actually to perform some act of disarmament. *A* will quite likely consider the act to have disadvantageous consequences. *A* expects to benefit, not by its own acts of disarmament, but by *B*'s acts. Hence if *A* were to reason simply in terms of immediate interest, *A* might well decide to violate the pact.

But *A*'s decision need be neither prudent nor reasonable. For suppose first that *B* is able to determine whether or not *A* adheres to the pact. If *A* violates, then *B* will detect the violation and will then consider what to do in the light of *A*'s behaviour. It is not to *B*'s advantage to disarm alone; *B* expects to gain, not by its own acts of disarmament, but by *A*'s acts. Hence *A*'s violation, if known to *B*, leads naturally to *B*'s counter-violation. If this continues, the effect of the pact is entirely undone, and *A* and *B* return to their mutually disadvantageous arms race. *A*, foreseeing this when considering whether or not to adhere to the pact in the given situation, must therefore conclude that the truly prudent course of action is to adhere.

Now suppose that *B* is unable to determine whether or not *A* adheres to the pact in the particular situation under consideration. If *A* judges adherence to be in itself disadvantageous, then it will decide, both on the basis of immediate interest and on the basis of prudence, to violate the pact. Since *A*'s decision is unknown to *B*, it cannot affect whether or not *B* adheres to the pact, and so the advantage gained by *A*'s violation is not outweighed by any consequent loss.

Therefore if *A* and *B* are prudent they will adhere to their disarmament pact whenever violation would be detectable by the other, and violate the pact whenever violation would not be detectable by the other. In other words, they will adhere openly and violate secretly. The disarmament pact between *A* and *B* thus possesses two of the characteristics ascribed by the thesis to morality. First, accepting the pact and acting on it is more advantageous for each than making no pact at all. Second, in so far as the pact stipulates that each must disarm even when disarming is undetectable by the other, it requires each to perform disadvantageous acts—acts which run counter to considerations of prudence.

One further condition must be met if the disarmament pact is to possess those characteristics ascribed by the thesis to a system of morality. It must be the case that the requirement that each party perform disadvantageous acts be essential to the advantage conferred by the pact; or, to put the matter in the way in which we expressed it earlier, both *A* and *B* must do better to adhere to this pact than to a pact which is similar save that it requires no disadvantageous acts. In terms of the example, *A* and *B* must do better to adhere to the pact than to a pact which stipulates that each must disarm only when disarming is detectable by the other.

We may plausibly suppose this condition to be met. Although *A* will gain by secretly retaining arms itself, it will lose by *B*'s similar acts, and its losses may well outweigh its gains. *B* may equally lose more by *A*'s secret violations than it gains by its own. So, despite the fact that prudence requires each to violate secretly, each may well do better if both adhere secretly than if both violate secretly. Supposing this to be the case, the disarmament pact is formally analogous to a moral system, as characterized by the thesis. That is, acceptance of and adherence to the pact by *A* and *B* is more advantageous for each, either than making no pact at all or than acceptance of and adherence to a pact requiring only open disarmament, and the pact requires each to perform acts of secret disarmament which are disadvantageous.

Some elementary notation, adapted for our purposes from the mathematical theory of games, may make the example even more perspicuous. Given a disarmament pact between *A* and *B*, each may pursue two pure strategies—adherence and violation. There are, then, four possible combinations of strategies, each determining a particular outcome. These outcomes can be ranked preferentially for each nation; we shall let the numerals 1 to 4 represent the ranking from first to fourth preference. Thus we construct a simple matrix,[6] in which *A*'s preferences are stated first:

		B	
		adheres	*violates*
	adheres	2, 2	4, 1
A			
	violates	1, 4	3, 3

The matrix does not itself show that agreement is advantageous to both, for it gives only the rankings of outcomes given the agreement. But it is plausible to assume that *A* and *B* would rank mutual violation on a par with no agreement. If we assume this, we can then indicate the value to each of making and adhering to the pact by reference to the matrix.

The matrix shows immediately that adherence to the pact is not the most advantageous possibility for either, since each prefers the outcome, if it alone violates, to the outcome of mutual adherence. It shows also that each gains less from its own violations than it loses from the other's, since each ranks mutual adherence above mutual violation.

Let us now use the matrix to show that, as we argued previously, public adherence to the pact is prudent and mutually advantageous, whereas private adherence is not prudent although mutually advantageous. Consider first the case when adherence—and so violation—are open and public.

If adherence and violation are open, then each knows the strategy chosen by the other, and can adjust its own strategy in the light of this knowledge—or, in other words, the strategies are interdependent. Suppose that each initially chooses the strategy of adherence. *A* notices that if it switches to violation it gains—moving from 2 to 1 in terms of preference ranking. Hence immediate interest dictates such a switch. But it notices further that if it switches, then *B* can also be expected to switch—moving from 4 to 3 on its preference scale. The eventual outcome would be stable, in that neither could benefit from switching from violation back to adherence. But the eventual outcome would represent not a gain for *A* but a loss—moving from 2 to 3 on its preference scale. Hence prudence dictates no change from the strategy of adherence. This adherence is mutually advantageous; *A* and *B* are in precisely similar positions in terms of their pact.

Consider now the case when adherence and violation are secret and private. Neither nation knows the strategy chosen by the other, so the two strategies are independent. Suppose *A* is trying to decide which strategy to follow. It does not know *B*'s choice. But it notices that if *B* adheres, then it pays *A* to violate, attaining 1 rather than 2 in terms of preference ranking. If *B* violates, then again it pays *A* to violate, attaining 3 rather than 4 on its preference scale. Hence, no matter which strategy *B* chooses, *A* will do better to violate, and so prudence dictates violation.

B of course reasons in just the same way. Hence each is moved by considerations of prudence to violate the pact, and the outcome assigns each rank 3 on its preference scale. This outcome is mutually disadvantageous to *A* and *B*, since mutual adherence would assign each rank 2 on its preference scale.

If *A* and *B* are both capable only of rational prudence, they find themselves at an impasse. The advantage of mutual adherence to the agreement when violations would be secret is not available to them, since neither can find it in his own over-all interest not to violate secretly. Hence, strictly prudent nations cannot reap the maximum advantage possible from a pact of the type under examination.

Of course, what *A* and *B* will no doubt endeavour to do is eliminate the possibility of secret violations of their pact. Indeed, barring additional complications, each must find it to his advantage to make it possible for the other to detect his own violations. In other words, each must find it advantageous to ensure that their choice of strategies is interdependent, so that the pact will always be prudent for each to keep. But it may not be possible for them to ensure this, and to the extent that they cannot, prudence will prevent them from maximizing mutual advantage.

IV

We may now return to the connection of morality with advantage. Morality, if it is a system of principles of the type characterized in the thesis, requires that some persons perform acts genuinely disadvantageous to themselves, as a means to greater mutual advantage. Our example shows sufficiently that such a system is possible, and indicates more precisely its character. In particular, by an argument strictly parallel to that which we have pursued, we may show that men who are merely prudent will not perform the required disadvantageous acts. But in so violating the principles of morality, they will disadvantage themselves. Each will lose more by the violations of others than he will gain by his own violations.

Now this conclusion would be unsurprising if it were only that no man can gain if he alone is moral rather than prudent. Obviously such a man loses, for he adheres to moral principles to his own disadvantage, while others violate them also to his disadvantage. The benefit of the moral system is not one which any individual can secure for himself, since each man gains from the sacrifices of others.

What is surprising in our conclusion is that no man can ever gain if he is moral. Not only does he not gain by being moral if others are prudent, but he also does not gain by being moral if others are moral. For although he now receives the advantage of others' adherence to moral principles, he reaps the disadvantage of his own adherence. As long as his own adherence to morality is independent of what others do (and this is required to distinguish morality from prudence), he must do better to be prudent.

If all men are moral, all will do better than if all are prudent. But any one man will always do better if he is prudent than if he is moral. There is no real paradox in supposing that morality is advantageous, even though it requires the performance of disadvantageous acts.

On the supposition that morality has the characteristics ascribed to it by the thesis, is it possible to answer the question 'Why should we be moral?' where 'we' is taken distributively, so that the question is a compendious way of asking, for each person, 'Why should I be moral?' More simply, is it possible to answer the question 'Why should I be moral?'

I take it that this question, if asked seriously, demands a reason for being moral other than moral reasons themselves. It demands that moral reasons be shown to be reasons for acting by a non-circular argument. Those who would answer it, like Baier, endeavour to do so by the introduction of considerations of advantage.

Two such considerations have emerged from our discussion. The first is that if all are moral, all will do better than if all are prudent. This will serve to answer the question 'Why should we be moral?' if this question is interpreted rather as 'Why should we all be moral—rather than all being something else?' If we must all be the same, then each person has a reason —a prudential reason—to prefer that we all be moral.

But, so interpreted, 'Why should we be moral?' is not a compendious way of asking, for each person, 'Why should I be moral?' Of course, if everyone is to be whatever I am, then I should be moral. But a general answer to the question 'Why should I be moral?' cannot presuppose this.

The second consideration is that any individual always does better to be prudent rather than moral, provided his choice does not determine other choices. But in so far as this answers the question 'Why should I be moral?' it leads to the conclusion 'I should not be moral.' One feels that this is not the answer which is wanted.

We may put the matter otherwise. The individual who needs a reason for being moral which is not itself a moral reason cannot have it. There is nothing surprising about this; it would be much more surprising if such reasons could be found. For it is more than apparently paradoxical to suppose that considerations of advantage could ever of themselves justify accepting a real disadvantage.

V

I suggested in Section II that the thesis, in modified form, might provide a necessary, although not a sufficient, condition for a moral system. I want now to consider how one might characterize the man who would qualify as moral according to the thesis. I shall call him the 'moral' man—and then ask what would be lacking from this characterization, in terms of some of our commonplace moral views.

The rationally prudent man is incapable of moral behaviour in even the limited sense defined by the thesis. What difference must there be between the prudent man and the 'moral' man? Most simply, the 'moral' man is the prudent but trustworthy man. I treat trustworthiness as the capacity which enables its possessor to adhere, and to judge that he ought to adhere, to a commitment which he has made, without regard to considerations of advantage.

The prudent but trustworthy man does not possess this capacity completely. He is capable of trustworthy behaviour only in so far as he regards his *commitment* as advantageous. Thus he differs from the prudent man just in the relevant respect; he accepts arguments of the form 'If it is advantageous for me to agree[7] to do x, and I do agree to do x, then I ought to do *x*, whether or not it then proves advantageous for me to do *x*.'

Suppose that *A* and *B*, the parties to the disarmament pact, are prudent but trustworthy. *A*, considering whether or not secretly to violate the agreement, reasons that its advantage in making and keeping the agreement, provided *B* does so as well, is greater than its advantage in not making it. If it can assume that *B* reasons in the same way, then it is in a position to conclude that it ought not to violate the pact. Although violation would be advantageous, consideration of this advantage is ruled out by *A*'s trustworthiness, given the advantage in agreeing to the pact.

The prudent but trustworthy man meets the requirements implicitly imposed by the thesis for the 'moral' man. But how far does 'moral' man display two characteristics commonly associated with morality—first, a willingness to make sacrifices, and second a concern with fairness?

Whenever a man ignores his own advantage for reasons other than those of greater advantage, he may be said to make some sacrifice. The 'moral' man, in being trustworthy, is thus required to make certain sacrifices. But these are extremely limited. And—not surprisingly, given the general direction of our argument—it is quite possible that they limit the advantages which the 'moral' man can secure.

Once more let us turn to our example. *A* and *B* have entered into a disarmament agreement and, being prudent but trustworthy, are faithfully carrying it out. The government of *A* is now informed by its scientists, however, that they have developed an effective missile defence, which will render *A* invulnerable to attack by any of the weapons actually or potentially at *B*'s disposal barring unforeseen technological developments. Furthermore, this defence can be installed secretly. The government is now called upon to decide whether to violate its agreement with *B*, install the new defence, and, with the arms it has retained through its violation, establish its dominance over *B*.

A is in a type of situation quite different from that previously considered. For it is not just that *A* will do better by secretly violating no matter what *B* does, but it will do better if both violate than if both continue to adhere to the pact. *A* is now in a position to gain from abandoning the agreement; it no longer finds mutual adherence advantageous.

We may represent this new situation in another matrix:

		B	
		adheres	*violates*
	adheres	3, 2	4, 1
A			
	violates	1, 4	2, 3

We assume again that the ranking of mutual violation is the same as that of no agreement. Now had this situation obtained at the outset, no agreement would have been made, for A would have had no reason to enter into a disarmament pact. And of course had A expected this situation to come about, no agreement—or only a temporary agreement—would have been made; A would no doubt have risked the short-term dangers of the continuing arms race in the hope of securing the long-run benefit of predominance over B once its missile defence was completed. On the contrary, A expected to benefit from the agreement, but now finds that, because of its unexpected development of a missile defence, the agreement is not in fact advantageous to it.

The prudent but trustworthy man is willing to carry out his agreements, and judges that he ought to carry them out, in so far as he considers them advantageous. A is prudent but trustworthy. But is A willing to carry out its agreement to disarm, now that it no longer considers the agreement advantageous?

If A adheres to its agreement in this situation, it makes a sacrifice greater than any advantage it receives from the similar sacrifices of others. It makes a sacrifice greater in kind than any which can be required by a mutually advantageous agreement. It must, then possess a capacity for trustworthy behaviour greater than that ascribed to the merely prudent but trustworthy man (or nation). This capacity need not be unlimited; it need not extend to a willingness to adhere to any commitment no matter what sacrifice is involved. But it must involve a willingness to adhere to a commitment made in the expectation of advantage, should that expectation be disappointed.

I shall call the man (or nation) who is willing to adhere, and judges that he ought to adhere, to his prudentially undertaken agreements even if they prove disadvantageous to him, the trustworthy man. It is likely that there are advantages available to trustworthy men which are not available to merely prudent but trustworthy men. For there may be situations in which men can make agreements which each expects to be advantageous to him, provided he can count on the others' adhering to it whether or not their expectation of advantage is realized. But each can count on this only if all have the capacity to adhere to commitments regardless of whether the commitment actually proves advantageous. Hence, only trustworthy men who know each other to be such will be able rationally to enter into, and so to benefit from, such agreements.

Baier's view of morality departs from that stated in the thesis in that it requires trustworthy, and not merely prudent but trustworthy, men. Baier admits that 'a person might do better for himself by following enlightened self-interest rather than morality'.[8] This admission seems to require that morality be a system of principles which each person may expect, initially, to be advantageous to him, if adopted and adhered to by everyone, but not a system which actually is advantageous to everyone.

Our commonplace moral views do, I think, support the view that the moral man must be trustworthy. Hence, we have established one modification required in the thesis, if it is to provide a more adequate set of conditions for a moral system.

But there is a much more basic respect in which the 'moral' man falls short or our expectations. He is willing to temper his single-minded pursuit of advantage only by accepting the obligation to adhere to prudentially undertaken commitments. He has no real concern for the advantage of others, which would lead him to modify his pursuit of advantage when it conflicted with the similar pursuits of others. Unless he expects to gain, he is unwilling to accept restrictions on the pursuit of advantage which are intended to equalize the opportunities open to all. In other words, he has no concern with fairness.

We tend to think of the moral man as one who does not seek his own well-being by means which would deny equal well-being to his fellows. This marks him off clearly from the 'moral' man, who differs from the prudent man only in that he can overcome the apparent paradox of prudence and obtain those advantages which are available only to those who can display real restraint in their pursuit of advantage.

Thus a system of principles might meet the conditions laid down in the thesis without taking any account of considerations of fairness. Such a system would contain principles for ensuring increased advantage (or expectation of advantage) to everyone, but no further principle need be present to determine the distribution of this increase.

It is possible that there are systems of principles which, if adopted and adhered to, provide advantages which strictly prudent men, however rational, cannot attain. These advantages are a function of the sacrifices which the principles impose on their adherents.

Morality may be such a system. If it is, this would explain our expectation that we should all be worse off were we to substitute prudence for morality in our deliberations. But to characterize morality as a system of principles advantageous to all is not to answer the question 'Why should I be moral?' nor is it to provide for those considerations of fairness which are equally essential to our moral understanding.

---

[1] David Hume, *An Enquiry Concerning the Principles of Morals*, sec. ix, pt. ii.

[2] Ogden Nash, 'Kind of an Ode to Duty.'

[3] Kurt Baier, *The Moral Point of View: A Rational Basis of Ethics* (Ithaca, 1958), p. 314.

[4] That this, and only this, is what he is entitled to claim may not be clear to Baier, for he supposes his account of morality to answer the question 'Why should we be moral?' interpreting 'we' distributively. This, as I shall argue in Sec. IV, is quite mistaken.

[5] The thesis is not intended to state Baier's view of morality. I shall suggest in Sec. V that Baier's view would require substituting 'everyone can expect to benefit' for 'it is advantageous to everyone'. The thesis is stronger and easier to discuss.

[6] Those familiar with the theory of games will recognize the matrix as a variant of the Prisoner's Dilemma. In a more formal treatment, it would be appropriate to develop the relation between morality and advantage by reference to the Prisoner's Dilemma. This would require reconstructing the disarmament pact and the moral system as proper games. Here I wish only to suggest the bearing of game theory on our enterprise.

[7] The word 'agree' requires elucidation. It is essential not to confuse an advantage in agreeing to do x with an advantage in saying that one will do x. If it is advantageous for me to agree to do x, then there is some set of actions open to me which includes both saying that I will do x and doing x, and which is more advantageous to me than any set of actions open to me which does not include saying that I will do x. On the other hand, if it is advantageous for me to say that I will do x, then there is some set of actions open to me which includes saying that I will do x, and which is more advantageous to me than any set which does not include saying that I will do x. But this set need not include doing x.

[8] Baier, *op. cit.*, p. 314.

NOTES ON THE CONTRIBUTORS

R. EDGLEY is a Professor of Philosophy at the University of Sussex.

G. E. M. ANSCOMBE has been Professor of Philosophy at Cambridge since 1970, where she is a Fellow of New Hall.

G. H. VON WRIGHT is a Research Professor in the Academy of Finland, and Professor at Large, Cornell University, since 1965.

A. J. P. KENNY is a Fellow of Balliol College, Oxford.

J. R. SEARLE is a Professor of Philosophy in the University of California at Berkeley.

B. A. O. WILLIAMS is Knightbridge Professor of Philosophy at Cambridge, and a Fellow of King's College.

G. HARMAN is a Professor of Philosophy at Princeton University.

R. CHISHOLM is a Professor of Philosophy at Brown University.

J. RAZ, the editor of this volume, is a Fellow of Balliol College, Oxford.

D. R. P. WIGGINS is Professor of Philosophy at Bedford College in the University of London.

T. NAGEL is a Professor of Philosophy at Princeton University.

G. R. GRICE is a Reader in the School of Social Studies, University of East Anglia.

P. R. FOOT is a Senior Research Fellow of Somerville College, Oxford.

D. P. GAUTHIER is Professor of Philosophy at the University of Toronto.

SELECTED BIBLIOGRAPHY

1. BOOKS MAINLY ON THE PROBLEMS OF PRACTICAL REASONING

CASTAÑEDA, HECTOR-NERI, *Thinking and Doing*, Reidel, 1975.
EDGLEY, ROY, *Reason in Theory and Practice*, Hutchinson, London, 1969.
GAUTHIER, DAVID P., *Practical Reasoning*, Oxford, 1963.
—— (ed.), *Morality and Rational Self Interest*, Englewood Cliffs, N.J., 1970.
KÖRNER, STEPHAN, *Experience and Conduct*, Cambridge U.P., 1976.
—— (ed.), *Practical Reason*, Blackwell, Oxford, 1974.
NAGEL, THOMAS, *The Possibility of Altruism*, Oxford, 1970.
NORMAN, RICHARD, *Reasons for Action*, Blackwell, Oxford, 1971.
RAZ, JOSEPH, *Practical Reason and Norms*, Hutchinson, London, 1975.
RICHARDS, DAVID A. J., *A Theory of Reasons for Action*, Oxford, 1971.

2. ARTICLES AND BOOKS CONTAINING MATERIAL ON PRACTICAL REASONING AND RELATED ISSUES

ABELSON, R., 'Because I want to', *Mind*, 74 (1965), 540.
ALSTON, W., 'Moral Attitudes and Moral Judgments', *Nous*, 2 (1968), 1.
ANSCOMBE, ELIZABETH, 'von Wright on Practical Inference'.
BAIER, K., 'Good Reasons', *Philosophical Studies*, 4 (1953), 1.
——, *The Moral Point of View*, Cornell, U.P., 1958.
——, 'Reasons for Doing Something', *J. of Phil.* 61 (1964), 198.
BLACK, M., 'Some Questions Concerning Practical Inference', *Caveats and Critiques*, Cornell U.P., 1975.
BOND, E. J., 'Reasons, Wants and Values', *Canadian J. of Phil.* 3 (1974), 333.
BRANDT, R., 'Rationality, Egoism and Morality', *J. of Phil.* 69 (1972), 681.
BRUNTON, J. A., 'Egoism and Morality', *Phil. Quar.* 6 (1956), 260.
——, 'The Devil is not a Fool or, Egoism Revisited', *American Phil. Quar.* 12 (1975), 321.
BURCH, R. W., 'Reason Giving and Action Guiding in Morality', *Southwestern J. of Phil.* 4 (1973), 29.
CARLSON, G. R., 'Ethical Egoism Reconsidered', *American Phil. Quar.* 10 (1973), 25.
COOPER, N., 'Oughts and Wants', *Proceedings of Aristotelian Society*, Supp. vol. 42 (1968), 143.
DAVIDSON, D., 'How is Weakness of the Will Possible', in J. Feinberg (ed.), *Moral Concepts*, Oxford, 1969.
FALK, W. D., 'Action Guiding Reasons', *J. of Phil.* 60 (1963), 702.
FOSS, J., 'A Rule of Minimal Rationality: The Logical Link between Beliefs and Values', *Inquiry*, 19 (1976), 345.
VAN FRAASSEN, B. C., 'Values and the Heart's Command', *J. of Phil.* 70 (1973), 5.
FRANKENA, W. K., 'Obligation and Motivation in Recent Moral Philosophy', in A. I. Melden (ed.), *Essays in Moral Philosophy*, Washington U.P., 1958.

GAUTHIER, D. P., 'The Impossiblity of Rational Egoism', *J. of Phil.* 71 (1974), 439.
——, 'Reason and Maximization', *Canadian J. of Phil.* 4 (1975) 411.
GEACH, P., 'Kenny on Practical Reasoning', *Logic Matters*, Blackwell, Oxford, 1972.
GRIFFITHS, A. P. and PETERS, R. S., 'The Autonomy of Prudence', *Mind*, 71 (1962), 161.
HALL, W. E., 'Practical Reason(s) and the Deadlock in Ethics', *Mind*, 64 (1955), 319.
HARE, R. M., *The Language of Morals*, Oxford, 1952.
——, *Freedom and Reason*, Oxford, 1963.
——, 'Practical Inferences', *Practical Inferences*, Macmillan, London, 1971.
HARMAN, G., 'Practical Reasoning', *Rev. of Metaphysics*, 29 (1976), 431.
JARVITZ, J. THOMPSON, 'Practical Reasoning', *Phil. Quar.* 12 (1962), 316.
JONES, P., 'Doubts about Prima Facie Duties', *Phil.* 45 (1970), 39.
KALIN, J., 'Two Kinds of Moral Reasoning: Ethical Egoism as a Moral Theory', *Canadian J. of Phil.* 5 (1975), 323.
LEMMON, E. J., 'Moral Dilemmas', *Phil. Rev.* 71 (1962), 139.
LESSER, A. H., 'Aesthetic Reasons for Acting', *Phil. Quar.* 22 (1972), 19.
LOCKE, D., 'Reasons, Wants, and Causes', *American Phil. Quar.* 11 (1974), 169.
MACINTYRE, A., *Against the Self Image of the Age*, Duckworth, London, 1971, Chs. 14–17, 21.
MACKIE, J. L., *Ethics*, Penguin, London, 1977.
MAYO, B. 'Commitments and Reasons', *Mind*, 64 (1955), 342.
MEDLIN, B., 'Ultimate Principles and Ethical Egoism', *Australasian J. of Phil.* 35 (1957), 111.
MEIKLE, S., 'Reasons for Action', *Phil Quar.* 24 (1974), 52.
MELDEN, A. I., 'Reasons for Action and Matters of Fact', *Proceedings and Addresses of the American Phil. Association*, 35 (1961–2), 45.
MILO, R. D., 'The Notion of a Practical Inference', *American Phil. Quar.* 13 (1976), 13.
MOTHERSILL, M., 'Anscombe's Account of the Practical Syllogism', *Phil Rev.* 71 (1962), 448.
NORRIS, S. E., 'The Intelligibility of Practical Reasoning', *American Phil. Quar.* 12 (1975), 77.
QUINN, W., 'Egoism as an Ethical System', *J. of Phil.* 71 (1974), 456.
RACHELS, J., 'Wants, Reasons and Justification', *Phil Quar.* 18 (1968), 299.
——, 'Reasons for Action', *Canadian J. of Phil.* 1 (1971), 173.
RESHER, N., 'Practical Reasoning and Value', *Phil. Quar.* 16 (1966), 121.
RORTY, A., 'Wants and Justifications', *J. of Phil.* 63 (1966), 765.
SCRUTON, R., 'Attitudes, Beliefs and Reasons', in J. Casey (ed.), *Morality and Moral Reasoning*, Methuen, London, 1971.
SHOPE, R., 'Prima Facie Duty', *J. of Phil.* 62 (1965), 279.
SILVERSTON, H. S., 'Practical Reasons and Universality', *Australasian J. of Phil.* 52 (1974), 146.
SNARE, F., 'Wants and Reasons', *Personalist*, 53 (1972), 395.
——, 'The Definition of Prima Facie Duties', *Phil. Quar.* 24 (1974), 235.
SOLOMON, W. D., 'Moral Reasons', *American Phil. Quar.* 12 (1975), 331.
SOSA, E., 'On Practical Inference and the Logic of Imperatives', *Theoria*, 32 (1966), 211.
——, 'On Practical Inference with an Excursus on Theoretical Inference', *Étude de logique juridique*, ed. Ch. Perelman, *Logique et Analyse*, 215, vol. 4 (1970).
STURGEON, N. L., 'Altruism, Solipsism and the Objectivity of Reason', *Phil. Rev.* 83 (1974), 374.

TRIGG, R., 'Moral Conflict', *Mind*. 80 (1971), 41.
WALACE, J. D., 'Practical Inquiry', *Phil. Rev.* 78 (1969), 435.
WALTON, K. A., 'Rational Action', *Mind*, 76 (1967), 537.
WHEATLEY, J., 'Reasons for Acting', *Dialogue*, 7 (1969), 553.
WOODS, M., 'Reasons for Action and Desires', *Proc. of Aristotelian Society*, Suppl. vol. 46 (1972), 189.
VON WRIGHT, G. H., 'Practical Inference', *Phil. Rev.* 72 (1963), 159.
——, 'The Logic of Practical Discourse', in R. Klibansky (ed.), La Nuove Italia Editione, Firenze, 1968, *Contemporary Philosophy*, vol. 1, p. 141.

INDEX OF NAMES

(not including authors mentioned only in the Bibliography)